Word Grammar

RICHARD HUDSON

Basil Blackwell

For
Gay, Lucy and Alice

Basil Blackwell Publisher Limited
108 Cowley Road, Oxford OX4 1JF, England

Basil Blackwell Inc.
432 Park Avenue South, Suite 1505
New York, NY 10016, USA

British Library Cataloguing in Publication Data

Hudson, Richard, 19
Word grammar.
1. Semantics
I. Title
422   PE1576

ISBN 0-631-13186-8

Typeset by Getset (BTS) Ltd, Eynsham, Oxford
Printed in Great Britain by
Redwood Burn Ltd, Trowbridge

Contents

Preface

This book is about a linguistic theory, word grammar, which is radically different from a theory I advocated in print in 1976, daughter-dependency grammar: notably, it has no place for constituents larger than words or for syntactic features, and it presents language structure as a special case of general cognitive structure. I gather from various friends and colleagues that the world sometimes disapproves of people who change their minds in this way, so I should like to offer the world an apology for littering the intellectual landscape with yet another theory. My only excuse is that it is very difficult to be right first time. I am sure that word grammar is a great improvement on daughter-dependency grammar, so I hope it will survive longer.

I wrote a draft of a completely different book, with the same title, in 1982, and I had extremely helpful comments on either the whole or parts of it from the following colleagues: Noam Chomsky, David Katz, Tokumi Kodama, Jim McCawley, Barbara Prangell, Neil Smith, Mark Steedman, Maureen Taylor, Willy Van Langendonck, Peter Wason, Yorick Wilks, Deirdre Wilson and Mary Wood (plus a number of anonymous publisher's readers). I am most grateful to all of them, and hope they agree that the present book is better than the one they helped to demolish.

I also take this opportunity to acknowledge a grant from the SSRC which allowed me to concentrate for a short three months on the analysis of English grammar underlying the theory.

1

Introduction

A THEORY OF LANGUAGE STRUCTURE

Language as a network

Word grammar is a theory of language structure. At the most general level, it consists of generalization (1):

(1)   A language is a network of entities related by propositions.

For example, we might take the entities to include words and phonemes, connected by propositions such as 'The word *rat* consists of /r/ followed by /a/ followed by /t/,' and 'The phoneme /a/ is an instance of the category ''vowel'' '; in these examples, the two propositions refer to the entities 'the word *rat*', 'the phoneme /r/', 'the phoneme /a/' and 'the phoneme /t/', and 'the category ''vowel'' '. Further, the two propositions between them connect the word *rat* to the category 'vowel', though indirectly. The two propositions and the five entities to which they refer make up a (very small) subnetwork within the total network of English, and we could diagram this subnetwork as in (2):

(2)

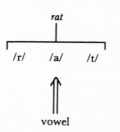

This diagram uses a set of conventions which I shall explain shortly, but the main point of it is to show how the relations among entities in a grammar may be presented as a network. A little imagination leads from this little subnetwork to the monster network that would be needed for the whole language.

This very general claim does not obviously distinguish word grammar from any other available theory of language structure. Some theories are explicitly formulated in terms of networks, the obvious example being stratificational theory (see Sullivan 1980 for a recent summary). However, it makes no difference whether a theory refers explicitly to the notion of 'networks' or not, because all the available theories of language structure can be interpreted in such a way that they are compatible with (1). For example, a phrase-structure rule can be seen as a proposition about a mother category and its daughters ('a sentence consists of . . .'); a transformation as a proposition about adjacent phrase-markers in a derivation; a lexical entry as a proposition about the syntactic, phonological and semantic structures that are compatible with one another as structures for the same word; and so on. Ever since the notion of 'well-formedness condition' became common-place in transformational theory (following McCawley 1968a), it has been possible to interpret a grammar in this way, and similar remarks apply to other theories, *mutatis mutandis*. Moreover, any grammar must define a structure in which every entity is related to every other entity directly or indirectly, so it constitutes a network in the sense of (1).

Nevertheless, even at this very general level there are two respects in which (1) does distinguish word grammar from at least some other theories.

(a) In the sense in which I intend the word 'proposition', it does not apply to *procedures*. That is, in terms of the distinction which cognitive scientists commonly make between procedural and declarative knowledge, I see a language as consisting (entirely) of *declarative* knowledge, expressed as propositions. I am aware that the opposite view is widespread among cognitive scientists, including some scholars for whose work I have great admiration (J.R. Anderson 1976, Miller and Johnson-Laird 1976, Winograd 1975, Small 1980, among others); but I have seen no persuasive arguments against the position that we linguists generally take for granted, namely the declarative view of language. (In this respect the cognitive grammar of Lakoff and Thompson 1975 is quite exceptional.) At the same time, though, I recognize the need for procedures that make use of language as part of the solution for practical problems; for example, when you buy a ticket you have to perform various actions, some of which are linguistic. These procedures are what I call 'schemata' in Hudson 1980a, and I shall assume (at least for the purposes of the present book) that they are a separate part of one's knowledge from the language itself. At any rate, I recognize this interface as an interesting and important area for future research.

(b) The view of a language as a network does not commit one to analysing the language as a pair of lists: a list of *rules*, and a list of lexical *entries*. This is of course how a transformational grammar is structured, and likewise most other kinds of grammar, with a few exceptions which include stratificational grammar again, space grammar (Langacker 1982), and lexical generative grammar (Diehl 1981). The list view is a specific interpretation of the network claim, and implies two distinctions which are in fact rather hard to make. One of the distinctions is that between one lexical entry and another – the notorious distinction between polysemy and homonymy being the main culprit. So far as I know, no satisfactory suggestion has yet been made for deciding where the boundaries of a lexical entry lie (Lyons 1977:550 surveys the state of the art), so we have no general principle for deciding, for example, whether *horn* involves just one lexical entry or two in the two meanings 'horn of an animal' and 'musical instrument' (or, worse still, 'part of a motor-car'). My view is that we are trying to make a distinction which corresponds to no kind of reality, so the search for principles on which to base it is bound to be fruitless. The network approach allows us to sidestep the issue completely: we have a set of word-forms, and a set of word-meanings which are related to the word-forms in a complex way, as part of the network. Once we have established these connections, there is no motivation for then going on to chop up the network into discrete chunks called 'lexical entries'.

The other distinction which is generally assumed is that between rules and lexical entries. However, the distinction was absent from the earliest version of transformational grammar (Chomsky 1957), was then denied, or at least blurred, in generative semantics (e.g. McCawley 1968b), and has never been accepted in stratificational grammar. Evidently it is less obvious than one might think if one were to judge by most current discussions in the transformational literature, and elsewhere too. Moreover, there is a generally unrecognized transition area between typical 'rules' and typical 'lexical entries' where their respective properties are mixed up in a confusing way. For example, there are a reasonably large number of constructions which are tied to particular words, such as *What about . . . ?* Should this be treated by means of a rule, on the ground that such sentences contain patterns which are not permitted by other rules (e.g. *What about the unemployment figures?* contains no verb)? Or should it be included in the lexicon, as a lexical entry, on the ground that it is an idiosyncratic pattern restricted to the word *what* or *how* followed by *about*? Once again, I know of no general principles to which we could refer in deciding questions like this, so I feel that the only reasonable conclusion to be drawn is that we are trying to draw a distinction (rule versus lexical entry) which has no reality. (Other examples of constructions like *What about . . . ?* are mentioned in Lyons 1968:178, Baker 1979 and Carroll 1978; it is easy to extend their lists with examples like *If it weren't for . . ., Not that . . ., If only . . ., No sooner . . . than . . ., The more . . . the more . . ., More fool . . . for . . .-ing . . .,* etc.)

The distinctive characteristic of word grammar, then, is that it is less restrictive than many other theories in that it does not impose on the grammar the requirement that it consist of a list of rules and a (distinct) list of lexical entries. The network structure is compatible with a more diffuse organization than this, and I have argued that such diffuseness is a good thing because it seems to correspond to the reality of language data. Of course, in general one does not boast of the flexibility and power of one's theory of language, because we are all trying to restrict flexibility in order to make claims about language that are as precise as possible. However, it goes without saying that we should put the restrictions of our theory in the same places as language itself is restricted; and what I have tried to show in the above is that the places where other theories restrict language structure, by requiring boundaries, are places where no boundaries actually exist.

Linguistic entities

We can now be more precise about the entities which occur in the network (and in the next subsection we shall do the same for the propositions). What is a linguistic entity, as far as word grammar is concerned? The theory is called this precisely because the notion 'word' is central to the answer. I am aware of the problems that arise in defining the word, especially if we are aiming at an operational definition which will tell us in all cases, for all languages, how to recognize a word boundary. Nevertheless, it seems to be widely agreed among linguists these days that most, or perhaps even all, languages make use of units which could reasonably be called words. Moreover, any reasonably sophisticated theory of language must take account of cliticization, which I take it involves two words, one of which is contained in the other, so we may expect uncertainty about word-boundaries in precisely these cases. For instance, how many words are there in *We're* (as in *We're ready*)? Similar problems can again be expected from compounding, where two words are combined to form one (e.g. *chocolate box*). We shall have something to say about both these phenomena on pp. 48 – 52, but in the meantime my purpose is to suggest that the problems of identifying word boundaries in these uncertain cases should not prevent us from taking the word as the pillar on which this theory rests.

Assuming, then, that we all know (roughly) what we mean by 'word', the following are the kinds of entity which are referred to in a word grammar:

(a) Single words, which may be taken at any degree of generality (though the different degrees are, of course, kept clearly distinct in the grammar); thus the following would all be treated as entities in a grammar for English:

(i)   the word *ran*, with final *b* due to assimilation to a following bilabial (as in *ran back*);
(ii) the word *ran* (irrespective of final consonant);
(iii) the word *run* (irrespective of tense – i.e. the 'lexeme' *run*, in the terminology of Lyons 1977:19);
(iv) the word-type 'past tense verb';
(v)   the word-type 'verb';
(vi) the entity 'English word' (it is this entity that brings together all the parts of a grammar for English, as opposed to other languages – a distinction which clearly needs to be made, especially if we want to study bilingual speakers);
(vii) the entity 'word' (which unifies all that we have to say about language in general).

(b) Parts of words, whether these parts correspond to morphemes or to phonological segments (we shall see on pp. 52 – 7 that this distinction is in any case somewhat unclear), and as I have just pointed out, the parts of a word may also include smaller words. Once again, these parts may be taken at any degree of generality, from the particular allophone or allormorph up to the general classes like 'vowel'.

(c) Strings of words involved in co-ordinate structures, whether as conjuncts or as the whole co-ordinate structure. Some of these strings are 'incomplete', in that they could not occur outside a co-ordinate structure, hence the special connection between word-strings and co-ordinate structures. For example, we recognize all the bracketed strings in the following as linguistic entities, to which the grammar may refer:

({John collects books} and {his wife, records})

The whole of chapter 5 is devoted to the discussion of co-ordinate structures.

(d) Word-meanings – more generally, any element in the semantic structure. It makes little difference whether or not we say that word-meanings are strictly speaking part of the linguistic network as such, because they are one of the two main points at which the (linguistic) network of words makes contact with the (non-linguistic) network of general cognitive structures, and the interface by definition belongs to both networks. In any case, the view for which I shall argue in this book is that the linguistic network is just part of a larger network, without any clear differences between the linguistic and non-linguistic beyond the fact that one is about words and the other is not; so I cannot see any empirical issue at stake in deciding whether word-meanings are part of language or not. The main point is that there are propositions which link words to word-meanings, so we need to take account of these propositions in the theory of language structure.

(e) Elements of the utterance-event, by which I mean the participants of the utterance-event (speaker, addressee), the time, the place and various other factors. For some words, we need to refer to one or more of these elements – for instance, we need to say that *pussy* and *cat* are different with respect to the constraints they place on speaker or addressee (*pussy* being used only by or to young children). Once again, I see no point in arguing about whether or not such elements are really part of the language; since they are part of the interface between words and the rest of the world, they could be taken as part of both. Moreover, if everything is basically contained in a single grand network, it makes little difference what we decide.

Two features of that list of entities are particularly noteworthy: first, there is no mention of phrases, clauses or sentences, as the word constitutes the upper boundary (apart from the units of co-ordinate structures). Chapter 3 will take up this controversial claim, and justify it. Second, the discussion shows that I am not concerned to define the boundaries of language, in contrast with many other linguistic theories. If we assume that words and their parts are indisputably linguistic entities, then there are two ways in which we could use this assumption as the basis for delimiting language, according to whether we concentrate on the entities or on the propositions that relate them. If we focus on entities, we could say that the language network includes words and their parts (and co-ordinate structures), and nothing else – i.e. excluding word-meanings and elements of the utterance-event. If on the other hand we focus on propositions, we could say that a proposition is linguistic if it refers to a word (or word-part or word-string), in which case word-meanings and so on would be included in the language network, on the ground that they are referred to by some propositions that also refer to words. I see no reason why we should force ourselves to make this choice, because nothing seems to follow from it: I shall try to show that there is little or nothing that we can say about the network centred on words which we could not also say about other parts of the general network.

Propositions connecting linguistic entities

Word grammar allows just five types of proposition to refer to words. (For simplicity, I shall ignore word-parts and word-strings in the following discussion, since they are cumbersome to refer to, and in any case the propositions in which they are involved represent a subset of the types which can refer to words.) Each type of proposition may be identified by means of a particular function, or predicate expression, so we can represent the different propositions as *formulae*. For example, one of the predicate expressions we shall use is 'composition', which refers to the part – whole relation. This is the predicate contained in the proposition that relates the word *rat* to its constituent parts, /r/, /a/ and /t/. A fairly standard formulation of this proposition would put the predicate in front of a pair of brackets, with its arguments inside the brackets;

(1)   composition (*rat*,[/r/ + /a/ + /t/])

However, this is not the notation that I shall use for formulae, though I should find it somewhat hard to produce solid evidence that my notation is better. Instead, I make use of a different notational tradition, that of tagmemic grammar (e.g. Pike 1982), which I also used in earlier theory, daughter-dependency grammar (Hudson 1976a). In this tradition, relations are expressed in terms of 'slots' (corresponding to the predicate expression) and their 'fillers'. This tradition needs to be supplemented, however, because a slot and a single filler cannot express anything more than a one-place predicate, whereas all the propositions in word grammar express relations and involve two arguments. So I have followed the convention of tying the slot to one argument as its 'possessor', with the filler as the other argument. This notation corresponds to a prose statement: 'the . . . of . . . is . . . .' For example, in the case of *rat* it corresponds to 'the composition of *rat* is /r/ + /a/ + /t/.' To show the 'possessor' of the slot, I shall put it in brackets after the name of the slot (a widespread convention, found in Kac 1978 for example), and I connect the slot and its filler by a colon, which can be verbalized as 'is'. Thus, in place of (1) above, we shall use (2):

(2)   composition(*rat*): /r/ + /a/ + /t/

However, it is helpful to have a notation for *diagrams*, to represent the same propositions. For example, we have already seen how the composition of *rat* can be shown diagrammatrically (in the diagram of (2) on p. 1. One of the advantages of diagrams is that they make the network property of the grammar easier to grasp, whereas formulae have to be presented as a list.

The five types of proposition, then, are as follows (in none of the diagram conventions is the vertical dimension relevant):

(a) *Composition*. This relates the word to its parts.

Diagram:

(Here, as elsewhere, *w* stands for the word concerned.)

(b) *Model*. This relates the word to the more general entity of which it is an instance; for example, *rat* is an instance of a noun. We shall discuss this relation in more detail in the next section.

Diagram:
w
↑

(Here *m* stands for the model.)   m

(c) *Companion*. These propositions relate the word to the other words with which it occurs, and will later be supplemented by more specific propositions which distinguish various grammatical relations, notably 'modifier', 'head' and 'subject' (see chapter 3 for further discussion).

Diagram: w ——————— c   or   c ——————— w

(The *c* stands for 'companion'.)

(d) *Referent.* All the connections between a word and the semantic structure are established via the word's 'referent'. Chapter 4 will explain why I assume that every word has a referent, with a small handful of exceptions (e.g. *and*).

Diagram:

(Here and elsewhere I shall use the asterisk to distinguish a word's referent from the word itself.)

(e) *Utterance-event.* A word is linked to its speakers, addressees, times and places of utterance via the event of uttering the word, which I shall call the 'utterance-event'. These relations are somewhat complex, so I shall devote most of chapter 6 to them and largely ignore them till then.

Diagram:

To give a clearer idea of the relation between the two notations, here is an account of the part of the grammar which is responsible for the verb *pop,* as in *The balloon popped.* First we have it expressed in formulae, with a prose translation on the right which is not part of the grammar, but just a guide for the reader:

(3) composition(*pop*):	$p_1 + p_2 + p_3$,	*Pop* consists of three phonemes of which the first is an instance of
model(p_1):	/p/,	/p/,
model(p_2):	/o/,	the second is an instance of /o/,
model(p_3):	/p/,	and the third is another instance of /p/.
model(*pop*):	verb	*Pop* is an instance of a verb.
companion(verb):	c,	Verbs (e.g. *pop*)

c < verb

referent(*pop*):   pop*,

    model(pop*):   event,
    changer(pop*):   c*

take a companion which precedes them. *Pop* refers to pop*, which is an instance of an event, and involves a 'changer', namely the referent of the companion c.

I think the analysis should be self-explanatory, but there are some details which I shall discuss and justify in later sections. For the moment we are concerned primarily with notation, rather than content.

Now we can present the same information in terms of a diagram, using the conventions that I have just introduced:

(4)

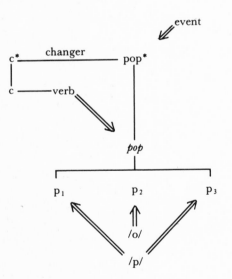

This diagram should be self-explanatory too, except for one point: I have written the word 'changer' on top of the line which connects c* to pop*. In doing so I am anticipating a convention which I shall introduce later, when we need to distinguish different semantic relations from one another, to supplement the relation 'companion'.

There are no other types of proposition than these in a word grammar, except for a couple of very elementary ones which always appear as conditions on other propositions, rather than as formulae in their own right. These deal respectively with *identity* and temporal *order*. In formulaic notation, we can by-pass the slot-filler notation in both cases, and use conventional symbols in between the related entities, = in the case of identity, and < for order. Thus we might have two entities, A and B, represented in the grammar as distinct entities, but we might then want to say that they are in fact one and the same entity, meaning that everything which is true of one is also true of the other. We can express this identity by writing 'A = B' in a formula, or by stretching the equals sign as a long double line in a diagram. (The double line with an arrow is in fact just a modification of this convention, to show the asymmetrical 'identity' relation between an instance and its model.)

An example of a part of the grammar in which identity needs to be expressed is the part which describes the equative verb *be*, as in *That's John*. This verb identifies the referent of the subject with that of the complement, so in the structure for *That's John* we should find something like 'That* = John*'. Many parts of the grammar make a somewhat different use of the identity relation, however, in order to express *partial* identity. One such case is the part responsible for gapping (as in *John had porridge for breakfast, and Bill, toast*), which simply requires the second conjunct (the part after *and*) to be interpreted as though it were the same as the first conjunct, except for the two overt elements (*Bill* and *toast*), which are substituted for the corresponding parts of the first conjunct. To formalize this kind of partial identity, we use the 'A = B' notation. Chapter 5 on co-ordinate structures, will explain how this applies to gapped structures, but we shall also use the ' = ' notation at other points for expressing partial identity.

Lastly, we have the question of temporal order, for which we have the symbol < mentioned above. This is to be taken in its mathematical sense 'less than', and can be used in this sense in some parts of the grammar (e.g. the parts dealing with the meanings of gradable adjectives, where we can say that *X is big* means 'X has a size such that the normal size is less than the size of X'). In the case of temporal order, we can imagine points of time as being represented by integers which increase with time, so we can show that one time A is earlier than another time B by writing 'A < B'. We shall exploit this possibility in dealing with the semantics of tense, but also in relation to temporal order of words in utterances. So if we want to say that the subject precedes its verb, then we can write the equivalent of 'subject < verb'. (We have precisely this rule formulated in (3), where the subject is represented as c, a companion of the verb.)

To summarize, we find the following types of proposition in a word grammar: composition, model, class, companion, referent and utterance-event (these are the main ones), plus identity (total or partial) and 'less than'. We also have two sets of notations for representing these types of proposition, according to whether we are using formulae or diagrams to represent the structure of the language. Between them, these propositions serve to link every linguistic entity to every other one, though in some cases the links are very indirect, so we may define the network of a language either by means of a diagram, or by means of a set of formulae. Of course, there are conceptual problems for any linguist who tries to capture anything bigger than a very small part of the total network, because the complexity increases alarmingly (though not exponentially, since there is a great deal of modularity). Each of the notations has its advantages and its snags, but for anyone interested in computerization, the formulaic notation is clearly the better of the two.

Levels and components

Most theories of language structure rest heavily on the notions 'level' and 'component', where 'level' refers to the separate structures that can be found in a sentence (semantic, syntactic, phonological, etc.) and 'component' refers to the separate parts of the grammar which are responsible for these structures. I think one of the reasons why linguists have in the past put such emphasis on these differences is because they offered the hope of modularity in the system – so we can concentrate on the phonology without worrying about the syntax, and so on. However, it is clear from the literature that most of the boundaries concerned are as problematic as those we considered earlier (e.g. polysemy versus homonymy).

In contrast, word grammar puts relatively little emphasis on levels and components, and there is certainly nothing comparable with the organization of a transformational grammar into blocks of rules which can be applied in sequence (first the phrase-structure rules, then the lexical rule, then the transformations, and so on). As a matter of fact, it is possible that this difference is simply a matter of style of presentation, rather than of the contents of the grammars concerned, because a transformational grammar (for example) in which all rule-ordering was intrinsic would presumably generate exactly the same structures if the component boundaries were abandoned, so that all rules were stored in a common pool. It all depends on whether the components are actually needed in order to prevent (say) a phonological rule from applying before a syntactic one, and that is a matter of debate at the moment.

The main level-boundary which is reflected in word grammar is that between words and their meanings. The grammar makes this boundary absolutely clear, because words and their referents are taken as distinct entities, with distinct names in the grammar, and they are related to one another by the formula 'referent(x): y'. Any name which can replace *x* must be a word (or word-part), and any which can replace *y* cannot be a word or word-part. There is thus never any uncertainty as to whether a given *entity* is a word or a referent, and the only *propositions* about which there is any uncertainty are precisely those of the form 'referent(x): y', whose task is to link the semantic and lower levels to one another. This boundary is of great help to the practising linguist, as it allows one to work on the semantics without simultaneously working on the syntax, and vice versa.

As far as the other traditional level-boundaries are concerned, however, there is less clarity. The relevant proposition-type is 'composition', dealing with part – whole relations, but we have already seen that the parts of a word may be other words, or morphemes, or phonological segments – for *in*, the constituents are presumably phonological segments, but for *dogs* they are morphemes, and what about *geese*? Moreover, the relation between a compound word and its component words is just the same kind of relation (composition) as that between a word and its component morphemes, and as that between a morpheme and its component phonological segments, so the diagram for the structure of an example like *wishing well* would presumably be as follows:

(1)

wishing-well

There is no natural division here into levels of sentence-structure, nor would the corresponding parts of the grammar show any natural division into components. The most we can say is that some of the entities (*wishing-well, wishing, wish* and *well*) are instances of words, and others (/w/, /i/, etc.) are instances of phonemes, with a residue of unassigned elements (namely, *ing*). I shall explore the differences between this distinction and the traditional 'level' distinction on pp. 52 – 7.

The modularity of a word grammar does not depend on division by levels and components, then. Instead, it derives from the fact that each proposition is assigned to just one entity, as its 'possessor', and that each entity may be the 'possessor' of a large number of different propositions. For example, a large number of propositions are assigned to the very general entity 'word', and another large set to 'English word', and another to 'verb'. Each of these sets of propositions is unified by virtue of this shared entity, but internally fairly disparate because different propositions refer to different aspects of word-structures – some to referents, others to morphology, and so on. It is true that we are not used, as linguists, to seeing language divided up on these lines, but with a little familiarity the practising linguist can find this organization just as helpful as the traditional one.

MODELS AND INSTANCES
How to inherit from a model

One of the fundamental relations in this theory is that between an instance and the entity, or 'model', of which it is an instance. This is the relation between *run* and 'verb', but it is also the relation between *ran* and the lexeme *run*, and so on (through all the pairs in the list on p. 5 – 6). Each more specific entity is an instance of the more general one, which is taken as the model for it, and the relation between them is formalized in terms of the 'model(x): y' formula. Since every word is an instance of some model, and every word (or word-type) is, ultimately, an instance of the category 'word', the relation of instantiation provides a hierarchy which brings together every word in the language. This is the 'skeleton' of the network, to which all the other types of relation are added.

The relations I have just been describing are traditionally described in terms of sets and members – 'word' is the name of a set, whose members may be subclassified into part-of-speech classes like 'verb', which may be further subdivided on two dimensions, on the one hand into lexemes like *run* and on the other hand into inflectional categories like 'past tense'. The reason for grouping individuals into sets is of course so that we can make generalizations across all the members of a set, by making the generalization about the set as a whole, but the same effect can be achieved by making use of the type – token relation between an instance and its model, without invoking sets at all. Thus, instead of taking 'verb' as the name of a class of words, whose internal structure is that of a *set* (an unordered list of members), we can take it as the name of a generalized word-type whose internal structure is that of a *word* (with a composition, a referent, and so on). We can make any generalizations that apply to verbs as a whole by applying them to this word type, and then they will be shared by any words which are instances (tokens) of the model 'verb'.

The difference between the set-theoretic approach and the instanti-ation approach is a subtle one and it is hard to find differences which could provide the basis for arguments one way or the other. One difference, however, is that the instantiation approach is more general, in that it covers cases of the type – token relation as well as traditional set-member relations. For instance, the relation between a set and a and a particular instance of this word, used on a particular occasion, would not normally be described as the relation between a set and a member of the set, in contrast with the relation between *in* and 'preposition'. This extra generality in the instantiation approach is an advantage, because we shall see that the two kinds of relation have the same general properties. Moreover, it is very unclear where the dividing line should be drawn – for example, is *ran* an instance of the type *run*, or a member of the set of forms in the paradigm of *run*? (This is yet another example of a distinction which is traditionally hard to make, but which word grammar avoids altogether.)

I think that it may be possible to find other benefits of the instantiation approach and that it allows us to refer directly to the 'typical' properties (e.g. that it avoids the logical problems of fuzzy sets), but I think it is enough at present to have pointed out the relation between the two approaches. I shall now take the instantiation approach for granted, and show what can be done with it.

Let us first see how this approach can be made to work. Let us assume (for the present subsection) that we know that some entity I is an instance of some other entity M (for 'model'). What this entails (by definition) is that I has all the properties of M, plus some others. For example, *pop* has all the properties common to all verbs, such as that of having a subject, and of inflecting by adding /t/ in the past tense; but it also has properties unique to it (e.g. it consists of /p/ + /o/ + /p/). Similarly, a particular instance of *popped* has all the properties of the type *popped* (e.g. it refers to a previous event of popping, it is pronounced /p/ + /o/ + /p/ + /t/), plus the property of having been uttered by some specific person on some specific occasion (information which would be included in the utterance-event slot). We can formulate this definition quite precisely, as the 'inheritance-of-properties principle' (Beaugrande and Dressler 1981:91).

(1)   *Inheritance of Properties Principle*
If I is an instance of M, then I inherits all the properties of M;
i.e. any proposition which applies to M must also apply to I,
mutatis mutandis.

This principle is of great benefit not only to the practising linguist (who can use it for making generalizations), but also to the practising speaker/hearer, because the latter gains access to all the information they have already about the model as soon as they link the instance to the model. So for example, when we learn a new word, all we need to do is to work out its part of speech, and we immediately gain access to a mass of information about how to inflect it, how this affects its meaning, how to combine it with other words, and so on.

Another principle makes the system even more useful, by allowing great flexibility. This principle allows the properties of the model to be overridden by properties of the instance, where the latter are specified in advance. We can call it the 'priority-to-the-instance principle', but it is already well known to linguists under the name of the 'proper-inclusion principle'. Pullum (1979) attributes this principle to various linguists, including Panini, S.R. Anderson and Sanders, and explains it as follows (1979:82): 'When a special case and a more general case are being tested for applicability, the general case should be considered to be applicable only if the special case is not.' The most obvious examples of this principle in operation are irregular inflections; e.g. given a general entry covering regular inflections, and a specific entry covering just the lexeme *run*, you apply the latter where it conflicts with the former (e.g. with regard to the past-tense form).

In terms of the instantiation approach, the principle can be formulated as follows:

(2)   *Priority to the Instance Principle*

The inheritance-of-properties principle does not apply to any
property of M which conflicts with a known property of I.

In the example just given, since you already know that the past tense of
run is *ran*, you ignore the general rule for verbs which predicts *runned*, on
the ground that the past tense of *run* cannot be *runned* and *ran* at the same
time. Similarly, if you already know that auxiliary verbs allow their
subjects to invert, then you ignore the proposition about verbs in
general which requires their subjects to precede them. We shall see this
principle applying at a great number of points in the grammar.

What the priority-to-the-instance principle means, of course, is that
some instances of a given model will be 'better' instances than others,
because some will conform to the model better than others do. Thus *stun*
is a more typical ('better') verb than *run*, because its inflections are
regular; auxiliary verbs are less typical than main verbs because they
override the regular rules for positioning subjects (*inter alia*); *enough* is a
less typical adverb than *sufficiently*, because *enough* is exceptional in
following the adjective that it modifies (*big enough*, not **enough big*); and
so on. We shall see later that the similarities to the 'prototype' view of
cognitive psychology are not coincidental, but for the present I shall just
point out the connections with the views of Lakoff on 'Linguistic
gestalts' (1977) and Ross on 'Non-discrete grammar' (e.g. 1973).

I am not suggesting that word grammar is the only kind of grammar
that can formalize irregularities, since that would be absurdly untrue.
However, I think word grammar compares favourably with other
theories in the manner in which it treats irregularities. Take a fairly
standard transformational treatment for an exception, which makes use
of 'rule features' to suppress the normal application of rules. This
implies that two different kinds of thing have to be learned: the normal
rule, and a rule feature. The word grammar treatment, in contrast,
requires the learner to learn two different instances of the same kind of
thing: the general pattern, and the specific pattern which overrides it.
Both patterns have the same status in the grammar, except that one is
attached to a more general entity than the other – e.g. both are
propositions about inflections, or about the position of the subject, or
whatever. My guess is that the word-grammar assumption is more
likely to be right.

As we shall see in the next subsection, the priority-to-the-instance
principle also covers a somewhat different range of phenomena, namely

cases where the normally expected properties of a word are overridden
by the requirements of the *context*. This is very common, of course. For
example, the final consonant of *in* can be assimilated to the consonant
at the start of the next word (compare *in bed, in front, in case*). This change
will be effected by a very general proposition, attached to the entity
'word', but taking account of the surroundings of the word. Of course,
this general rule cannot in itself take priority over the specific entry for
in, because that would be to turn the priority-to-the-instance principle
on its head. But the point is that the general rule only applies to *in* when
it is used in a particular context, which means that it applies not to *in*,
as represented in the grammar, but rather to an *instance* of *in*; so the
priority-to-the-instance principle comes into force, and the context
takes priority.

Since the priority-to-the-instance principle is just a condition on the
application of the inheritance-of-properties principle, we can merge
them into a single principle, the 'selective-inheritance principle':

(3)   *Selective Inheritance Principle*
    If I is an instance of M, then any proposition which applies to
    M must apply to I as well (with 'I' substituted in it for 'M'),
    provided this proposition does not contradict any proposition
        which is already known to apply to I.

This principle is not to be seen as part of the grammar for any
particular language for two reasons. One reason is that I assume it
applies to all languages, because I assume that all languages allow
lexical irregularities and contextual influence. On this assumption, the
relation between model and instance could not be otherwise than as
stated in the selective-inheritance principle, because this is the only way
in which deviations can be permitted. And of course I also assume that
all languages allow generalizations across words, so we must allow
instances to inherit properties of models because these are precisely the
contents of our generalizations. The second reason is that I shall try to
show on pp. 39 – 41 that the selective-inheritance principle is not
restricted to language, but applies to other things as well.

I take it that the selective-inheritance principle has some explanatory
value, since it brings together a very large number of different
phenomena under a single principle, and even allows a functional
explanation for this principle, as I have just suggested. I should like to
emphasize this claim, in order to balance the fact that I have denied so

many of the boundaries that linguists often refer to when they talk about 'explanations'.

How to find a model to inherit from

In the preceding subsection I concentrated on the relations between instances and their models within the grammar – i.e. within the stored knowledge about language that an individual has. I did occasionally mention the relations between uttered instances and their stored models, and these are what I want to focus on now. We shall take the point of view of a hearer, and ask how the hearer finds the right models for the things heard. I start, then, with the assumption that when we understand any part of our experience (and not just our linguistic experience), we do so by linking the particular experience to our stored knowledge, and analysing the former as a particular instance of parts of the latter. I think this assumption is uncontroversial. In the following, I shall have little to say about the particular mental processes which take place in the hearer's mind – this is the province of the psychologists. Rather, I shall suggest the general principles which control these processes.

Let us assume that the hearer approaches a particular utterance armed with a grammar for the language concerned, plus the selective-inheritance principle; and that they actually want to understand the utterance, with all this entails in terms of mental effort. The aim will be partially achieved once all the linguistic entities in the utterance have been linked, as instances, with stored linguistic entities; the other part of the operation will involve pragmatic inferencing which takes the hearer well beyond the stored knowledge of words and their parts. So we can present the hearer with three separate tasks:

(a)   decide which stored entity is the model for each perceived entity;
(b)   exploit the information in the stored entity, especially as regards its semantic and contextual implications;
(c)   draw any relevant conclusions from the output of the second operation.

These three tasks are intertwined in a complex way, as we all know, but I shall focus on the first one.

The problem for the hearer is that the known properties of the instance are never the same as those of its model. This is partly due to the fact that (by definition) the instance is more specific than its model, so more information is known about it (e.g. when and where it occurred, and in which linguistic context it occurred); so the hearer must select a particular subset of the observed properties, and then look for a model which has that subset of properties. However, even this is never possible, because some of the properties of the model cannot be matched by known properties of the instance, precisely because the referent of a word is not something which you can observe directly in the utterance. So all you know about the instance is its observable properties (and possibly even only a subset of them, if there is interference), plus some guesses as to what its referent might be.

A third problem for the hearer is that even the observable properties may not be reliable, because they may be deviant. This is an automatic consequence of the selective-inheritance principle, because this allows the normal properties of a word to be overridden by the requirements of the context, so the hearer may hear ɪn/, and have to work out that this is meant as an instance of ɪn/. Worse still, the part of the context which leads to the deviation may be non-linguistic, and not even covered by any specific stored information. For example, if I am at my dentist's, and he has his hand in my mouth, then any attempt by me to say *in* is likely to end up without any consonant at all, so the dentist, as hearer, has to make allowance for this deviance, and nevertheless allow my grunt to count as an instance of *in*.

The general principle seems to be that the hearer should maximize the benefits of the effort expended. For example, given that the hearer is aiming to understand what the speaker intends, then there is no point in following up a guess which is very unlikely to be the interpretation intended by the speaker. (Of course, there is always the possibility that the hearer may be looking for a quarrel and may actually try to look for unintended meanings; which goes to show that the processing of language is controlled by the intentions of the processor, and not just by automatic machinery in the hearer's head.)

In more specific terms, this general principle of maximizing benefits presumably means that the hearer takes as a model the stored entity which has most in common with the observed entity – that is, which shares the most propositions (after substituting the observed entity's name for the stored one's). This is the 'best fit' principle of Winograd 1976. When you hear a word which is not exactly the same in its pronunciation as any word already known to you, then you probably opt for the word to which it is most similar, taking account not only of its pronunciation but also of its guessed unobservable features. However, at this point we are entering the territory of experimental psychology, where a number of distinct hypotheses about processing could be formulated and tested. How long do you wait (in terms of microseconds, or in terms of information available) before you start to look for a model? How does the search proceed – by gradually narrowing down a range of possibilities, or by starting with a single guess, and then extending the search if the first guess draws a blank? Questions like this are of great interest, but well beyond my competence.

A THEORY OF UTTERANCE AND SENTENCE STRUCTURE
Sentence and utterance

It is orthodox in linguistics to make a distinction between 'sentences' and 'utterances', the former being 'types', and the latter 'tokens'. The same utterance can never occur twice, because every utterance is tied to some particular point in time, like any other event that happens. In contrast, the same sentence can 'occur' twice, in that it may be presented by two different utterances. Sentences are 'abstract' objects defined by grammars (in much the same way as our number system 'defines' the number 725), in contrast with utterances which are concrete, or at least specific and time-bound. This distinction is of course tied up with that between 'competence' and 'performance', since sentences are said to be in some sense 'constructs of' competence (Smith and Wilson 1979:287), while utterances belong to performance.

When put in such general terms, the contrast seems clear, but in practice it is like some of the other contrasts that we have considered: difficult to apply. ('It is important, but in practice exceedingly difficult, to maintain this distinction [between sentence and utterance] at all times in the study of meaning' – Levinson 1983:19) If we have a word with two meanings, does the sentence contain both of them, as alternatives, because the resolution of ambiguity is a matter of performance, or just one of them? How much phonetic detail should be specified in relation to the sentence? All assimilations? E.g. is there a sentence corresponding to *What's your name?*, in which the three consonants in the middle are collapsed into a single phonetic segment,

[c]?And what about intonation, absolute pitch, voice-quality, and the kind of phonetic detail and variation studied by Labovian sociolinguists? The problems are well known.

Another objection to the sentence/utterance distinction is that it is hard to see how it should apply if we take seriously the mentalist approach to language that many linguists accept (and which I too accept, as should be clear by now). If the aim of a linguist is to characterize the mental constructs involved in language, then two things follow. One is that the linguist is interested in utterances not so much as physical events, but rather as mental constructs that speakers and hearers produce as interpretations of these events. But which of these things should we call the 'utterance', from the linguist's point of view? If we say that the utterance is the event itself, then we are left without a name for the mental construct that counts as its interpretation, because we cannot call this a sentence on the ground that it is time-bound and evanescent. But if we use 'utterance' to refer to the mental construct, in what sense is this less abstract than the kind of thing which is called a sentence? Admittedly it is more specific, being tied to a particular time and place, but that is a different matter. A difference in specificity does not point to a categorical difference such as that usually assumed between sentences and utterances.

The second consequence of accepting the mentalist approach is that utterances and sentences both turn out to have the same status in relation to stored knowledge: neither of them is part of it, but both of them can be related to it by computation. The difference between them is just a matter of degree: how many steps in the computation are there between the contents of the mental grammar and the structure concerned? If we take as an example a slip of the tongue like *You've tasted the whole worm* for *You've wasted the whole term* (Clark and Clark 1977:275), then the thing said is an utterance, but the thing intended is (presumably) a sentence, and the latter is the link between the former and the grammar. But both the structures have to be worked out by the speaker and hearer, and the only difference between them is in the amount of calculation required.

My view of the sentence/utterance split is that it is neither useful nor definable, and should be ignored. Word grammar allows an alternative way of making the distinctions that this contrast was meant to make, but presents them as a continuum rather than a binary contrast. On the one hand, we have our stored knowledge, which we might reasonably call 'competence' (though I have many reservations about the distinction between what counts as linguistic competence and what does not – see pp. 31 – 41, 131 – 7 and Hudson 1980a). On the other, we have mental structures that people construct by referring to this competence, and which consist of parts each of which is an instance of some entity in competence. These mental entities differ from one another in two respects:

(a) They contain different amounts of information about non-linguistic context, so that a decontextualized example presented in a linguistics book has nothing but the most general information about the kinds of utterance-event in which it could occur, in contrast with a particular example on a particular occasion, where the utterance-event is fully specified.

(b) They contain parts which show different degrees of deviation from the stored norms, with spoonerisms and things said with the dentist's hand in one's mouth at or near one extreme of deviance.

Neither of the differences just mentioned allows a clear division between two categories which we could call 'sentence' and 'utterance'. Moreover, in both cases, the relation among the entities on the continuum defined is the same: instantiation, relating instances to their models. In one case, the differences reflect the fact that an instance is more specific than its model, and in the other they derive from the fact that an instance may deviate from its model. So even if we knew nothing about how language is actually used, we might predict, on the basis of the selective-inheritance principle, that both of these continua would exist. I see no advantage in going further, and imposing the distinction between 'sentence' and 'utterance' on these contrasts. Indeed, as a final shot I might add that I suspect there is a closer connection between the sentence/utterance contrast and the written/spoken contrast than many linguists recognize – writing being standard ('correct', 'normal'), permanent, decontextualized and neutral as to phonetic detail. It is interesting to notice that linguists have never seen a need to develop a name for written sentence-tokens ('written utterance' still sounds like a contradiction), and that they have rarely taken seriously the problems of identifying 'sentence' boundaries in spoken language (e.g. is *Go away I'm busy* one sentence or two? Matthews 1981:29).

Strings of words

In order to avoid making the distinction between sentence and utterance, we can refer simply to 'strings of words', or 'word-strings', and discuss in terms of them the issues which are elsewhere raised in connection with sentences. The most general question is, what is the nature of the structure that strings of words have? To focus the following discussion, we should recall the kind of answer which would be given in terms of transformational grammar: a string of words is structured on several different levels (phonology, syntax, etc.), and the way a grammar defines its total structure is to define a derivation, or ordered set of structures, with at least one structure for each level (and, as of 1981, at least three structures for syntax; Logical form, D-structure and S-structure: Chomsky 1981:29). Furthermore, each of the structures generated has the form of a phrase-marker, and there is a great deal of overlap between different structures in terms of the labels that are attached to nodes (e.g. all the syntactic structures include labels also found in the phonological structures, because these are introduced by lexical insertion).

The structures generated for word-strings by a word grammar are different from a transformational 'derivation' in ways that parallel the differences between the two types of grammar. We have already seen that a word occurring in a word-string must be taken as an instance of some word contained in the grammar (and likewise for entities other than words, *mutatis mutandis*), and that the properties of the word in the word-string are simply a copy of those of the stored word, plus some extra properties (and possibly some deviations). It therefore follows that the structure assigned to a word-string has the same kinds of characteristic as we find in the parts of the grammar from which the structures are inherited; and since the grammar as a whole is a network, this must also be true of the structure of a word-string. More specifically, it must be a network of entities connected by propositions, and the propositions concerned must be propositions of the types which I listed earlier (on pp. 8 – 12). Furthermore, each word in the string is itself taken as an instance of some model in the grammar, and this relation is expressed by the 'model(x): y' type of formula, which is itself part of the network; so the structure which we generate for a string of words is not only similar to the structures found in the grammar network, but it is in fact linked into this network by the instantiation connections, and the two structures can be part of one big network, whose 'edges' are made up of more or less transitory instances. The fact that our grammars change through time shows that the boundary between the permanent store and the transitory periphery is permeable.

Take as a simple example the word-string *Balloons pop*. The first word is an instance of the word *balloon* as contained in the grammar, but since it is a different entity from its model, it must have a different name. The convention I shall use is to name words in a word-string by giving each one a number, with the numbers increasing through the string. In contrast, we can use the written form *balloon* as the name of the corresponding stored entity, and similarly for the stored entity *pop*. (I have already applied this convention, in fact, in the structures (3) and (4) on pp. 9 and 10.) Diagrammatically, then:

(1)

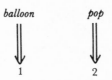

To expand the connections one step, we can add the fact that words 1 and 2 are not only instances of their respective lexemes, but also instances of the inflectional classes 'plural' and 'present', respectively:

(2)

This diagram shows that 1 is an instance of plural and of *balloon*, so by the selective-inheritance principle it must combine the properties of both of these models – the 'lexical' information from *balloon*, plus the 'grammatical' information from 'plural'; and similarly for 2 in relation to *pop* and 'present'. (You may find it helpful to think of the double arrow which I use for linking instances to models as a channel through which properties flow, in the direction of the arrow-point.)

Now we can show that the instantiation relation between the uttered words (1 and 2) and their models is just a continuation of the hierarchy of instantiation round which the whole grammar is built. Both *balloon*

and 'plural' are instances of 'noun', and *pop* and 'present' are instances
of 'verb':

(3)

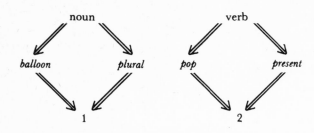

Furthermore, each of the two general word-types is an instance of
'word', so by adding these links to the diagram, we tie it all together,
and show at a very elementary level the skeleton on which the rest of the
grammar will be built.

(4)

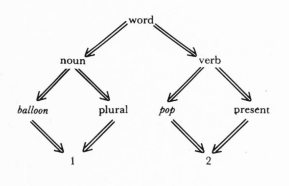

Inherited properties

We can now flesh out the example a little by showing how, in practice,
the mechanics of property-inheritance work. One mechanical point is
that the properties which are inherited by an instance are not technically
the same as the corresponding properties of the model, for the obvious
reason that properties are expressed as propositions, and a proposition
about the model is distinct from a proposition about the instance. So we
have an automatic change to make in any proposition that is inherited,
whereby the name of the model is replaced wherever it occurs by the
name of the instance. For instance, if we assume that one of the
properties of 'word' is that 'referent(word): word*', then this property
can be inherited by 'noun' as 'referent(noun): noun*', and by *balloon* as
'referent (*balloon*): balloon*', and so on. Everything else in an inherited

proposition stays the same. Suppose, for example, that we specify the referent of *balloon* (i.e. balloon*) as an instance of the general non-linguistic prototype BALLOON; this condition on the referent of *balloon* will automatically carry over to the referent of 1 as well, so this will also have to be an instance of BALLOON.

An interesting and important question arises if we assume this mechanical copying of propositions with minimal changes. If we want our grammar to mirror the structure of the speaker/hearer's knowledge (as I do), then we need to know which of two assumptions is correct: that inherited properties are calculated each time they are needed, or that they are calculated as soon as they are available for calculation, and then stored. For example, the diagram in (4) implies that inherited properties are calculated rather than stored, because it shows that *balloon* is an instance of 'noun', but not of 'word'. If inherited properties were stored, as properties of the inheriting instance, then *balloon* would indeed be shown as an instance of 'word', because this is one of the properties which it would inherit from 'noun'.

The question is familiar to linguists from discussions of the nature of redundancy rules. The currently standard view, I think, is that of Jackendoff (1975), according to which all redundant information is fully specified in the lexicon, for each lexical item concerned, so the redundancy rule simply picks out the generalization which makes this information redundant. If we were to extend this approach to word grammar, then the more general entries would act as redundancy rules picking out generalizations about information which is already fully specified in relation to less general entries (viz., the inherited properties). In contrast, it was earlier thought that redundancy rules make information available about particular lexical items which would *not* otherwise be available, from their respective lexical entries.

I take it that the question is ultimately an empirical one, and we are concerned here with two different claims regarding the structure of linguistic knowledge. On the other hand, I think we are still a very long way indeed from being able to answer the question, either in general or in relation to particular items of information. Each position seems plausible in relation to a different range of facts.

We could argue for the ready-stored redundant information on the ground that some regular (and therefore redundant) information about inflectional morphology could easily be stored in relation to particularly common lexical items; for example, after you have calculated for the thousandth time that *played* is the past tense of *play*, it must be at least tempting to store this fact away for future use. Moreover, when you learn a new lexeme, you must learn it in one of its particular inflected forms, so it is at least possible that you store this form as well as any information you have derived from it about the root of the lexeme. Though neither of these observations counts as evidence, at least they show that the ready-stored information view is plausible.

At the same time, we could show that the other view is plausible too, by pointing out that we probably would not bother to work out a particular inflected form of a new lexeme until we actually needed it. Moreover, we can be sure that at least one set of inherited properties are calculated and not stored, namely those of uttered words. Such words are (by definition) not stored, so their properties must be calculated. At least some experimental evidence seems to support the claim that some inflected forms are calculated (e.g. Mackay 1974), though alternative interpretations could be put on the results. Similarly, inherited information about non-linguistic entities has been shown to take longer to retrieve than non-inherited, idiosyncratic, information (Collins and Quillian 1969), so it would be surprising if the same were not true of language too.

The only reasonable conclusion seems to be that some predictable information is stored, and some is not; and at present we are not in a position to decide which is which (a similar conclusion is expressed in McCawley 1977). This leaves the linguist in a difficult position, as a searcher after psychological reality, but life (and linguistics) must go on, so I shall assume the *minimum* of storage, as a general policy. As far as psychological reality is concerned, then, my grammars will provide a base-line below which we must assume that mature speakers of the variety concerned will not sink. However, even this is too much to take for granted, in a sense, because I shall assume the *maximum* of generalization: i.e. any generalization that I can spot, I shall include in my grammar by means of a general entry, meaning that the information provided by the generalization will not be provided by the more specific entries which it covers. For example, I shall assume that there is a general category of 'auxiliary verb', to which various bits of information are attached which are true of the individual auxiliary verbs. But it would be quite possible to speak English fluently without ever having made this generalization in one's grammar, but having learned all the right facts about the individual verbs. So for such speakers, my grammar is predicting less stored information than they actually have in their heads.

In spite of these difficulties and uncertainties, the following principle can be extracted from my practice (and from that of many other linguists, I think):

The Linguist's Economy Principle
Never record any property more than once in relation to any entity.

That is, once you (the linguist) have decided there is a generalization to be made, you make it in relation to the relevant general category (e.g. 'auxiliary verb'), and then suppress any mention of it in more specific entries which can inherit the information from the general one. I think the grammar that a linguist produces should then at least help to define the limits within which actual competence grammars can be located, though we cannot make more specific empirical predictions.

When we apply this principle to the grammar fragment for *Balloons pop*, we can supplement the skeleton which I gave earlier (see p. 26) by adding properties to the entities.

(2)

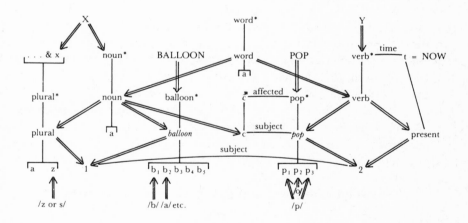

By applying the selective-inheritance principle to this diagram, we can calculate that the word-string consisting of *Balloons pop* has the following structure, in addition to the structure of its particular utterance-event (which I have ignored). I hope it is clear by now that the structure for *Balloons pop* is just an expansion of part of the grammar network given in (2), with the predictable properties added to 1 and 2.

(3)

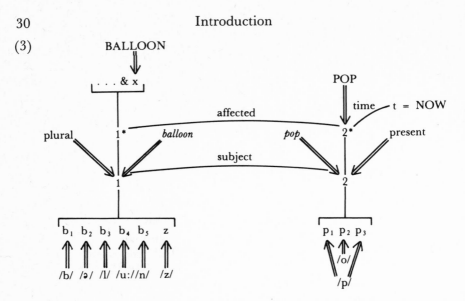

One final point about the way in which properties are inherited. It will be seen from (2) and (3) that the words 1 and 2 are linked to one another in two ways. First there is what we might call their 'stored' relations, as shown in the grammar. One such relation is what would traditionally be called their 'paradigmatic' relation, reflected in the instantiation hierarchy (they are both instances, ultimately, of words). Another is the relation shown between *pop* and the category 'noun', via the former's subject (named c in (2)); in prose, the grammar says that *pop* takes as subject a word which is an instance of 'noun'. We might call this a 'stored syntagmatic' relation. Apart from their stored relations, however, there are temporary relations, between 1 and 2 as such, in that 1 is shown as the subject of 2. This relation is just a particular instantiation of the general, stored, relation between *pop* and whatever its subject is.

The important consequence of seeing the relations between uttered words in this way is that we can then take the structure of a whole uttered string of words as nothing but the sum of the structures of the individual words. After all, according to word grammar the structure of a word is a set of propositions, and these propositions include some which refer to co-occurring words (what I called 'companions'). So once we have given a full list of the propositions that refer to all the words in a particular string, there is nothing else to add about the structure of that string. In other words, as already mentioned on pp. 6 – 7, according to word grammar the structure of a string of words need not make reference to any units larger than words – phrases, clauses or sentences. This is a controversial claim, which will receive the discussion that it deserves in chapter 3.

To summarize the word grammar theory of utterance and sentence structure, my position is as follows:

(4)   The structure of an uttered word W is a set of propositions inherited from the stored word(s) of which W is an instance.

(5)   This structure includes instantiation links between W and the stored grammar, so the structure of W forms part of a total network of entities linked by propositions, in which some of the entities are relatively permanent, and others (such as W) are relatively temporary.

(6)   In view of (4) and (5), no distinction need be drawn between the properties of uttered words and those of stored words.

(7)   The structure of an uttered word-string is the sum of the structures of the words in the string.

A THEORY OF LANGUAGE AS A MENTAL PHENOMENON
Language as a mental phenomenon

Throughout the discussion so far, I have been taking it for granted that language is a mental phenomenon – a kind of knowledge, plus the exploitation of this knowledge in behaviour. Some linguists object to linguistic discussions with a mentalist bias, on the grounds that linguists should concentrate on studying the patterns in 'language itself', and leave it to the psychologists to take over from us when we have worked out the linguistic structures whose psychological properties need to be investigated. I have some sympathy with such a view to the extent that it is based on a distrust of linguists who are misled by vague psychological theories (e.g. those about connections between the structure of a language and the national temperament of its speakers), but I should like to present here some reasons why we should view language as a mental phenomenon.

(a) Language is a property of the *individual*. If you want to find out the facts of an unanalysed language, you must find an individual who knows that language, because the facts only 'exist' in the minds of individuals, and if all the individuals who know the language die, then the language 'dies' with them. Furthermore, if you find two individuals who speak 'the same' language, you are certain to find differences between them if you push the analysis far enough (Ferguson 1979); once again, this is due to the fact that language is a property of the individual (the result of each individual's observations of their unique experience of language). Putting it crudely, the place where you look for the data of linguistics is in the individual human being (in contrast with, say, meteorological data, which you look for in the sky, and geological data, which are in the ground).

This view contrasts with the traditional view that language is a property of the community (against which I have argued on sociolinguistic grounds in Hudson 1980a: 25, 183). I strongly suspect that this view arises at least in part from the fact that our professional ancestors spent two thousand years writing grammars for standard languages, which are a rather special kind of language in that one could reasonably take them as a property of a community. This is precisely because the community (or a section of it) interferes in a fairly conscious way in the normal linguistic processes, and creates a variety which is relatively immune to individual variation because it is codified (in dictionaries and grammars), taught explicitly in schools, and published. Most languages are not 'fixed' in this way, and it would be quite wrong to build a general theory of language on the assumption that standard languages are typical. The normal pattern is for each individual to learn their language from their particular network of friends and relations, and to try hard to make their own language as similar as possible to these models (if need be, by learning different languages or varieties for use with different groups). Larger aggregates, whether linguistic ('language X', 'dialect X', 'register X') or social ('speech community X') are popular fictions, and not categories which are sufficiently clear to be used by linguists in their analysis. (I have argued this case in Hudson 1980a, chapter 2.)

In relation to the goals of transformational linguistics, as defined by Chomsky, I am partly in agreement and partly not. The part I agree with is the aim of studying individuals and building a general theory of the structure of the individual's knowledge of language. What I reject, on the other hand, is the apparent attempt to have it both ways, by preserving the belief that language is a property of the community. In Chomsky's famous definition of the goals of linguistic theory (1965:3), he refers to the notion of 'an ideal speaker – listener, in a completely

homogeneous speech-community, who knows its language perfectly
. . .'. What does it mean to know the language of one's speech
community perfectly? Surely we all know our own language (in the sense
of idiolects) perfectly, by definition? And why assume there is such a
thing as a speech community which has a language (as its communal
property)? If one accepts the view that language is a property of the
individual and *not* of some putative community, then all the reference to
speech communities could have been omitted from Chomsky's
definition of linguistic theory, and the prescriptive overtones of the
existing definition would disappear.

An advantage for the linguist of taking language as a property of
individuals is that it puts individual differences into a much healthier
perspective. If you think a language is a property of a community, then
it comes as something of a disappointment to discover that individuals
differ. These differences figure in one's thinking as a problem and a
source of discomfort, because one imagines the language to be a single
homogeneous structure for the whole community. On the other hand,
individual differences are in no sense problematic if you see each
'language' as the property of one individual. On the contrary,
interesting questions then arise as to the relations among individuals
and their grammars, which can be pursued by those interested in such
things (sociolinguists, historical linguists, social psychologists, students
of language acquisition, etc.).

The relevance of this discussion of individuals and communities is
that individuals have minds, but communities do not (at least, I do not
believe they do, nor do most of my colleagues). Accordingly, it makes
no sense to advocate a mentalist approach to language if language is a
property of a community, but it is a very reasonable suggestion for those
who see language in relation to individuals, because one can then take
the next step, which is to say that a language is a property of the
individual's mind.

(b) The data of linguistic analysis includes *judgements* (regarding
grammaticality, or degree of formality, or naughtiness, or synonymy,
or whatever). It makes no difference in principle whether these
judgements are our own or those of an informant, or whether we use
them on their own or to supplement recordings of spontaneous speech.
Moreover, the judgements may lead to an analysis which conflicts with
whatever can be observed more directly, and in at least some such cases
we would give priority to the judgements as data on which to build our
theories. One fact is that every individual is capable of making mistakes

(in relation to their own grammar, of course – I have already excluded 'community grammars' and standard languages from consideration); and a second fact is that most linguists are concerned to study the system underlying actual speech, so they would want to distinguish errors from other cases. But it is only if you have a supply of judgements at hand that you can do this.

The need for judgements regarding the deviance of spontaneous speech arises naturally from the theory of word grammar, since the possibility of deviance is inherent in the system. The linguist hearing a particular form used would always need to know whether this form is a direct copy of the model on which it is based, or whether it is deviant in some respect, and such information can best be supplied by comments from an informant (preferably the speaker themself). What I have been describing is normal practice among descriptive linguists, but it rests firmly on the assumption that the patterns we want to analyse are those that the speaker knows, and which (we hope) are reflected in their judgements, and that the observation of natural speech is only one way of gaining access to this knowledge.

If judgements are essential in the study of forms (which can be observed), how much more essential are they in the study of meanings (which cannot). Of course, we can guess what a speaker means by an expression, and this is indeed how we learn most of our meanings, but we always face the danger of being wrong, and the linguist deprived of judgements runs the same risk, in this respect, as the ordinary speaker/hearer/learner. It has been observed that we are likely to be much less aware of differences in meaning than of differences in form, precisely because we can easily guess wrongly (see for instance Labov's discussion of the terms *mother-wit* and *common-sense*, 1972:118), so linguists must always beware of imposing their own interpretation on observed speech.

(c) The study of meaning is inseparable from the study of individual *knowledge of the world*. This claim is fundamental to word grammar, and I shall discuss it more fully below (especially in chapter 4), but it does not depend on arguments internal to the theory of word grammar. One argument is that it is very hard in practice to distinguish between 'dictionary meaning' and 'encyclopaedic meaning', and although a great many scholars take this distinction for granted, none of them has been able to justify it to my satisfaction. (See Haiman 1980 for a good critical discussion.) As with the other boundaries that I have discussed, we need to be sure that we are not on a wild-goose chase before building this one into our thinking, and my opinion is that we are indeed on a wild-goose chase.

Another argument is that we cannot assume that there is some 'community' norm for the meanings of linguistic expressions, which we could take as the linguistic meaning, leaving other parts of meaning to vary from individual to individual. To make this assumption seems to involve a very prescriptive view of language (such as I have already rejected), and in any case there is no empirical support for it. (Just consider the meanings of words like *rule* and *system* among linguists; is there a single 'true' community meaning for these words, and if so, how could we find it?)

In a sense, the argument that world-knowledge is inseparable from meaning is a continuation of the previous argument, that judgements are essential data in linguistic analysis. What I am claiming is that you cannot study the meaning of an expression unless you know how it is taken by the particular individual whose language you are studying, so presumably that individual's judgements are crucial data. However, I am also going further than when I made the general point about judgements, because I am claiming now that the judgements will tell us specifically how the expressions concerned relate to other parts of the informant's *knowledge*. For example, if we wanted to know exactly what the verb *pop* meant, for a particular person, we should be exploring the relations between that word and the structure of the person's knowledge of events. Moreover, we might find that the relevant facts were somewhat imprecise (e.g. I am not sure quite what I do mean by *pop*, though I could supply examples of typical instances), but the linguistic analysis should reflect this vagueness faithfully if it is to avoid prescriptivism. Any theory which tries to analyse meanings without reference to meaners is (in my view) doomed to circularity, prescriptivism or failure.

I shall now take it for granted, then, that when we are studying language we are studying a mental phenomenon, and that the observable data that we use (spontaneous speech and judgements) are just clues to the structures that we really want to model, which are mental structures.

The uniqueness of language

If language is a mental phenomenon, then we must inquire into its relations to other mental phenomena. In particular, how similar is the structure of language to the structures of other types of knowledge? Two radically different views can be found among linguists (apart from the view that the question is either uninteresting or unresearchable). The Chomskyan view is that language is sufficiently distinct in its structure to be referred to as a separate mental 'organ', and because of this assumption there is very little attempt, in Chomskyan linguistics, to find or exploit similarities between linguistic and non-linguistic knowledge. In contrast, some linguists are attracted to emphasize the similarities between language and non-language (e.g. George Lakoff writes (1977): 'For me the most interesting results in linguistics would be those showing how language is related to other aspects of our being human'). It is interesting to speculate about why linguists choose one or the other of these positions, and it may well be that personal temperament counts for as much as academic arguments. It is probably clear by now that I sympathize with Lakoff more than with Chomsky on this issue, but I hope that word grammar will allow us to investigate it more fruitfully than has been possible hitherto.

The question is where the onus of proof lies, on those who believe language is different from non-language, or on those who believe it is similar. I think the answer must be that it lies with the advocates of differences, provided we can assume that language is an instance of knowledge. Conveniently, this assumption is not at issue, since Chomskyan linguists (including Chomsky, of course) accept it. But if two things are both instances of a single category (e.g. 'knowledge'), then we can (and do) assume that both of them share all the properties of this common model – after all, that is simply a generalization of the principles which I discussed in connection with linguistic models. There must of course be some difference between the two related things, otherwise they would not be distinct, but we need not assume any differences beyond those which lead us to distinguish them in the first place.

Applied to linguistic and non-linguistic knowledge, this argument means that we should start by assuming that the two have the same properties, except for whatever distinguishes 'linguistic' from 'non-linguistic' by our definition of these terms. We have assumed so far that 'linguistic' knowledge is knowledge of 'linguistic' entities, and linguistic entities (according to pp. 4 – 7) are words or their parts. So we can say that non-linguistic knowledge is any other kind of knowledge. Given this definition of the categories, then, we should assume that there is *no* difference between linguistic and non-linguistic knowledge, beyond the fact that one is to do with words and the other is not.

This is what we should take as our null hypothesis, and if there really are further differences between the two kinds of knowledge, then we can refute the null hypothesis by discovering them. But oddly enough, those who argue that language is unique have not taken this approach. Instead, they have assumed uniqueness, and written their grammars accordingly. The evidence for uniqueness then consists of the various peculiar characteristics that these grammars have, and which are hard to parallel outside language. Clearly, we cannot draw any conclusions from the discovery that it is possible to analyse language in a way that makes it look unique. What we need is evidence that it is *not* possible to analyse language in a way that makes it look like everything else. But since advocates of uniqueness have not tried to argue in this way, the best we can say is that the debate will be interesting when they do, but it has not yet started.

Word grammar and structures outside language

The relevance of all this to word grammar is that this theory generalizes beyond language, and allows us to analyse language structure as a particular case of knowledge structure. I shall now justify this claim, starting with non-linguistic structures that are used as meanings. There was a time when many linguists would have agreed with Ferdinand de Saussure (1916/1959:111):

> Psychologically our thought – apart from its expression in words – is only a shapeless and indistinct mass. Philosophers and linguists have always agreed in recognising that without the help of signs we would be unable to make a clear-cut, consistent distinction between two ideas. Without language, thought is a vague, uncharted nebula. There are no pre-existing ideas, and nothing is distinct before the appearance of language.

In contrast, many linguists would now agree (as I do) with Jackendoff (1978:203): 'the theory of semantics of a natural language is simply a subpart of the general theory of conceptual structure; the well-formedness rules for semantics are a subset of those for concepts; and the semantic structures derived from projection rules are a particular class of concepts.' I gave reasons above for accepting this view of the relation between meanings and concepts (see p. 34), so I will not go into the matter again. The conclusion, then, is that the semantic structures which a word grammar generates are not only similar to general conceptual structures, but they are *instances* of such structures. (For further discussion, see pp. 131 – 61.)

What about the structures which we generate for words themselves, and the machinery by which they are generated? We listed five types of propositions which can refer to linguistic entities (pp. 7 – 12): composition, model, companion, referent, utterance-event. In addition we recognized the elementary proposition types 'identity' and 'order', or 'inequality'. Can such concepts refer to non-linguistic entities? If we find a concept-type that is restricted to referring to words, this would be evidence for a general structural uniqueness in language. Let us consider them one at a time.

Identity is very common between non-linguistic entities – for example, when we discover that the postman and the scoutmaster are in fact one and the same person, we link the relevant names in our minds by the 'identity' proposition. Similarly for partial identity – if for example we try to imagine to ourselves what a well-known face would look like with the hair done differently. *Order* is equally common – wherever two events are related in time in our minds, we are invoking the 'order' proposition, and its generalization to any 'inequality' occurs whenever we know which of two entities is the bigger. So the elementary proposition types are certainly not unique to language.

Composition is the relation between any whole and its parts, so 'composition (x): y' could have x standing for a bicycle and y for its parts, and so on. *Model* is the relation between an instance and its model, so the x and y in 'model(x): y' could stand for 'bicycle' and 'my bicycle' respectively (or for 'my bicycle' and 'my bicycle today', respectively, where the latter entity is specified for position, having a flat tyre, and so on).

Companion links two things which co-occur, e.g. thunder and lightning, the lady next door and her dog, house and dustbin. The relations between the co-occurring things can be of various types, of course, and there are two which are of particular importance in language (see chapter 3): the asymmetrical relation called 'dependency', between 'heads' and their 'modifiers', and the relation between a subject and its predicate. As Chomsky has observed (1981:10) it is unlikely that we shall be able to find non-linguistic examples of the 'subject' relation, although it is certainly worth looking hard for them; but dependency relations are common outside language, in much the same sense as they have when applied to language. For example, a dustbin depends on a house in much the same way as an adjective depends on a noun (you do not expect a dustbin without a house, and the dustbin is located in relation to a house, not vice versa).

We are left just with *referent* and *utterance-event* for which to find non-linguistic uses. If we take our definition of 'linguistic entity' seriously, then this should be easy, because we can go outside the realm of words into other semiotic systems. If we assume that the word *yes* has a referent, then a nod of the head must have one too; and if the word *three* does, so does a gesture with three fingers held up. Similarly, if the word *Cheerio!* is tied to a particular kind of utterance-event (and a particular occurrence of it is tied to a particular utterance-event), then the same must be true of a wave of the hand. (There is a little more discussion of similarities between linguistic and non-linguistic behaviour in Hudson 1980a:134) At the very least there is a prima-facie case for claiming that neither 'referent' nor 'utterance-event' is tied exclusively to words.

Models and prototypes

Another place where we could look for features unique to language would be in the principles governing the use of models (see pp. 14 – 21). We have seen that the structure of language is based on a skeleton of relations between instances and their models, and that the properties of the model are 'selectively inherited' by their instances. Is the same true of non-linguistic entities? Clearly it is. Evidence (if evidence were needed for something so self-evident) comes from the research on prototypes by Rosch (e.g. 1976) and her associates, and also a great deal of other work done by cognitive scientists (e.g. Schank and Abelson 1977). A robin is an instance of a bird, and is a less deviant instance than a penguin; moreover, we might deduce from the knowledge that penguins are birds the conclusion that they must lay eggs (though I for one have never seen a penguin egg, let alone a penguin laying an egg). Furthermore, we can have deviant robins, and even deviant instances of particular robins. The similarities to the relations among linguistic entities are obvious. (I shall point out another such set of similarities between language and non-language on p. 100.)

I have not applied the term 'prototype' to the entities in word-grammar structures because I prefer not to make the identification too close. For one thing, those who discuss prototypes include some people who believe that some concepts are prototypes, and others are not, the difference being reflected in the internal structures of the concepts concerned (e.g. Pulman 1983:151). In contrast, for me entities all have the same status in this respect, and the 'fuzziness' of a prototype-based concept lies not in its internal structure but rather in the deviations which the world allows between it and its instances. Where a lot of deviation is possible, there will be a lot of fuzziness, and it may be that the amount of deviation possible depends on the number of distinct properties that each entity has, and on the extent to which these are in fact independent of each other.

Another difference between the entities of word grammar and prototypes is that prototypes are generally distinguished from the categories to which they belong; thus the prototypical bird (e.g. a robin) is a member of the category 'bird'. In contrast, I have avoided distinguishing between categories and their members, for reasons that I explained in connection with *run* and 'verb' on p. 15. (The views of Rosch on this matter are explained clearly by Pulman 1983:150.)

A third difference is that some psychologists distinguish between 'prototypes' and 'schemata', the latter being less completely specified than the former (J.R. Anderson 1980:133). For example, a prototypical bird might be specified in all respects as a robin, with all the properties of robins, whereas a schema for 'bird' would leave some properties unspecified. The entities of word grammar are certainly schemata, and not prototypes, in this respect, because models always have fewer properties than their instances.

Finally, there is a difference in relation to the notion of 'family resemblances', which are problematic for prototype theory (e.g. Pulman 1983:105). The problem is that some entities seem to be applicable to a range of instances which have no properties in common at all (e.g. what do all instances of furniture have in common? or all games?). If a prototype is defined by shared features, how can 'furniture' or 'game' be a prototype? In word grammar, there is only one problem, namely how to choose between the two alternative analyses of such cases.

One analysis says that there is indeed one property which is shared by all instances of furniture, namely the fact that you can apply the word *furniture* to them. This analysis puts the relations between, say, tables and cupboards on all fours with the relations between the horn of a cow and the hooter of a car: if it were not for the shared word, there would be no reason for linking them. But the word exists, and they are linked. In other words, 'family resemblances' are just a special case of what is traditionally called polysemy.

The other analysis exploits the fact that properties may be overridden, and that this applies to *all* properties, there being no distinction between 'defining' or 'essential' properties and others. This being so, there is nothing to stop us from taking all the properties of all the instances of a 'family resemblances' case, and combining them into a set of properties (linked by 'or' as well as by 'and') for the model. For example, we might take the properties of furniture to include 'for sitting on' or 'for keeping things in'; and we might even include 'made of wood', without mentioning other possibilities, and leave it to the entries for particular instances to override this property where necessary. And of course we could in fact combine the two analyses by including among the properties of furniture the fact that it can be called *furniture*.

In conclusion, then, the phenomena which led to the development of prototype theory can be accommodated by a theory based on the relations between instances and their models such as the one assumed in word grammar. But this theory avoids some of the problems that arise for prototype theory as such.

Conclusions

Word grammar should be seen as part of a more general theory of knowledge structure, at least part of which is already widely accepted by psychologists and linguists. Most generally, the whole of knowledge is a network of entities related by propositions (a generalization of the definition of language which I gave on p. 1). For this view, compare the following passage from Clark and Haviland (1977): 'the listener represents the content of conversations, as well as other knowledge, in a relative permanent memory. This knowledge consists of a set of propositions interrelated by indices which show which propositions are embedded in which, which entities are identical, and so on.' Similarly, it is now widely accepted that knowledge is represented in an abstract code, such as could be represented in terms of propositions; J.R. Anderson (1980:123) describes this discovery as 'one of the major accomplishments of modern cognitive psychology'.

I have shown that the knowledge which we call 'linguistic' is also exploited in rather similar ways to the way in which we exploit non-linguistic knowledge, at least as far as the use of models is concerned. This conclusion is supported by a great deal of reputable linguistic opinion – for example, Bierwisch (1981) points out the similarities between the errors we make in speaking and those we make in other kinds of activity. Furthermore, linguistic and non-linguistic knowledge can interfere with one another in speaking, as witness what Cutler calls 'environmental contamination' (1981) – e.g. if I mean to say the word *ruler* but say *ribbon* instead because I am looking into a drawer full of typewriter ribbons. And of course linguistic entities are closely connected with non-linguistic ones which serve as their referents.

Where do these conclusions leave our original question about the uniqueness of language? In some respects, we have already pushed the discussion forward (to the extent that the conclusions are valid), by showing that there are considerable similarities between language and non-language, so it certainly cannot be the case that *everything* in language is unique. However, we have also improved our chances of discovering whatever traits of language are unique by providing a common analytical framework for linguistic and non-linguistic knowledge. It would clearly be hopeless to look for points of comparison where there was no way of deciding what was comparable with what; but we can now ask some quite specific questions (e.g. are any of the specific instances of the 'companion' proposition unique to language – the 'subject' relation, for example?). Moreover, I think the rules of the game are a little clearer, if my suggestion is accepted that language and non-language be assumed to have similar structures until differences are proved.

I hope to show that word grammar leads to positive and productive work on language, and is not just a matter of pulling down familiar partitions (though this is certainly part of what the theory leads to). So I should like to dissociate word grammar from the kind of linguistic research which 'has been guided by the belief that the system is fairly chaotic, or that language is so intertwined with other aspects of knowledge and belief that it is a mistake even to try to isolate a faculty of language for separate study' (Chomsky 1981:14). We should certainly try to find properties unique to language, but we may fail, and if we fail then we can claim to have made a most significant discovery: that language is as it is just because it is an instance of knowledge, and that is the way knowledge in general is.

2

Morphology and Lexical Relations

MORPHOLOGY AND SYNTAX

Affixes and models

This chapter will be concerned with what I called above the paradigmatic relations among words – relations they have irrespective of whether or not they occur in the same sentence. The first two sections concentrate on morphological relations, and in the third the discussion broadens out to bring in other relations as well. By 'morphological' relations I mean those which involve the internal composition of the related words, and we shall have to discuss not only affixation but also other less straightforward types of relation. To start with, however, we can pretend that the only way in which words may be morphologically related is by virtue of the presence or absence of affixes.

I think it is widely accepted among linguists nowadays that the analysis of a word in terms of affixes and roots – what I call its morphological analysis – is separate from its analysis in terms of syntactic categories or semantic categories. The following discussion will rest on this assumption, so I shall briefly explain why we need to accept it.

(a) In some cases, the morphological analysis may bear no relation at all to either of the other two analyses. A particularly clear case is the word *understand*. It seems very reasonable to assume that some speakers are aware of the relation between *understand* and *stand* – indeed, I for one am certainly aware of it, and so are you – so we must at least allow ourselves to show this morphological relation. But it seems to be nothing but a morphological relation, since there is no corresponding connection between the meanings of the two words (such that we could, for example, say that the meaning of *stand* is included in that of *understand*), nor is there anything in their respective syntactic structures to show any more connection between them than there is, for example, between *stand* and *comprehend*. The network for this part of the grammar will therefore be the following:

(1)

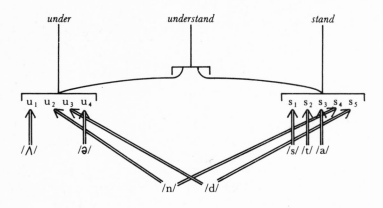

The point about this diagram is that there are *no* connections between the morphemes *under* and *stand* into which I have divided *understand*, and anything else in the structure of this word. Nor are there any links between *understand* and the other two words, except for the morphological links.

(b) Even where an affix can be related to some syntactic or semantic category, this relation need not be a simple one: the same affix may be related to more than one category, as alternatives (e.g. *-s* in English is related either to 'plural' or to 'present'); an affix may be related to a bundle of syntactic categories (as in typical inflecting languages); words of the same syntactic category may differ as to whether or not they contain a particular affix (e.g. the past tenses of *pit* and *put* differ with respect to the suffix *-ed*); and so on. The discrepancies between morphological and syntactic (or semantic) analyses are well known, and point fairly uncontroversially to some version of the 'word-and-paradigm' analysis advocated by linguists such as Matthews (1974) and S.R. Anderson (1977).

Having shown that there is no necessary connection between morphological structure and other properties, the fact remains that often there is a connection, however complex. How are these connections to be shown in a word grammar? We have just seen, in connection with *understand*, that morphological structure is shown in the 'composition' property, whereas the other properties are distributed through various other properties, so we have to find a means to bring these various properties together.

Let us start with the regular singular/plural contrast in English nouns, where we have to relate the -s suffix to the syntactic feature 'plural' and to the semantic structure for a plural noun. I have made no mention of syntactic features so far in my explanation of word grammar, because we do not need them as a part of the theory. Instead, we make use of the relation between instances and their models, which we have already seen to apply to the relation between subclasses and classes. The relation between 'plural' and 'noun' is thus that between an instance and its model, just like the relation between 'noun' and 'word', and parallel to the relation between *boy* and 'noun'. (For example, in the analysis of *balloons* on p. 26, I showed *balloons* as an instance of *balloon* and also of 'plural', and the latter two are both instances of 'noun'.) Thus, where other linguists would say '*balloons* has the feature [plural], I would say '*balloons* is an instance of (the entity) ''plural'',' and where others would say '[plural] represents a subcategorization of N (or [noun])', I would say '(The entity) ''plural'' is an instance of (the entity) ''noun''.'

One of the attractions of this kind of treatment is that it reflects our feeling that a plural noun is a kind of deviation from the normal, or unmarked, state of a noun. We can show the normal pattern for both morphology and semantics in relation to the 'noun' entity, and let 'plural' introduce some special deviations. Indeed it is possible that we could go further, by not distinguishing the singular from the noun itself. That is, we should replace the 'singular/plural' distinction by a privative opposition between 'plural' (a special kind of deviation from the norm) and normal. The only thing that would prevent us from adopting this analysis would be a rule which had to refer to the category 'singular', to the exclusion of 'plural'. We could not formulate such a rule simply in relation to 'noun', because there would be no way to prevent 'noun' from being instantiated as 'plural'. So far as I know, there are no such rules in English, and I shall formulate the grammar accordingly.

The plural is 'marked', then, with respect to its morphological structure, in that its morphological structure includes that of the lexeme (viz., the root). However, this morphological markedness is also paralleled in the semantic structure, because I assume that the plural noun refers to a set whose members individually count as instances of the same model as the singular. In the little grammar on p. 29 I gave a semantic analysis for plurals which brought out this marked status of plurals (to be justified on p. 199), and showed how this particular part of the morphology could be related to syntactic and semantic structures: the morphology is related directly to the syntactic categories 'plural' and 'noun', and these in turn are related to the semantic structures. I repeat here the relevant part of the grammar, with a minor change to make it clearer:

(2)

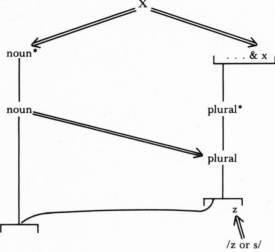

The point of this discussion of plural nouns is to show how syntactic features can be replaced, and how the word-grammar alternative can simplify the analysis of a clearly privative opposition. I am not of course suggesting that all morphological oppositions are privative, but non-privative oppositions can be handled in the same way, *mutatis mutandis*. For example, I assume that the singular/plural contrast in Latin would be equipollent, so that the category 'singular' would need to be distinguished from the category 'noun', just as 'plural' would. If the only way to distinguish syntactic categories was by means of binary distinctive features, there would be no way to distinguish the English and Latin patterns, but word grammar does allow us to distinguish clearly between privative and equipollent contrasts.

A further advantage of using models is that they can be linked in a network, allowing a very flexible system of cross-references. This degree of flexibility seems to be necessary in morphology, even when we are dealing with the morphology of a language like English. The problem must be familiar to any linguist who has tried to make sense of the English verb and its morphology. If you classify verbs according to their morphology, you get a classification which conflicts with the one you need for syntax (and semantics); but it really makes very little sense to ask which of these classifications is the 'right' one, because they are both right. For example, the morphology brings together categories that are syntactically as diverse as past tense and passive participle (e.g. *baked* for both), and the syntax brings together verbs with no ending and with *-s* (both present tense), and combines both of these with verbs containing *-ed* (all of them being tensed verbs). What we need is a way of having it all ways, so that we can make whatever generalizations are needed. So far as I can tell, the following network is just what is required.

(3)

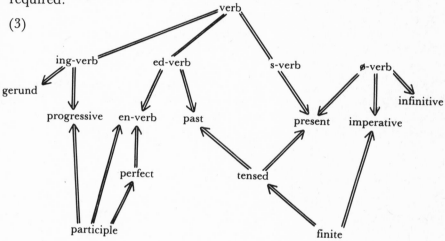

In this network, the top line of categories are directly linked to the morphology of the regular verb, so it is in reference to them that the regular affixes will be defined. Then comes a row of further distinctions, some of which are reflected in the morphology of some irregular verbs – notably, some verbs distinguish 'en-verb' from 'past' (e.g. *taken* versus *took*), and one distinguishes present from imperative and infinitive (viz., *am/is/are* versus *be*). Below this line we have a set of increasingly general categories, by which the finest categories are regrouped on a non-morphological basis. We could make use of these categories in order to express facts such as that modal verbs must be tensed, or that participles may be used as postmodifiers of nouns, like relative clauses.

It could be objected that the morphologically based categories are redundant, because the syntactically based ones already make all the distinctions that are necessary (namely, the finest categories). All we need is a set of morphological statements which would link each affix to a subset of these fine categories. The trouble with an analysis along these lines would be that it would leave too much freedom for irregular morphology. On the basis of the network as it stands, we can predict that certain kinds of irregularity will be more common than others: irregularities which respect these categories should be more common than irregularities that introduce new groupings. The prediction is confirmed by the facts, since there are many examples of the former type, but few of the latter. Thus *take* exploits a larger than usual number of the distinctions that are available, as does *begin*. Moreover, we might predict that if a verb is irregular in having the same form for two categories which are not covered by a distinctive super-category, then they are more likely to have no affix at all than to have some affix distinguishing them from the basic form; and this turns out to be true as well – for example, verbs like *cut* which have identical forms for 'ed-verb' and for 'Ø-verb' in fact have no affix at all in either case. The analysis predicts, then, that no verb will generalize the *ed* suffix to the present and imperative, or the *ing* suffix to the past tense.

Clitics

The following suggestions are particularly tentative, as clitics are notoriously complicated; they are hard to identify with certainty, and once you have identified them, they are hard to fit into a general theoretical framework. I shall take as a general, and rather rough, definition of 'clitic' a word which is part of the composition of some larger word (its host), but which is also syntactically related to the latter as a companion (or in some cases, as a companion of a companion of a . . . companion). Many such words are phonologically affix-like (with no independent stress), but I shall not build this into the definition, as I think it may be a separate parameter.

Examples of clitics are the French object and subject pronouns (e.g. *je* and *le* in *Je le connais*, 'I know him'), the weak forms of English auxiliary verbs (e.g. *'s* in *John's here*) and the interrogative particle *-ne* of Latin (e.g. *Romulus-ne domum aedificavit?*, 'Did Romulus build a house?'). The reason for saying that items like these are clitics is that they behave in ways similar to morphemes inside a word. For example, the French clitic pronouns cannot be co-ordinated, in contrast with full noun-phrases (e.g. *Je connais Jean et Marie*, 'I know John and Mary', contrasts in its grammaticality with the ungrammatical *Je le et la connais, follow (as pointed out e.g. by Perlmutter 1971, Warburton 1977). For French verbs, this would mean that we should need to provide a larger word containing both the verb and its clitic pronouns (see pages 86 – 7 for an analysis). Thus the clitics are treated like affixes in some respects, but they are also treated like separate words in other respects – e.g. the object pronoun is an object in just the same sense as a full noun-phrase, and if a verb requires an object this requirement will be satisfied just as well by a clitic as by any other kind of object.

It seems to be generally assumed that the word in whose structure a clitic is located must be provided by the other word, the 'host', but I think this need not be so. In any generative grammar, such as word grammar, we have to know where the structure containing the clitic comes from, in the sense that the structure for French verbs (presumably) comes from the general entry for verbs. (This is supported by considerations such as that verbs are the only word-class which take clitic pronouns, and that one subclass of verbs, imperatives, have a different structure for clitics from the rest.) There is no reason, a priori, why this structure should not be provided by the clitic itself, and I believe this is often the case. Take the weak auxiliaries in English as an example. It is often suggested that these are cliticized to the subject (for a recent review of the evidence, see Kaisse 1983), and I see no reason to question this analysis, but it would be very difficult to formulate the rules in such a way that the subject provides the structure into which the clitic fits. Instead, we can make use of the entry for auxiliary verbs, and provide a word to contain both the auxiliary and the preceding word.

The kind of structure which we need to generate is illustrated in (1):

(1)

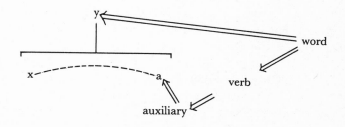

Here *a* stands for the auxiliary verb, and *x* for the word to which it is cliticised; *y* is the word made up of these two words. Thus, if we ask how many words there are in *he's*, the correct answer is three: *he*, *'s* and *he's*. The dotted line shows that x need not be directly related to a, as it is in *he's*. For example, consider *The man at number five's away*. Here *'s* is cliticised to *five*, which is related to it via five intervening companions (*number*, *at*, *man* and *the*). Thus use of dots is the same as we saw in the representation of a set (in (2) on p. 46), and stands for an indefinitely long series of instances of the type specified (in this case, companions). Dots are an important notational convention which I shall exploit a good deal.

The same structure could be described in terms of a formula:
(2) composition(y): x + a, model(a): auxiliary,
                                  companion(. . . . a): x
Here too the dots have the same meaning.

Compounds

What I have to say about compounds is as tentative as the above remarks about clitics, but it is worth sketching the broad outlines of a possible treatment within the word-grammar framework. The basic facts about compounds are reasonably straightforward, though I recognize that there are serious research problems that need to be investigated. A compound is a word whose composition consists of a string of two words. Syntactically, the compound may take its categorization from one of its component words, and in English this is the normal pattern, the relevant word being the second of the two. Thus, *blackbird* and *coal black* are a noun and an adjective respectively. Semantically, a compound may or may not be compositional, so the component words of *ladybird* have no more connection with the meaning of the whole (what Americans call *ladybug*) than did the component morphemes of *understand*. However, a compound like *biscuit box* is compositional, so a generalization needs to be made about the relations among the semantic structures involved.

Where a compound is in some respect idiosyncratic, the relevant features may be specified in the entry for the compound itself, and these features will automatically override the features to be expected on the basis of general rules. So *ladybird* will be listed (presumably) with the following structure. It will be seen that the structure does indeed show a remote connection between the referents of *ladybird* and of *bird* and *lady*, though the compound is not strictly compositional. This is one of the attractions of word grammar, in contrast with other theories that make compositionality an all-or-nothing matter.

(3)

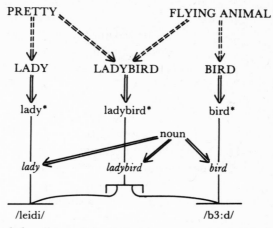

(I have simplified the diagram by missing out the instantiation relation between the phonological segments and their respective phonemes; now that the principle is established, I shall continue to simplify the analyses in this way where this relation is irrelevant.)

More regular compounds can be listed with their structures complete as well, of course, but we also need a general rule to make the general pattern explicit. A very simple rule can be written which covers the English type of compound (where the 'head' is second), and if further restrictions need to be added, this can be done by imposing conditions on the parts of the rule (e.g. it may be that we need to prevent the second element from being a verb, provided we can take examples like *meat-eating* as adjectives).

(4)

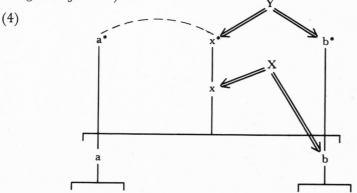

In words, any pair of words *a* and *b* may be put together, forming a compound x, but the classification of the compound must be the same as that of the second word, b, and the referent of the compound must be an instance of the same non-linguistic model as the referent of b. The semantic contribution of the first word, a, is made by its referent, a*, which acts as a semantic companion (of a companion . . .) of x*, the referent of the compound. (For example, the referent of *biscuit* in *biscuit box* defines the thing contained by x*.)

This entry illustrates another attraction of word grammar, namely that entities can be represented as variables, which allows cross-category generalizations. For example, by representing the word-class of the compound by X, we allow it to range over 'noun', 'adjective' and any other word-class in the grammar; moreover, it can be more specific, such as 'plural noun', as well. It is easy to impose conditions on the variables, as I have just explained; for example, we can require X not to be 'verb' if need be. Similar remarks apply to the variable Y, standing for the non-linguistic model of the referent of the compound and its head. When we combine this source of generality with the generality provided by the broken line connecting a* to x*, we can produce very general rules indeed.

Compounds and clitics are similar in that in both kinds of construction a word contains another word (or words) among its constituents. In both cases, it is hard to decide where the boundary between syntax and morphology lies, because we could be on either level, according to how we interpret our definitions of the levels. Widely accepted definitions would be: 'Syntax is the level which deals with relations between words' and 'Morphology is the level which deals with the internal structures of words.' Clitics and compounds satisfy *both* of these definitions, so we could locate the structures concerned on either or both of the levels. It seems best, in view of this uncertainty, not to make too much depend on getting the morphology/syntax boundary right, and one of the characteristics of word grammar is that very little depends on it (as I explained in the discussion of levels and components on pp. 12 – 14).

MORPHOLOGY AND PHONOLOGY
Morphemes and phonemes

In the American structuralist tradition, a distinction was made between phonological segments – i.e. phonemes, as far as that tradition was concerned – and morphemes. Phonemes and morphemes were located on different levels of analysis, and represented different kinds of abstraction, so they were distinguished whether or not they were different in length. Thus the suffix of *dogs* would be a morpheme consisting of a single phoneme. Since the morpheme *-s* and the phoneme /z/ belonged to different levels of analysis, the relation between them was not one of composition (a part and its whole), but rather of 'realization'. This distinction is fundamental to several theories, most notably stratificational grammar, and has its classic formulation in Hockett (1961). I have already said that I reject the distinction between the levels of morphology and phonology, along with that between morphology and syntax, but it is worth commenting briefly on this particular distinction.

Let us assume, for simplicity, that the phonological structure of a language may be described in terms of a set of phonemes, as 'normalized' speech sounds, and that particular sounds which occur in words of the language are instances of these phonemes. This gives the kind of structure that we have assumed so far, as in the following structure for *cat*:

(1)

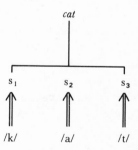

(The symbols 's₁' and so on are arbitrary, but *s* can be taken to stand either for 'segment' or for 'sound'.) Given this kind of analysis, it is possible to identify any sound segment as such, because it will be linked, as an instance, to a phoneme, and all the phonemes will (ultimately) be linked, as instances, to the entity 'sound segment':

(2)

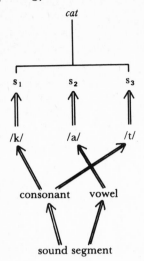

This being so, there is never any uncertainty as to whether or not some entity is a phoneme, or sound segment. By implication, then, any constituent of a word which is not a phoneme must be a morpheme, if we want to classify word-parts as either one or the other. So I am not denying that a distinction may be made between phonemes and morphemes.

What I am denying is that there is any need for a distinction in the grammar between the levels of analysis called 'morphemic' and 'phonemic', like that made by Hockett and his followers. For example, a word like *cats* can be taken as having two parts, the second of which is not a morpheme but rather a phoneme – an analysis which is incompatible with the strict division of levels of American structuralism.

This view is just an extension of the previous discussion, where I showed that the elements out of which a word may consist need not all be of the same type (e.g. they may be words which can occur on their own, or bound morphemes such as affixes). I am now claiming that the parts of a word may be phonemes or morphemes, and that these may be mixed up together (e.g. in *cats* the first part is a morpheme and the second a phoneme). In other words, a word may consist of any entity which (ultimately) is a string of one or more speech sounds – an unexciting conclusion in a sense, though it leads to the prediction that at least memorized phrase-length strings can be parts of words, and this prediction is controversial (but probably right – see for example the evidence in Botha 1981).

Abandoning the level-distinction between morphology and phonology has a number of advantages, and (so far as I can see) no disadvantages. One is that it simplifies the rules that need to be stated, because we can relate the second part of *cats* directly to the phoneme /s/, instead of going through a redundant 'plural morpheme' (redundant, because we already show that *cats* is plural by saying that it is an instance of the word-type 'plural', as shown in (2) on p. 46). Once the notion 'syntactic feature' (or its equivalent in word grammar, word-type entity) is adopted, the classical morpheme (as opposed to morph) loses much, or perhaps all, of its point. Another is that it allows generalizations in which the functions of phonemes and morphemes are combined in one element; for example, a phonotactic statement for the English word ought to show that if /s/ occurs as the last of four consonants in a word-final cluster, then it is always a separate morpheme. A third advantage is that languages without morphology pose no special problems, since we are not committed to postulating a completely pointless and redundant level of analysis for such languages.

As for the distinction between word and morpheme, this has no particular importance, now that we have seen that words can occur as parts of other words. Certainly there is no requirement that every word be analysed into one or more morphemes, as we have just seen. However, word grammar does oblige us to distinguish between words and non-words, because every word is ultimately linked, by instantiation, to the entity 'word', just as every sound-segment is linked to 'sound segment'. For example, *rocking* is a word, and so is its first part, *rock* (since *rocking* is formed by adding *-ing* to the lexeme *rock*, and the latter is a (generalized) word). The question is, what is *-ing*? Clearly it is too big to be a phoneme, and traditionally it would not be a word, so it must be a morpheme. We can express this analysis in word grammar by leaving the *-ing* sequence without any model at all – i.e. it is neither a word nor a phoneme, but we need not postulate a special category in the grammar on a par with 'word' and 'phoneme' in order to accommodate it. Similarly, we shall have to postulate strings of words which have no model when we come to deal with co-ordinate structures (e.g. *Jim, vodka* in *John drinks wine and Jim, vodka*), so we have a precedent for such *ad hoc*, model-less entities. Other analyses are of course possible, and are worth investigating (e.g. that 'word' could be extended even to cover bound affixes), but for the present I shall assume the position just stated. That is to say, a word grammar will give a general definition for 'word', and also one for 'sound segment', but will make no generalizations about 'morpheme'.

One final comment on the notion 'sound segment'. I have conducted the discussion so far on the assumption that something like the classical phoneme is part of the structure of a language, an assumption that is still widely held by linguists who are otherwise inclined to the principles of generative phonology (e.g. Smith 1973). In terms of word grammar, this means that I am assuming that we have an inventory of normalized sound-segments as part of our language network, corresponding to phonemes like /t/ or /l/, and particular sounds are taken as instances of these phonemes (with various allophonic deviations permitted). However, an attraction of word grammar is that it allows us to have the best of both worlds, in that we can also have the benefits of a feature analysis of sound segments. This is possible because each phoneme may itself be taken as an instance of a number of more general categories, each corresponding to one of the phonological features of generative phonology (and similar theories). For example, we shall presumably need to recognize categories like 'consonant', 'vowel', 'voiced', 'fricative', and so on. Classification would be done in the usual way for word grammar, by treating the relevant phonemes as instances of the more general category.

One difference between this approach and a purely feature-based approach is that we can produce an inventory of phonemes for a particular language, to show which combinations of features are actually used (e.g. in Arabic the combination corresponding to a /p/ phoneme is not used, so it would not appear in the list). Presenting the facts in this way is more satisfactory than the alternative of using redundancy rules to mark generalizable gaps, as this is also the way in which the lexicon is used, as a list of the actual words which exploit the total range of possible words. Another difference is that each of the categories referred to has a similar status to the phonemes themselves, in that it represents a particular type of sound; so there is no need for any of the categories to be based on a single property, whether articulatory or acoustic; so an entity like 'vowel' can be defined in terms of a complex combination of properties, just as the phoneme /t/ is. Moreover, we can expect to find more or less typical vowels, just as we find more or less typical instances of /t/; and of course this expectation is fulfilled.

I have hardly begun to explore the potential of word grammar in the field of phonology, and I am aware of a large number of major questions that need to be answered – for example, can a system such as the one just outlined define parameters of variation, such as 'place of articulation', which are so important in many assimilation rules? How, if at all, can we adapt it to deal with non-binary contrasts such as 'tongue height'? Is there a universal set of phonological categories, and if not, does it matter?

Allomorphy

In the first section I explained how affixes can be introduced, but I have not yet said how we can deal with variations in their phonological content from word to word – with allomorphy, in other words. I shall now outline treatments for three different kinds of allomorphy:

(a) idiosyncratic, where a word contains an allomorph not found elsewhere (e.g. *oxen*);

(b) phonology-conditioned, where a morpheme has different allomorphs in different phonological environments (e.g. *cats* versus *dogs* versus *horses*);

(c) class-conditioned, where words fall into a number of large classes each of which takes a different allomorph (e.g. Latin conjugation and declension differences; German *Hirshe*, 'stags', versus *Hirten*, 'shepherds').

(1)

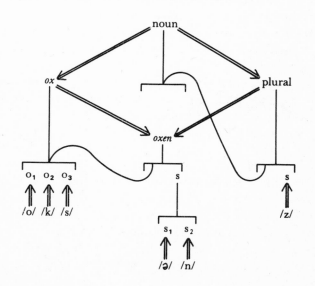

(a) *Idiosyncratic.* This is the easiest kind of allomorphy, because there is no problem of generalizing across words. Let us assume that the general entry for nouns is similar to the one in (2) on p. 46. This entry allows plural nouns to contain a suffix, which we can call *s*. All the entry for an irregular noun like *ox* needs to do is to supply the irregular composition for *s*, which will override the normal requirements. And of course the only thing about *ox* that is irregular is its morphology, so there is no need to specify the semantic structure for the plural – this can be left to the general entry for nouns. By the selective-inheritance principle, we know that the plural of *ox* should inherit the properties of both *ox* and 'plural', since it is an instance of both; so it inherits all the semantic properties of 'plural' (not shown above), but it does not inherit its morphological properties, since there are contradicted by its own specified properties (*s* cannot both be an instance of /z/ and be composed of /an/).

(b) *Phonology-conditioned.* This kind of allomorphy is typically very general in its application, so that the same kind of variation is found in a number of different affixes, and these affixes occur in a variety of word classes. Our example will be the well-known pattern of variation in the English alveolar suffixes written *-(e)s* and *-(e)d*. In both cases, an epenthetic vowel is inserted if the root ends in a consonant similar to the suffix itself, and in both cases the voicing of the suffix is affected by that of a consonant at the end of the root. The suffixes occur both in nouns and in verbs, and *-(e)s* is found in both (as plural and as present-tense agreement marker), not to mention its use as a 'genitive' marker (written *'s* or *s'*). Moreover, *-(e)d* is used not only as a past-tense and participle marker, but also as a device for forming adjectives out of nouns (*bearded, blue-eyed*).

We can start the analysis by selecting one of the variants in each case as the basic or underlying one, so that all we need to account for is deviation from this form. The natural choice is the voiced consonant without epenthetic vowel: /z/ and /d/ respectively. (This is the form which is found after vowels, where the voice of the suffix is least likely to have been altered by assimilation.) So we now need two rules, one for devoicing assimilation (as in *cats* or *walked*), and the other for the epenthetic vowel (as in *horses* and *wanted*).

For each of these rules, we postulate a particular subclass of words, namely that subclass to which the rule concerned applies. Let us call the subclass for devoicing 'devoicing-word'. As a subclass, this is connected to the category 'word' as an instance, and it will inherit all the latter's properties unless these are overridden by its own properties. One of the general properties of words, in English, is that they may or may not contain a suffix, which we can continue to represent as *s* for 'suffix'. To show optionality in word grammar, we pair the element concerned in a disjunction with *Ø* (following the practice of stratificational grammar). One property of devoicing words is that they must contain this suffix *s*, or to be more precise, an instance of it – an instance, because this is where the allomorphic variation is located. So we have an instance of *s*, labelled *s'*, which has all the properties of *s* except for being voiceless, like the consonant just before it. The diagram is as follows:

(3)

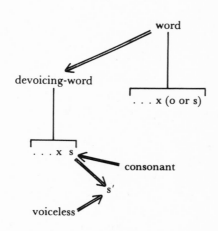

The treatment of the epenthetic vowel is somewhat similar. Again we postulate a subclass of words, called 'epenthesizing-word', and again we exploit the suffix element *s*, and also the *x* which stands for the segment just before the suffix. This time, however, *x* means 'the segment which would be final if there were no suffix'. This is important, because *x* is separated from the consonant of the suffix by the epenthetic vowel, where the latter occurs. The condition for the occurrence of the epenthetic vowel, then, is partly that there should be a suffix, but more precisely the suffix should be similar to *x* in its phonological properties: if the suffix is /d/, then *x* must be an alveolar stop, and if it is /z/, *x* must be an alveolar or palato-alveolar fricative. This part of the condition can be expressed by having a variable P (for 'phonetic' or 'property', or both), and requiring both *x* and *s* to be instances of this variable entity. The identity of P can vary (as just described), but whatever it is, it must be the same for *x* and for *s*. Diagrammatically, then:

(4)

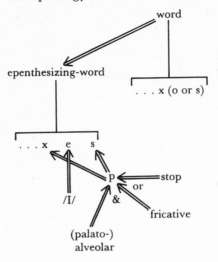

This pushes the diagrammatic notation to its limits, and somewhat past them in one respect: the variable P brings together a set of phonological features which should be defined as '(palato-)alveolar and (stop or fricative)' – or perhaps even '((palato-alveolar or alveolar) and fricative) or (alveolar and stop)'. Such sets can be defined by means of brackets in the formulaic notation, but not in diagrams of the kind I am using.

One attractive characteristic of this analysis is that it does not force us to assign the epenthetic vowel to the suffix as a morpheme. The suffix is still the single consonant, /d/ or /z/, represented by s, and the epenthetic vowel is shown as a direct constituent of the word. This contrasts with any analysis which makes use of morpheme boundaries to trigger such rules, since the vowel must be inserted either before or after the morpheme boundary. I think it would be hard to find psycholinguistic evidence for either position, and it is quite likely that we avoid the choice as speakers and learners, so it is good to be able to avoid it as linguists too.

It could be objected to my analysis that the word-categories 'epenthesizing-word' and 'devoicing-word' are *ad hoc*, because these categories are not referred to by any other rules of the grammar (in particular, they clearly have no relevance to syntax or semantics). However, similarly *ad hoc* categories are already well established in morphology, in the form of 'conjugations' and 'declensions'; and in any case I see no reason for accepting the general principle that every category must have more than one use in the grammar.

(c) *Class-conditioned.* The third type of allomorphy is the kind associated with conjugations and declensions, where (say) nouns can be assigned to four different classes, each requiring a different set of allomorphs (and, indeed, of morphological structures – e.g. in Beja one conjugation has prefixes where another has suffixes; see Hudson 1974). To take a simple example, in German various allomorphs are possible for the plural suffix, according to the class of noun to which it is attached, so nouns like *Hirsch*, 'stag', add *-e*, while those like *Hirt*, 'shepherd', add *-en*. If we call these two classes 1 and 2 respectively, we can diagram the relations as follows:

(5)

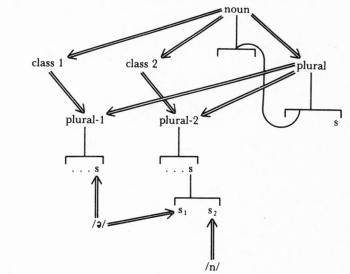

I hope this needs no comment, apart from the rather obvious remark that the diagram notation would be unmanageable for a full analysis of a morphological system like that of most inflecting languages. Once again the formulaic notation would be much preferable, although it does not present the relations in quite as direct a way as do diagrams.

Variation within the root

I have shown how we can deal with allomorphic variation in affixes, but such variation also occurs inside the root, and it is this that we must now explore. I shall show again how it can be handled without recourse to 'processes' such as could be described by means of rewrite rules, though we shall again preserve the distinction between 'underlying' or 'normal' and 'deviant' forms. I shall discuss the following three types of variation in the form of a root:

(a)   Suppletion, where there is no similarity between the forms concerned (e.g. *go/went*);

(b)   vowel change, where there is partial similarity between the forms, but the differences cannot be generalized (e.g. *foot/feet*);

(c)   generalizable vowel changes (and other changes in the phonological structure), such as is found in semitic languages.

(a) *Suppletion.* The entry for a suppletive word like *went* would simply make no connection at all to the basic form, *go*. Here is the relevant part of the grammar network:

(1)

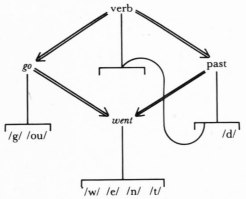

This network treats *went* and *go* as distinct word-forms, neither of which in any sense contains the other or is derived from the other; but since *went* is an instance of *go*, it inherits all the latter's properties other than its phonological shape. I take it that such an analysis is exactly what we need for suppletion.

(b) *Idiosyncratic vowel change.* The analysis for *foot/feet* must be different from that for *go/went*, because *foot* and *feet* are not totally unrelated in form: they both have the same consonants, and it is only the vowels that are different. This partial similarity must be shown, but there is no need to invoke a 'rule' to relate the two forms, because no other noun has this particular vowel alternation. Another requirement of the analysis is like that for *go/went*: we must avoid postulating a suffix, contrary to the regular pattern. This is the subnetwork that we need:

(2)

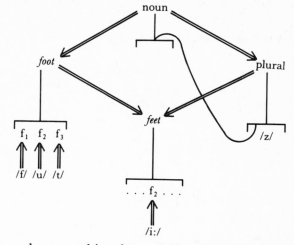

The difference between this subnetwork and the last one is that the only part of the phonological structure that is specified for *feet* is the vowel. Since the rest is unspecified, it will be inherited, as required, from *foot*.

   (c) *Generalizable vowel change.* Considerable interest has been expressed of late in semitic morphology, where vowels express inflections and consonants (generally speaking) express the lexical content. This has been one of the main testing grounds for the 'autosegmental' approach to morphology (McCarthy 1981), which in some ways is similar to word grammar. In particular, we can divide up the phonological structure of a word into a number of different parts on a morphological basis, and we can do this even when the parts overlap. For example, McCarthy quotes the classical Arabic form /ktatab/, 'he wrote', and shows how it can be analysed as follows:

/k . . . t . . . b/ 'write'
/. . . t . . ./ (i.e. the first of the two *t*'s) Class VIII
/. . . a . . . a . . . / perfect

A morpheme-based approach has difficulty in providing a satisfactory analysis for such cases, precisely because it requires a strict division between morphological and phonological structure, whereas we need to refer to the phonological structure (defined in terms of consonants and vowels, for example) in order to state the morphological structure. The main difference between the autosegmental approach and mine is that the former appears to maintain the morpheme as an essential unit of analysis, whereas I have abandoned it, as I explained earlier. However, there are other more particular differences too, such as the fact that McCarthy invokes a transformational type of rule for inversion, which again produces a distinction between 'deep' and 'surface' structures which is absent from word grammar.

I shall now show how the form /ktatab/ could be generated in a word grammar of classical Arabic. (A detailed analysis of the morphology of Tunisian Arabic has been prepared within the framework of an earlier version of word grammar; see Chekili 1982.) First we produce a generalized abstract phonological structure for verbs in general

(3)

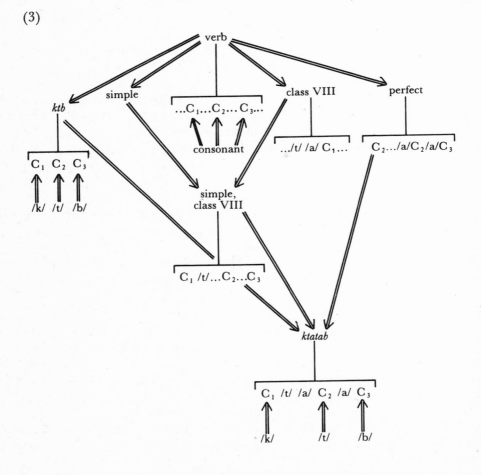

(actually, for triliteral verbs, but we can ignore other types of verbs without distorting the picture seriously). This will consist of '. . . C_1 . . . C_2 . . . C_3 . . .', allowing for prefixes, suffixes and internal vowels and other bits and pieces to be inserted as appropriate. This formula is exploited in the entries for particular verbs such as 'write', because they simply identify the phonemes that act as models for C_1, C_2 and C_3 respectively. Oversimplifying somewhat, the category 'perfect' requires /a/ to be inserted between C_1 and C_2, and also between C_2 and C_3; and class VIII is responsible for the /t/ after C_1, although it is normally marked by a prefix /ta/. We can assume a subcategory 'simple' which interacts with 'class VIII' to produce this deviation from the normal order (this is instead of McCarthy's permutation transformation). Thus the form /ktatab/ inherits the combined properties of the verb 'write', and the subclasses 'simple', 'class VIII' and 'perfect'. The diagram in (3) shows how it all works.

I hope this example shows the lines along which an analysis of semitic morphology would run. It was sufficiently complex to suggest the degree of flexibility which word grammar offers, in an area where flexibility is all-important.

LEXICAL RELATIONS
Similarities, regularities and redundancy rules

One of the advantages of a network analysis is that each entity appears only once in the network, so if two words are both related to this entity in some way, this shared relationship will be completely explicit in the grammar. For a trivial example, it is easy to see that the grammar relates every word containing the phoneme /p/ to every other such word, because the entity /p/ will be connected, by instantiation, to every sound segment for which it is a model. More importantly, if two words have some element of meaning in common, this will be brought out by the network, as will any other kind of partial similarity. We have seen a great number of examples of such shared entities, and there is no need to provide further ones. One of the attractions of the diagrammatic notation that I have been using so far is that it makes such connections obvious, because each entity is (in principle) shown just once in the diagram, by a single labelled node. (We have in fact had to make some exceptions to this principle to avoid intolerable complexity in the diagrams; for example, the diagrams on pp. 57 – 61 all contained more than one node representing the same entity, the suffix *s*.)

I shall aim to show how this simple fact about word grammar helps to reveal the structure of the lexicon, without recourse to the 'redundancy rules' which are so often invoked, but so rarely discussed, in the transformational literature. (The most important published discussions of which I am aware are Jackendoff 1975 and Hust 1978; but the unpublished Diehl 1981 contains some penetrating observations.) It is quite difficult to be sure what function redundancy rules are meant to fulfil, but a fairly widely held view is that of Jackendoff (1975), in which they are required to characterize the notion 'distinct but related lexical entry'. That is to say, we start with the orthodox assumption that the lexicon is 'simply an unordered list of lexical formatives' (Chomsky 1965:84), and not a network; then we discover that some of the lexical entries which we have separated off from one another are in fact partially similar to one another, so we need some kind of mechanism for bringing out these relations between 'distinct but related lexical entries'.

There is an obvious similarity between this train of argument and the one which led to the adoption of transformational rules. You make an assumption, you find it produces undesirable consequences, but instead of abandoning the initial assumption and trying something different, you patch up the theory by adding machinery for dealing with the unwanted consequences. In one case, the initial assumption is that the grammar must contain phrase-structure rules, and the patching machinery is the apparatus of transformations (as I argue in Hudson 1976a); in the other the assumption is that the lexicon is a list of separate lexical entries, and the patching machinery is the redundancy rule. In both cases, there are alternative assumptions which are worth exploring before we jump to the conclusion that extra machinery is necessary. In the case of lexical relations, the alternative is to assume that 'the entire lexicon of a language is viewed as a continuous graph relating all entries of the language' (Raskin 1981).

In order to explain how word grammar can handle lexical relations we shall have to differentiate among a number of different types of relation:

(a) (Partial) homonymy (e.g. *stand*, 'tolerate', 'be upright'; *stand/understand*);

(b) (Partial) synonymy (e.g. *radio/wireless; thief/steal*);

(c) Idiosyncratic similarities in both form and meaning (e.g.

male/female);

(d) General but irregular similarities in both form and meaning
(e.g. *decide/decision*);

(e) General and regular similarities in both form and meaning
(e.g. *final/non-final*).

This classification ignores certain parameters, notably syntax, but the
apparatus available in word grammar is capable of accommodating
such relations as well.

(a) *(Partial) homonymy.* Let us assume that the word *book* may have
two different types of referent, one concrete, the other abstract
(Chomsky 1970:218), and that this constitutes an example of polysemy,
as Chomsky suggests. To reflect this analysis, all we need to do in a
network is to have a single entity for the word-form *book*, and assign it
two different referents, each with a distinct non-linguistic model. There
are various possibilities for the semantic structure, if we wish to relate
these referents more closely; for example, we might treat one as an
instance of the other (such an analysis would certainly be appropriate
for the two meanings of *dog*, one with its sex specified and the other
without). But the main point is that we can show that the two referents
are linked by a shared word-form in a completely explicit way in a
network, by listing the word-form concerned just once:

(1)

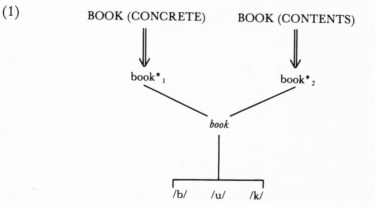

In a case like the two meanings of *stand* ('tolerate' and 'be upright'),
the semantic differences are accompanied by syntactic differences (one
is transitive, the other intransitive), so we need to distinguish the two
word-forms at the point where syntactic facts are stated. However, we
can still treat the form itself as one entity, by listing it just once, and
considering the two syntactically different uses of it as different

instances; or if we want to show that one use is basic, and the other derived, we can treat just one use as an instance, and attach all the syntactic information about the basic use directly to the model itself. An analysis like this would be suitable for pairs like *walk* (intransitive) and *walk* (transitive). I have not yet explained how to treat syntax in a word-grammar network, so I cannot give a complete network for the relevant facts, but here is a partial network, in which I assume that both the uses of *stand* are equally basic:

(2)

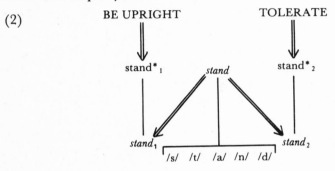

There is no need to specify the forms of the two particular uses of *stand*, since they will inherit the form of the model *stand*; so once again the grammar makes the formal connection between them quite explicit.

We have already seen how a word grammar would relate *stand* to *understand* (see (1) on p. 44), and similar partial overlaps in the forms of two words could be shown in the same way.

The main point of these examples is to show that word grammar can show formal connections between words without invoking the notion 'lexical entry' or 'lexical item'. There would be no objection of course to using these terms as part of our informal metalanguage, but there would be no point in trying to add boundaries between 'lexical entries' to the grammar, in addition to the relations already shown. Nor is there any point in arguing about the 'correct' definition of 'lexical entry', to help us (for instance) to decide which cases involve polysemy and which involve homonymy; as I have already mentioned (see p. 3) we simply do not know how to distinguish the two, so any definition will be as good as any other.

(b) *(Partial) synonymy*. If two word-forms share a single meaning, this connection may be shown in the same way as the connections in form, by representing the shared element concerned just once in the grammar, and allowing it to be exploited by the two words. A simple example would be a pair like *radio/wireless*, which are synonyms (any differences between them would be in the 'utterance-event' slot, in relation to factors such as the age of the speaker). We need to keep their referents distinct, in order to allow for sentences like *A radio is the same thing as a wireless*; so we connect them by linking them both to the same non-linguistic model, RADIO:

(3)

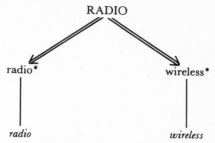

Similarly, the meaning of *steal* is contained in the semantic structure of *thief* ('one who steals') in just the same way as the meaning of *rob* is contained in that of *robber*. This connection too will be shown in the same way, by representing the meaning of *steal* just once, and then cross-referring to this entity from the entity representing the meaning of *thief*. The interesting thing about examples like the two just given is that the connections among the entities concerned are just as direct and clear as the connections involved in homonymy, but few linguists would consider showing the semantic connections by postulating a single lexical entry, to cover both *wireless* and *radio* (for instance). To the extent that the notion 'lexical item' or 'lexical entry' is discussed at all, the discussion is usually based on the assumption that the unifying factor is' form, so two forms as different as *wireless* and *radio* could not form a single entry. However, I know of no attempt to justify this assumption, and one suspects that the main reason for its popularity is that this is how traditional dictionaries are organized.

(c) *Idiosyncratic similarities in both form and meaning.* It is reasonable to assume that at least some speakers take the word-form *female* as *fe* plus *male*, on the analogy of *male*. However, the connection between form and meaning here is idiosyncratic, in that there are no other word-pairs that are related in form by the presence or absence of *fe-*. In a word-grammar analysis, these connections in form and meaning will be shown directly, in the ways just described. In other words, *male* and *female* are both partial homonyms (they share the form *male*) and partial synonyms (they share the meaning 'sexed', or some such). I think it is also reasonable to assume that the presence of *female* in a grammar that already contains *male* constitutes less 'new information' than does the presence of an unrelated word, such as *onion*. But if this is so, then the relation between *male* and *female* ought to be handled by a redundancy rule, according to Jakendoff's definition quoted above. This would mean a redundancy rule which would apply just to a single pair of words – but is this the kind of thing which proponents of redundancy rules have in mind? I suspect not, but it seems to be a consequence of the assumption that connections between separate lexical items must be shown by redundancy rule.

(d) *General but irregular similarities in both form and meaning.* A pair like *decide/decision* is like *male/female* in that there is a similarity in both form and meaning, such that the differences in form can be linked to the differences in meaning. We could bring out these similarities in the same way as we did with *male/female*, and this is indeed how *decide/decision* would be treated in a word-grammar analysis. However, in addition to this pair there are other pairs which show the same formal and semantic relations (e.g. *deride/derision, elide/elision*). It is reasonable to assume that for at least some speakers the connection between deride/derision and these other pairs is also shown in the grammar, as well as the connection between *decide* and *decision*. This can be done in a word grammar by postulating an abstract word-pair with the relevant relation, and linking *decide/decision*, along with the other pairs, to this abstract pair as a model. Here is the subnetwork for *decide/decision* and the abstract pair:

(4)

An abstract entry like this is similar to the entries we gave above for inflectional morphology, and is in the spirit of Diehl 1981 (who attributes the idea of using incompletely specified lexical entries to Gruber 1965). There is also an important difference, however: the abstract entities called *a* and *b* in the above diagram are *ad hoc* in the sense that they are not needed for any other purpose, whereas inflectional entries are attached to categories like 'noun'. Moreover, the different inflected forms are held together by their shared model (e.g. 'noun'), but there is no model shared by both *a* and *b,* or by both *decide* and *decision*.

As we all know, derivational patterns like the one that links *decide* and *decision* are irregular, and do not apply completely generally (e.g. *abide* is not matched by **abision*). There is no problem in showing this in a word grammar, because the abstract entry only applies to those words which are shown as instances of it. Thus there is no danger of overgeneration, nor any need to mark some words as exceptions to a general rule. Moreover, a word may be covered by the abstract entry even if its partner does not exist, because the partners are linked separately to their respective models. For example, *vision* is an instance of *b*, with the internal structure *v-ision* and a semantic structure like that for *decision*; but there is no need to postulate an 'abstract' verb *v-ide* to match it. All these problems that are avoided by word grammar arise in a theory which uses rules in order to bring out similarities between lexical entries. In contrast, it should be clear that there is no need for 'rules', as distinct from the network, in a word grammar.

(e) *General and regular similarities in both form and meaning.* Finally we come to pairs like *final* and *non-final*, whose relation is not only found in other pairs, but can be brought under a general rule which has no exceptions (assuming, that is, that any adjective can have *non-* added to it; for simplicity I shall ignore the possibility of adding *non-* to other kinds of words, such as *non-linguist*). These can be treated in a way similar to the above, except that the abstract entry will exploit the general entity 'adjective', so that it will automatically apply to any adjective. Because of this, there is no need to link individual adjectives to the abstract entry, nor need we list the individual forms with *non-* (although some of them may well be listed, of course). Here is the entry for *non-*:

(5)

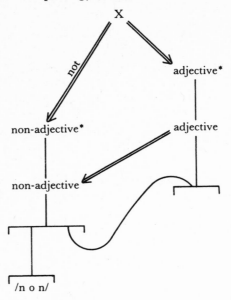

Any adjective will inherit from the category 'adjective' the ability to be matched by a form in *non-*, just as any noun inherits the ability to be plural.

We have seen how word grammar can handle a reasonably wide range of lexical relations, but it would be wrong for me to suggest that I already know how to deal with everything. For example, I am not sure at present how to deal with 'conversion', where an instance of one word-class may be used instead as an instance of another. However, I hope to have shown that word grammar compares favourably with the most popular current alternative, the transformational approach based on lexical entries and redundancy rules.

Creative innovations

All the discussion so far has assumed that whenever we utter a word when speaking English we have a model for it in our store of knowledge of English words. But this is not the case, of course – sometimes we are stuck for a word which expresses the content we intend, and we have to behave creatively in finding a solution to our communicative problem. This situation is familiar to linguists, who have earned themselves a reputation for being pathologically creative in the field of technical terminology. Various options are open to us: we can borrow a word from another language (e.g. *sandhi*), or we can use an existing word with a new meaning (e.g. *competence*), or we can create a new word out of existing material, using more or less original patterns (e.g. *etic, Chomsky-adjoin, semantax, construal*). When first used, none of these examples were instances of models already in English, so their users were going beyond their English resources.

The question is whether a grammar should contain a set of 'word-formation rules' in order to predict, or constrain, the production of new vocabulary items. My view has for some time been that it should not (Hudson 1976b), and I shall make no attempt to provide such rules in word grammar. I hold this view for a number of reasons:

(a) We may assume that humans have (varying degrees of) creative intelligence which allows them to find non-standard solutions to problems outside language; and it is unreasonable to suppose that this ability is switched off when the problems are linguistic ones. So we can take it that at least some cases of linguistic innovation are to be explained as the product of this general intelligence applied to language, and until we have evidence to the contrary, there is no reason to think that any cases of linguistic innovation require a different explanation.

(b) It would be most unusual to have a rule in one language which instructed one to borrow material from a different language, so generally speaking we can be fairly sure that at least one kind of innovation – borrowing – is not rule-governed. It is true that this may be an overstatement, because language X may contain rules telling its speakers how to deal with words that they borrow from language Y – e.g. how to adapt their pronunciations to reconcile them with the system of X; however the point is that at least some borrowing is not rule-governed.

(c) At least some examples of innovations are isolated, and do not represent any general pattern. For example, the sociologist Goffman has coined the noun *with*, on the basis of the preposition *with*, to mean 'a group of people who recognise that they are socially "together", and interact with one another'. So far as I know, there are no other noun/preposition pairs in this kind of relation, so Goffman was not applying a rule, nor (so far as I know) has his precedent led to the generalization of this pattern by other people.

(d) Even when there is a clear pattern to exploit, it may be 'unproductive', which might suggest that there was a word-formation rule once, but it is now 'dead' (this is a very popular assumption in word-formation studies). But even an apparently unproductive pattern may be the basis for sporadic innovations. For example, the suffix *-let* which produced forms like *piglet* and *booklet* in the past has been used recently in the words *notelet* and *starlet* (Quirk *et al.* 1972:994). So is the 'rule' alive or dead? If it is dead, then we must assume that some other process led to *notelet* and *starlet*, so the same process could be used in all the other cases too; but if it is alive, why do we not use it more often?

(e) Word-formation rules are peculiar rules, in comparison with other linguistic rules, in that when they apply they change the grammar, by extending its vocabulary. This means that there is a diachronic change between the states of the language before and after applying the rule, so word-formation rules are diachronic, not synchronic, if they are anything at all.

The conclusion, then, is that there is no need to provide for word-formation rules in word grammar. However, I should point out that the patterns traditionally described by word-formation rules, to the extent that they are relevant to synchronic grammar, are catered for in word grammar. Any partial similarity among stored lexemes can be shown in the various ways outlined in the previous subsection, and any generalizable patterns can be generalized, whether they are regular or not. Moreover, we have seen how completely regular and general patterns may be expressed, either in the case of derived forms like *non-final* (p. 71), or in the case of compounds (pp. 50 – 2).

3

Syntax

DEPENDENCY STRUCTURES

Companions, heads and modifiers

Traditionally, morphology and syntax are considered as branches of grammar, and word grammar also shows them as having a lot in common. In particular, they are both concerned with words, rather than with the referents of words, which distinguishes them from semantics; but they are also concerned with words in a different way from phonology, because they both contribute to the complex pattern of constraints on the ways in which words may be combined with one another in meaningful utterances. That is, we are in grammar when we find statements about what kinds of word may combine with what other kinds of word, and in what order, and with what effect on their meanings. In contrast, phonology tells us how the words are pronounced when they are put together, and so far as I know there are no phonological rules, as such, which say that some particular (phonologically specified) type of word must not combine with some other type. At this level of generality, the difference between grammar and phonology is fairly clear, but I have already pointed out pp. 52 – 7 that the distinction between phonology and morphology, at least as levels of analysis, is not clear.

What distinguishes syntax from morphology is the type of relation to which most of the rules refer. In our discussion of morphology, we only had to deal with two kinds of relation: the 'composition' relation, and the 'instantiation' one. In syntax, on the contrary, we shall have very little to do with the composition relation – this is probably the most controversial part of word grammar – though we shall again use the instantiation relation. The main relation in syntax is the 'companion' relation, between words which occur together, so we shall change from diagrams with vertical lines sitting on horizontal bars, to ones with horizontal arcs linking co-occurring words.

The relation of 'companion' is more than mere co-occurrence: it is a matter of co-occurrence sanctioned explicitly by the grammar. For example, in *She has brown eyes*, there will be entries in the grammar that specifically allow *she* and *has* to co-occur, but none which allows *has* and *brown* to co-occur; rather, *brown* is allowed to occur with words like *eyes*, and the latter are allowed to occur with words like *has*, so each of these pairs are 'companions' of one another, but *has* is not a companion of *brown*. The relations are shown in (1):

(1)   *She   has   brown   eyes*

It can be seen that the information given by this diagram is half-way between that given by a simple chain, which specifies nothing but temporal order, and that given by a phrase-marker, in which some words are shown as being more closely related to one another than others are. In particular, (1) excludes a direct relation between *has* and *brown*, but it is sufficiently vague to be applied to a wide range of different structures – for example, both the sentences in (2) could be given the same analysis as (1), in terms of companion-ship.

(2)   Try eating baked beans.
                            Baked beans I like.

This is clearly not yet good enough, as we must be able to distinguish sentences like these from one another, so it is customary to add *directionality* to the companion relation, so that one companion in each relation is labelled as 'head' to distinguish it from the other. This is customary in the European tradition of 'dependency theory', first formalized by Tesnière (1959), and it is on this tradition that the syntactic part of word grammar is mainly based. In recent years, the dependency tradition has been discussed more favourably in the Anglo-Saxon linguistics literature, especially in Britain (e.g. Matthews 1981, Atkinson *et al*. 1982, Herbst *et al*. 1980), but this is a new development, as the tradition has been generally ignored, with few exceptions (e.g. J.M. Anderson 1971, 1977, Haas 1973, Hays 1964, Robinson 1970). This is a great pity, as dependency theory offers a serious alternative to phrase-structure grammar, so it is important for us to explore their respective merits. A good deal of the discussion in the present chapter will be devoted to this comparison.

Once we have picked out one word in each pair as head, the three example sentences just quoted can be distinguished. The notation I shall use for showing the head in a structure diagram is an arrow-head pointing to the modifier. A diagram with the arrow-heads added can be called a *dependency structure*. The dependency structures for our three sentences are given in (3):

(3)
　　She　has　brown　eyes.　　Try　eating　baked　beans.　　Baked　beans　I　like.

If we are using formulaic notation, we use slots named 'head', so the formulaic equivalent of the diagram for *She has brown eyes* is the following:

(4)　　　　　　　　　head (*she*): *has*
　　　　　　　　　　head (*brown*): *eyes*
　　　　　　　　　　head (*eyes*): *has*

The directionality supplied by the 'head' notation is a supplement to the companion relations already shown by the arcs, so a headed arc is really equivalent to a cluster of separate propositions about the words concerned. Take the pair *brown eyes*, for example. *Brown* is a companion of *eyes*, but *eyes* is of course also a companion of *brown*, so we can extract two propositions about the companion relation, plus the proposition about *eyes* being head. Thus we could, in principle, expand (4) in a mechanical way by adding propositions such as 'companion (*she*): *has*', and so on. None of this need be expressed in a grammar, however, because the companion relation is completely redundant once the head relation is expressed. The rules and structures that we shall consider in this book will make hardly any reference at all to the companion relation as such (but see p. 124), but will refer a lot to the head relation. Moreover, we shall also use the term 'modifier' to refer to the other member of a companion relation, so we can even leave the head undefined if we have defined its modifier. (The term 'modifier' is less well established in the literature than 'head'; indeed, I differ from some dependency theorists, e.g. Allerton 1982, precisely in claiming that a single term is adequate for referring to the non-head member of a companion pair.)

What is the basis of the asymmetry between a head and its modifier? More concretely, how do we know which member of an established companion pair is the head? The most general answer is that it is the head that provides the link between the modifier and the rest of the sentence, rather than vice versa. For example, the position of *brown* in *She has brown eyes* is fixed in relation to *eyes*, and not vice versa (*brown* must precede *eyes*, *eyes*, as object, must follow *has*; its position after *brown* is just the converse of the latter's position before it, and it is this relation which is specified in the grammar). It will be recalled that we found similar asymmetries in many non-linguistic companion relations such as that between a house and its dustbin (p. 39) – the point being that if you conceptualize the normal position of your dustbin you see it in relation to your house, but not vice versa, so if your dustbin happens to be between your house and your friend's house, this is a consequence of the fact that your house is next to your friend's, and your dustbin is next to your house.

It is not just the temporal order of a modifier which is fixed relative to its head in an asymmetrical way. The same is true of various other properties of the modifier, and at least in the clear cases all the properties reveal the same direction of dependence (in other words, we can assume an entity called 'head', and another called 'modifier', in which all the properties are congruent; but particular instances of heads and modifiers may be deviant in one or more respects). I shall briefly mention the main types of property to which the asymmetry applies:

(a) temporal order (already illustrated);
(b) possibility of occurrence – whether the modifier may, or must, occur at all rests with the head, and not vice versa;
(c) inflectional selection (i.e. traditional 'government') – the head decides which inflectional form of the modifier occurs;
(d) lexical selection (alias 'collocation') – the head selects a particular, formally specified, word (e.g. *decide* selects the preposition *on*);
(e) semantic structure – the head provides a structure into which the modifier fits (e.g. *brown* defines the colour of the eyes, rather than *eyes* defining the application-range of *brown*).

We shall see a large number of examples of these types of asymmetry in this chapter and the following ones, so there is no need to go into more detail here. I should like to raise a general question about the connection between dependency and the companion relation. Is every companion relation between words a matter of dependency? The answer is by no means clear, but it may well turn out that some syntactic relations between companions are symmetrical, in which case the distinction between heads and modifiers will not apply to them. The kinds of construction that may be like this are those that are generally ignored by syntacticians of all persuasions, such as asyndeton and apposition (both discussed interestingly by Matthews 1981). I shall leave this question open, since I have nothing substantial to say about it, so although the companion relation can be replaced by dependency in some constructions, this may not be so in all constructions. However, all the constructions that I discuss here will be of the kind that do involve dependency, with the exception of the co-ordinate structures to be discussed in chapter 5.

The dependency chain

If we assume temporarily that every word (except the main verb) has just one head, then it follows that a dependency structure for a sentence must define a number of *dependency chains*, whose links are made up from simple dependency pairs. To show this we must take a somewhat more complicated example, such as the following:

(1)

Fathers   of few   children   have   any   fun

Here, as in other examples, I have to make various analytical assumptions for which I could provide justification, but I cannot provide the justification at this point as it would interrupt the general argument. On the whole, my assumed analyses could be replaced by other analyses without this making any difference to the general points that I am trying to explain. I hope the analyses will become somewhat easier to accept as the discussion proceeds, and as I have an opportunity to bring in some of the supporting arguments at appropriate places. Meanwhile, I must ask readers to bear with me, even when the analyses strike them as unorthodox to the point of perversion.

In structure (1), we can define two dependency chains leading from the main verb, *have*, to *children* and *fun* respectively. *Have* is the first head in both chains, and *children* and *fun* are their last modifiers. One of the points on which most dependency theorists are agreed is that the main verb is the word on which all the other words in the sentence depend, and I shall accept this general analysis too (except in main wh-questions, where the wh-word is the head of the main verb). This makes dependency analysis of sentence structure quite easy in most cases: you start with the main verb, and then trace the various dependency chains out from there. Moreover, in English the majority of dependency pairs have the modifier after its head, as in (1), so most dependency chains link adjacent words, with every arrow pointing to the right. (2) shows just how easy this kind of analysis can be:

(2)
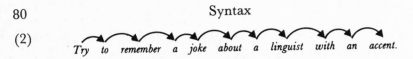

Try to remember a joke about a linguist with an accent.

The dependency chain has a number of uses, of which I shall just mention two here, with a promise of further references to it in later discussions. First, let us return to example (1), which is taken from Jackendoff (1977:60). The first interesting fact about this sentence is that *any* occurs in it, although normally permitted only in negative and interrogative contexts. Similarly, if we were to add a tag question, it would take the form *do they?*, suggesting that the sentence is negative. Putting these two facts together, we arrive at the conclusion that (1) is indeed negative. In order to state this fact in a dependency framework, we give a negative structure to the main verb, *have*, but at present we can leave the precise nature of this structure unexplored, the main point being that the negativity is a property of the word *have*. Now, it is obviously the word *few* that signals the presence of the negativity, and we have already seen that the presence of the word *any* is a consequence of the negativity, so we have to ask what the relation is among *few, have* and *any* such that the presence of *few* permits *any* to occur. Armed with dependency chains, we can give a simple answer: *few* causes some word 'up' the dependency chain to be negative, and *any* can occur provided that some word 'up' the dependency chain from it is negative. Since *have* is 'up' the dependency chain from both of them, it provides the link we were looking for. (The metaphor of heads being 'higher' than modifiers is sufficiently obvious for me now to stop putting quotation marks round 'up'.)

The second noteworthy fact about sentence (1) is, as Jackendoff points out, that it contrasts in grammaticality with (3):

(3)   *Fathers with few children have any fun.

In order to explain why this should be (something which Jackendoff admits to being unable to do) we need to refine the notion 'up the dependency chain', as far as *few* (or any other negative word) is concerned. The difference between sentences (1) and (2) is a semantic one, centring on the difference between the expressions *father of X* and *father with X*. In the former case, X is represented semantically within the semantic structure of *father*, because the meaning of *father* precisely involves a relation between a person (the referent of *father*), and some child, and it is this child which is specified by X; so X simply provides further detail about a variable already present in the semantic structure of *father*. In the other case, though, *with X* is equivalent in meaning to 'who has/have X', and X does not take up a ready-made position in the structure of X.

This analysis allows us to formulate the rule for transferring negativity up the dependency chain:

(4)   quantity(a*): q,   quantity(b*): q, q = (almost) zero
       X(a*): b*,

In words, the negativity of a modifier *b* transfers to its head, provided that the referent of *b* fills some slot which is attached directly to the referent of its head. The lexical entry for *father* will specify that the referent of the object of *of* does fill such a slot, so negativity will transfer; but it will not transfer across *with*, because this relates its object less directly to the referent of *fathers*. Once the negativity has reached *fathers*, as in *fathers of few children*, it can then transfer again, up the dependency chain, by exploiting (4) recursively, so *have* too becomes negative; and since this is higher in the dependency chain which contains *any*, the latter is covered by a negative word up its dependency chain. The entry for words such as *any* must therefore contain the following constraint:

(5)   quantity(h*): (almost) zero, head (. . . x): h,

where *x* stands for the word like *any*, and 'head (. . . x)' means 'the head of . . . *x*', with the usual interpretation for the string of dots (an indefinitely long series of the elements defined before or after the dots). This formula shows both how we can formalize the dependency chain, using ('head . . . x)', and why it is sometimes useful to do so.

Another use of the dependency chain is in typology, where we can distinguish languages which allow long chains (such as English) from those that only allow very short ones. This is the distinction made in phrase-structure terms between 'configurational' and 'non-configurational' languages (Hale 1981), but it has recently been reinterpreted in dependency terms by Blake (1983). A non-configurational language (what Blake calls a 'flat' language) is one in which word-order is very free within the clause, so that all the words which depend on a particular verb may occur in any order. Speaking of Kalkatungu, which is such a language, Blake reports: 'Not only can the verb and its arguments be arranged in any order, but where an argument is represented by more than one word, these words can appear in any order and may be scattered among the other words of the sentence.' However, 'where there are clearly two clauses in a sentence, words do not hop from one to another.' For example, we may take the following sentence:

(6) cipa-yi   tuku-yu   yaun-tu   yaṇi   icayi
    this-erg   dog-erg   big-erg   white-man   bite
    'this dog bit the white-man';

and we may literally put the words into any order we please, without producing an ungrammatical string.

Blake's interpretation of these facts is that the words for 'this', 'dog' and 'big' in (5) do not constitute a section of a single dependency chain, as their translation equivalents in English would, but rather they each depend directly on the verb 'bite'. The modifiers of a given verb may occur in any order, but those of different verbs cannot be mixed up together (this follows automatically from the principle of putting modifiers next to their heads, which is very general indeed in its application – see pp. 98 – 103). In contrast with English, then, a given semantic slot may be filled in Kalkatungu by the referents of more than one modifier – e.g. by the referents of 'this, 'dog' and 'big' in (5) – so the complexity of structure comes between the semantic and the syntactic structure in Kalkatungu, whereas it is in the syntactic structure itself in English. (We shall see that the semantic structure of a modifier, in English, is slotted into the semantic structure of its head, so that a single word's structure encapsulates the semantics of the whole of a dependency chain.)

My examples illustrate just two out of a wide variety of uses to which the notion 'dependency chain' can be put, and we shall meet other uses later.

Multiple heads and interdependence

The examples discussed so far have involved rather simple dependency chains, approaching the ultimate in simplicity of example (2) on p. 80, where each word had just one head and one modifier (except for the two ends of the chain). The only complication we have recognized has been that some words have had more than one modifier. Extreme examples of this possibility come from non-configurational languages, so the dependency structure of the sentence given in (6) above would be:

(1)

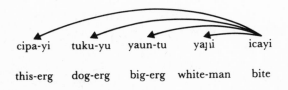

One thing on which all dependency theorists are agreed is that this possibility exists, and there has never been any attempt to limit the number of modifiers per word, except empirically (compare the binary tendency in the immediate-constituent tradition). We may call this pattern 'head-sharing', because several words all have the same word as head.

More controversial types of complication need to be recognized, however:

(a)   modifier-sharing, where one word acts as modifier for two different words;

(b)   interdependence, where A acts as head of B, but B also acts as head of A.

Modifier-sharing could also be called 'head-multiplying', because it involves one word which has more than one head. This kind of analysis seems to be advisable in constructions where transformationalists would invoke 'subject-raising' (or its current equivalent, such as 'Move-alpha'), which has the effect of allowing a single noun-phrase to act as subject of two verbs in the same sentence.

For example, it is well known that verbs like *seem* have a subject which must also be taken as subject of the infinitive (though in the semantics, this item is related only to the infinitive, and not at all to *seem*). Take a sentence like *John seems to like Mary. John* is clearly subject of *seems* (and therefore, like other subjects, a modifier), but it can be argued that it is also the syntactic subject of *like*, on various well-known grounds (e.g. if the subject is an 'idiom chunk', then it must be related to the rest of its idiom, namely the infinitive, at the syntactic level, not the semantic level, because this is the only level at which it exists; so *the cat* is subject of *be* as well as of *seems* in *The cat seems to be out of the bag*). Assuming then that *John* is syntactically (as well as semantically) related to *like*, in *John seems to like Mary*, we have no choice but to show this by a dependency structure like this:

(2)

John   seems   to   like   Mary

(I am following the now common practice of taking *to* as a subject-raising auxiliary verb, so it too has a syntactic subject which it shares with its infinitive; there is a discussion of this analysis in Hudson 1976a.) This, then, is an example of one word (*John*) which has more

than one head. In a more complex example, with more infinitives in the
dependency chain, the same word could have a very large number of
heads, but this need not worry us, except that the diagrams needed
would be rather complicated to look at.

Modifier-sharing is not restricted to subject-raising (and also
controlling) verbs, but is found in a wide variety of constructions. We
also find it in embedded interrogative clauses, such as *I don't know what
he said*. The word *what* depends on *know*, but it also depends on *said*. The
latter connection is obvious – *what* is object of *said* – but the former is
less obvious. One argument is that *what* can occur on its own, without
the rest of the interrogative clause, as in *He said something, but I don't know
what*. In this sentence, *what* must depend on *know*, because there is
nothing else for it to depend on, so we may assume that the same is true
even when there is something else to depend on. Another argument is
that if we take *what* as an instance of the more general category
'interrogative word' (also containing *whether*), then we have a simple
way of saying that verbs like *wonder* must take an interrogative clause as
their complement; they must take an interrogative word as their
modifier. Arguments such as this, then, lead us to analyse *what* as
modifier not only of *said*, but also of *know*. The dependency structure is
the following:

(3)
             I   don't   know   what   he   said

The second type of complex dependence is interdependence. There
are two different ways in which one can imagine interdependence, one
of which I believe need not be allowed for. This is the kind of
interdependence that would characterize some subtype of dependency
relation; thus we might imagine a classification of companion relations
into those with and those without dependency, and then the former
might be subdivided into those with asymmetrical dependency and
those with symmetrical dependency (i.e. interdependence). Such a view
of interdependence has been suggested by some dependency theorists
(e.g. Heringer 1970), but I can see no place for it, at least not in the
version of dependency theory which I am advocating here. After all,
what would 'symmetrical dependency' be, if not the same as pure
companion-ship without dependency?

Another type of interdependence does seem to be needed, however,
and indeed I have just used it (in the structure for *I don't know what he
said*). This is where two separate dependency relations both happen to
involve the same pair of words, but each relation treats a different word

as head. Take the last example, where the arc linking *what* to *said* has an arrow at each end, to show interdependence. These two words are linked in two ways. First, *what* is head, with *said* depending on it, because *what* is an interrogative word, as permitted by verbs such as *know* and *wonder*, and because interrogative words may (but need not) be followed by a finite verb (e.g. *said*). Hence the arrow pointing at *said*. Secondly, however, *said* is head, with *what* as modifier, because *what* is its object, and objects are always modifiers of the verbs to which they belong (for well-known reasons to do with transitivity, semantic structure and so on). This explains the other arrow, pointing at *what*. The significant point is that these arrows represent separate, and independent, relations, because the word on which the finite verb depends need not be its object, and indeed could be modifier of a different verb altogether (e.g. *I don't know what he said he was going to do*, where *what* modifies *do*). Thus there are interdependence relations in sentence structure, but these always reflect a pair of separate entries in the grammar.

To summarize, then, dependency theory needs to recognize the following configurations of dependency structure:

(a)   one word may have any number of modifiers, including zero;
(b)   one word may have any number of heads, including zero;
(c)   a pair of words may be interdependent as a result of a chance coincidence of two conflicting dependency constructions.

It is worth looking for further constraints on possible configurations; for example, I think it is unlikely that any single entry in the grammar will specifically sanction more than two heads for a single word, whereas it is common for entries to require just two heads (e.g. the entries for subject-raising and control verbs do just that.) If this is the case, it will be worth looking for a functional explanation, and if we fail to find one, then we shall have an instance of an arbitrary constraint which may turn out to be specific to language. Pending such discoveries, however, we can conclude that the range of dependency configurations actually found more or less exhausts all the logical possibilities.

Dependency within the word

All the discussion so far has rested on the assumption that dependency relations occur between words, but not between parts of words, so that dependency and composition (or, more generally, companion-ship and composition) are in complementary distribution: parts of a word are related by composition, separate words are related by dependency/companion-ship. We may now question this assumption, though no definitive answer will emerge at the end of the discussion.

On pp. 48 – 52 we discussed two parts of grammar where syntax and morphology are intermingled: clitics and compounds. In the case of clitics, it is very clear that there are dependency relations among the parts of a word. For example, consider the French sentence *Il le connaît,* 'He knows him.' Assuming that we take *il,* 'he' and *le,* 'him' as clitics (following the now established tradition), the whole expression must be a single word, containing the words *il* and *le.* But one of the main reasons for saying that *il* and *le* are words, rather than prefixes, is that they function syntactically like separate words, and each may be replaced by a full noun (e.g. *Jean* and *Pierre*), without affecting grammaticality, or other parts of the meaning. Thus, from a syntactic point of view, *il* and *Jean,* and *le* and *Pierre,* need not be distinguished (except perhaps in terms of class-membership); but *il* and *le* have to occur in the clitic position, just before the verb, whereas *Jean* and *Pierre* follow the usual rules of syntax: *Jean connaît Pierre.* Thus, if *Jean* and *Pierre* are modifiers of *connaît,* so should *il* and *le* be. Furthermore, if we do not recognize *il* and *le* as modifiers, and more specifically as subject and object respectively, then we shall have difficulty in reconciling the grammaticality of this sentence with the general rule that finite verbs (such as *connaît*) must have a subject, and the specific requirement that forms of *connaître* (e.g. *connaît*) must have an object.

Let us assume, then, that the dependency structures for *Jean connaît Pierre* and for *il le connaît* are similar, although the word orders are different. This similarity is shown in (1):

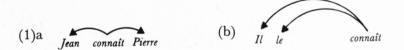

(1)a   *Jean   connaît   Pierre*   (b)   *Il   le   connaît*

But now we also want to distinguish the clitic pronouns *il* and *le* from the independent *Jean* and *Pierre.* The former behave like affixes, as we have already noted (page 49), so what we need is a larger word within whose structure *il* and *le* can be treated like affixes to *connaît:* the word *il le connaît.* This relation is shown in (2):

(2)

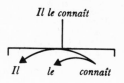

The only other fact about *il le connaît* that the analysis needs to show is that it is an instance of 'French word'; this is necessary because otherwise we should not be explaining the affix-like properties of *il* and *le*. Further classification (e.g. as a verb) is unnecessary and redundant, in view of all the information already available about *connaît* itself (which will be analysed in just the same way as in *Jean connaît Pierre*); so this ad-hoc, unstored word will be related directly to 'French word', as an instance. (There are precedents for such analyses even among stored words; for example, there seems little point in trying to assign some part-of-speech analysis to the English word *oh*, as in *Oh, is that so?*.) The main point of this discussion is that the dependency relations between *connaît* and the pronouns apply within a word.

Compounds too seem to suggest this kind of analysis, in which the second part of the compound (in English, that is) acts as head, and the first part as modifier. For example, in *furniture shop* the word *shop* provides the link between *furniture* and the rest of the sentence – it is because *shop* is a noun that the whole can occur where nouns can occur; if the whole were plural, the suffix would be added to *shop*, not to *furniture*; and semantically, a furniture shop is a kind of shop, and not a kind of furniture. This is a completely orthodox and traditional analysis, and if we accept it and the equally orthodox view that a compound is a single word, then we thereby accept dependency within the word. In this case, however, unlike the clitic case, we can and must classify the larger word (*furniture shop*) as a noun, in order to allow for the recursion typical of compounds.

(3)

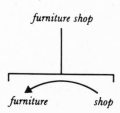

Some linguists (Williams 1981, Selkirk 1981) have recently suggested that we should extend this kind of analysis even to the relation between a root and its suffix, where the latter determines the syntactic category of the whole (e.g. in *beautify*, the head would be *-fy*, because this marks the word as a verb). I am not convinced that this step is necessary, at least not in a word grammar, because we can easily express the necessary generalization in other ways. For example, we could have a very general entry for English words which allows their stems to contain a suffix, and then list all the relevant suffixes as instances of this one suffix entity. Moreover, the Williams/Selkirk analysis is certain to raise problems when it comes to preventing suffixes from occurring on their own, as full words – if *fy* is a verb, why is it that it cannot occur in the positions normally available to verbs, e.g. **I will fy?* It seems better to take a conservative position on this issue.

On the other hand, there are reasons for entertaining a radical extension of the analysis given for compounds to other parts of the grammar too, at least in English. One of the curiosities of English is that different word-order rules apply in different areas of the grammar. As far as verbs and their modifiers are concerned, modifiers generally follow their heads, or else can occur equally easily before or after (as with some kinds of adverbial). There are exceptions, the most obvious being the position of the subject, but the general pattern is quite clear. As far as other word-classes than verbs are concerned, the same is generally true as well, but certain general classes of word regularly occur before their heads – adjectives precede their head nouns, adverbs precede their head adjective or adverb, and so on. And then, as we have just seen, compounds always have their heads after their modifiers. One could interpret these patterns as showing that English grammar provides two separate models for word-order: the verb, with its following modifiers, and the compound, with its preceding modifier. (One could go on to interpret the two patterns diachronically, of course, and see the verb as a source of innovation, with compounds preserving the old Germanic order, just as French clitics preserve the Latin order.)

Now we could remodel the grammatical analysis to take account of this informal interpretation, by greatly extending the scope of the notion 'compound' – by extending it, in fact, to include all constructions in which the modifier precedes its head. (We can exclude the subject from this reanalysis, because its position is fixed by other principles.) This would mean that analyses like that suggested above for *furniture shop* would be given also to expressions like *London shop* (where each word has a separate stress), and even to *expensive shop*. That is, *expensive shop* would be shown as a single word containing a modifier followed by its head. Similar analyses would be needed for examples like *very fast*, and even for *soon left* as in *John soon left*.

This reanalysis may seem perverse, in requiring us to stretch our ordinary understanding of the meaning of 'word', but it is hard to find solid reasons for rejecting it. Here are some points in favour of it:

(a) Once we have accepted that *furniture shop* is a single word, we have already stretched the normal meaning of 'word', since the latter is tied to writing and the fact is that we have a word-space between *furniture* and *shop*; so the layman's word only provides a very rough model for the meaning of 'word' as used by the linguist, and we need not feel bound to use this term in the layman's sense.

(b) The word-order rules for English would be extremely simple under the reanalysis:

(i)   most generally, a modifier follows its head;
(ii) some kinds of adverbial are exceptional in being free to come either before or after their heads;
(iii) the position of the subject (and various kinds of topicalized or otherwise front-shifted words) is fixed by other principles, so they precede their heads;
(iv) if a modifier and its head are both part of a word, then the modifier comes first;
(v)   there are odd lexical exceptions – e.g. *enough* follows its head.

(c) The reanalysis would explain why premodifiers cannot themselves have postmodifiers, which is otherwise an odd and arbitrary restriction; for example, *nice* may be postmodified by *to look at*, but not if *nice* itself premodifies a noun (e.g. **nice to look at scenery*). The reason for this restriction is that the parts of a word cannot be separated by other words which are not part of the same word – a natural restriction to put on part: whole relations in general (namely, that wholes should be continuous in space and time). And *to look at* cannot be part of the same word as *nice scenery*, because the composition of a word only provides a maximum of two places, and these places are already filled (by *nice* and *scenery*). On the other hand, if the first word has a premodifier, there is no problem because the two together constitute a single word, and only occupy one place in the larger word's structure; so *very nice scenery* is fine.

(d) Under the reanalysis it is easy to accommodate examples like *blue-eyed*, because *blue eye* is a word, therefore a single unit, therefore a possible first member of a word consisting of it plus *-ed*, and comparable with a simple word like *beard* (as in *bearded*). Under a more conventional dependency analysis, *-ed* would need to be added to a pair of words with no unifying factor other than the dependency relation between them; furthermore it would be hard to explain why *pretty-coloured* is fine, but *this-coloured* and *every-coloured* are not. The reanalysis does offer an explanation for this difference: *this colour* and *every colour* are not single words, because (as I shall argue in the next subsection) determiners (e.g. *this, every*) are not modifiers, but heads.

I offer this reanalysis as a possibility which deserves serious consideration, but a good deal more research will be needed before we can be sure how seriously to take it. Meanwhile, I shall assume more conventional analyses in the rest of this book, out of respect for most readers' probable scepticism. But I think we can take it as fairly well established that it is possible in principle for parts of a word to be in a dependency relation to one another.

Determiners as heads?

My subject here is not so much a general matter of principle as a point in the analysis of English, but it needs some discussion because my position is controversial, and the constructions involved occur in virtually every example sentence. The question is, how should we analyse the dependency relations between determiners and nouns? The traditional assumption is that the noun is head (hence the common term 'head-noun'), whereas I shall argue for the determiner being head. The main types of determiner that I shall consider will be quantifiers (*all, every, three*, etc.), articles (*a, the, some*) and various other words such as *this* and *which*. (Terminology in this area is extremely unsatisfactory and unhelpful.) What follows are some reasons for saying that when such words are followed by a noun, they are the head and the latter is the modifier.

(a) Many of these words (e.g. *all, three, some, this, which*) can occur on their own, with an understood noun, in positions otherwise available only to nouns (e.g. as inverted subject), so they must themselves be classifiables as nouns, unless we invoke some kind of deep structure in which the noun is present, and allow surface structure to deviate. Traditionally, they are called 'pronouns' when used on their own, and 'adjectives' or 'articles' otherwise, but it is hard to see any evidence that their class-membership is different in the two cases.

(b) Many of them can be followed by an optional *of* phrase (e.g. *all/three/which of the boys*), with the lexical noun in a clearly modifying position, inside the *of* phrase, and this fact has led other linguists (e.g. Jackendoff 1972, Hogg 1977) to adopt an analysis for at least some determiners similar to the one I am proposing here.

(c) The lack of lexical content in determiners is irrelevant, because there is no general requirement for heads to have more lexical-type meaning than their modifiers. Furthermore, there is a clear parallel in the verb system, where auxiliaries stand to 'main' verbs in much the same way as determiners stand to lexical nouns. It is now widely accepted that a main verb is syntactically subordinate to its auxiliary verb (Pullum and Wilson 1977 is a particularly important collection of evidence), and I have accepted this analysis in all my dependency analyses. So if one can accept the semantically empty *does* of *John does like syntax* as head of *like*, there should be no objection (at least on these grounds) to taking even *a* or *the* as head of a following noun.

(d) A case can be made (e.g. Sommerstein 1972, Postal 1966) for the analysis of *the* as an allomorph of *he, she, it* and *they*, none of which can occur before a lexical noun (in contrast with *we* and *you*, which can, as witness *we/you linguists*). This analysis makes it natural to take *the* either as head, or as the first of two nouns in apposition, whatever relation that implies (see the brief discussion of apposition on p. 78 above).

(e) This analysis explains why the determiner is always before any adjectival or other modifiers: if the lexical noun modifies the determiner, then its own modifiers must not be separated from it by the determiner (according to a principle of adjacency to be explained below). Otherwise there is no explanation for the total ungrammaticality of examples such as *big the boy*. The same conclusion holds even if we accept the compound analysis of premodifiers discussed in the previous subsection: if determiners were modifiers, they would be premodifiers, so again they should be able to occur in different orders relative to other premodifiers.

It is true that the adoption of this analysis raises some problems, notably the overlap between determiners and premodifiers (numbers can be taken as belonging to either), and the fact that lexical nouns are also optional after ordinary adjectives. These similarities between determiners and premodifiers suggest that we might hope to be able to find an analysis which makes the difference between them less radical than under the analysis I am proposing. On balance, however, I favour this analysis, and shall continue to assume it throughout this book.

CONSTITUENT STRUCTURE
Similarities and differences between dependency structure and constituent structure

There are considerable similarities between dependency structures and the more familiar constituent structures, as far as the information they convey is concerned. Indeed, the similarities are so great that Robinson (1970) has argued that the two kinds of structure are equivalent (both weakly and even strongly) – a conclusion which goes some way to explain the general neglect of dependency theory among linguists familiar with constituent structure. The general connection between dependency structure and constituent structure is that a constituent can be defined as some word plus all the words depending on it, either directly or indirectly (in other words, that word plus all the dependency chains leading up to it). For example, the structure for *The cat sat on the mat* would be as follows according to the two types of analysis, with the phrase-marker built in a mechanical way onto the dependency structure to show the simple relation between them:

(1)

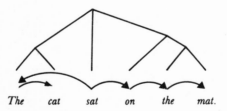

The   cat   sat   on   the   mat.

The phrase-marker is somewhat unorthodox in that it gives a three-way split into subject, verb and object, rather than the usual subject – predicate division; but it is no less a phrase-marker for that.

I should like to dispute the claim that dependency structure is equivalent to constituent structure. I know of three differences between them which all suggest non-equivalence:

(a) Constituent structure, in itself, lacks the information about the asymmetrical relation between the head and its modifiers which is available in dependency structure. It is true that recent developments in phrase-structure theory have been in the direction of making this information available through the labelling, either indirectly through the apparatus of $\overline{X}$ theory (Jackendoff 1977) or directly, via the label 'Head' (Gazdar and Pullum 1981). It is encouraging to see this increasing recognition of the importance of dependency relations, especially among linguists who are (apparently) unaware of the literature on dependency theory, much less influenced by it. However, the fact remains that without this special enrichment, constituency-based analysis does not show which words are heads and which are their modifiers.

(b) Conversely, constituent structure provides more 'information' than dependency structure, in that it provides extra nodes. For the six-word sentence *The cat sat on the mat*, the dependency structure provided just six nodes to which further information could be attached (i.e. six linguistic entities), whereas the constituent structure provided these six plus four more, one for each of the noun-phrases, one for the prepositional phrase, and one for the whole sentence. The question is whether these extra nodes are actually needed. The currently popular answer, based on $\overline{X}$ theory, is already nearer to 'no' than it would have been before the arrival of $\overline{X}$ theory, because the syntactic features on the head now have to be just the same as those on the phrasal node, so the latter cannot be used to carry extra features. The only information which distinguishes the higher nodes from their respective head nodes is carried by the number of bars, so we shall have to concentrate in the later discussion on the necessity for these bars.

(c) If we take constituent structure to be equivalent to a labelled bracketing, then it cannot provide the kind of analysis which I described above as 'modifier sharing' (see p. 83), in spite of the optimistic remarks of some linguists (e.g. Sampson 1975). In such an analysis there is no way in which *John* could be shown as belonging both to *seems* and also to *like*, in *John seems to like syntax*; the only solution is to provide two distinct structures, one for each of these relations, and link them by transformation.

As with the first difference, it would be possible to change the theory of constituent structure in order to make it more similar to dependency theory, and any such change would be welcome. An example of such a change is the suggestion of Rouveret and Vergnaud (1980), quoted with approval by Chomsky (1981:128). They suggest that every NP which is a sister of a particular verb should be explicitly linked to the verb by an index, which would presumably be exactly equivalent to a dependency arrow. Once this device, and all its attendant machinery, is introduced into a phrase-structure grammar, it would be very close in power to a dependency grammar; and it might well be possible to link a single noun-phrase node to two different verbs. However, the question which would then arise would be whether all the bits of phrase-structure theory which distinguished it from dependency theory (notably, higher nodes) were really necessary; and if the answer was no, then the resulting change would in effect mean that phrase-structure grammar had become dependency theory.

Some disadvantages, and dubious advantages, of constituent structure

It should be clear by now that word grammar makes no use of linguistic entities larger than words, with the exception of those needed for co-ordinate structures. To be more precise, a word grammar, as such, makes no reference to phrases, clauses or sentences, either by these terms or by any other name, but this need not prevent us from using such words as part of our metalanguage. There can be no objection to talking about 'the sentence *The cat sat on the mat*', or 'the phrase *the cat*', so long as this is not taken to imply that these units are part of the technical analysis which a word grammar would generate. The present subsection will present some reasons for accepting this highly controversial view.

(a) We start with the tradition. Many linguists have the impression, I think, that constituent structure (by which I shall mean here 'constituent structure above the word', of course) is part of our long grammatical tradition, but this is not so. For example, it was not recognized by Paṇiṇi (Kiparsky and Staal 1969), nor by Thomas of Erfurt and the other fourteenth-century modistae (Covington 1979). In fact, according to Percival 1976 it is possible to date its birth quite precisely: it was invented by the psychologist Wundt in the last decades of the nineteenth century, and borrowed from him by Leonard Bloomfield, who introduced it into American linguistics. So the grammatical tradition actually provides more support for dependency theory than it does for constituent structure.

(b) A positive disadvantage of constituent structure is that it makes strict subcategorization difficult or even impossible (according to how 'strict' is strict). For example, it is clearly necessary to refer in strict subcategorization to complementizers and tense (Hendrick 1981, Chomsky 1981:81), but strict subcategorization is only allowed to refer to sisters, and complementizers and tense are not normally analysed in such a way as to make them available for strict subcategorization. One could patch up the constituent structure approach in various ways: so Hendrick suggests relaxing the constraint that strict subcategorization only refer to sisters, and Chomsky suggests reanalysing sentence structure so that tense is a feature on the abstract element INFL, which should be taken as the head of its sentence, and therefore (presumably) available for strict subcategorization although still not a sister of the governing verb. In dependency structure, on the other hand, there is no problem, because the words that need to be referred to (the tensed verb and the complementizers) are in any case analysed as modifiers of the verb on which they depend. As Brame puts it, 'Once it is seen that all lexical selection is defined in terms of head selectors, then there is no longer any reason to incorporate trees and non-lexical categories' (1983:159) – in fact, trees and non-lexical categories simply get in the way.

To illustrate the difference between the two approaches, I shall give analyses for the sentence *I wonder who he saw*, showing how remote the interrogative pronoun is from *wonder* in the phrase-structure analysis, and how close it is in the dependency one. The point is that we must subcategorize *wonder* as a verb which takes an (optional) interrogative clause (i.e. an interrogative word plus its optional modifier, a finite verb).

(1)

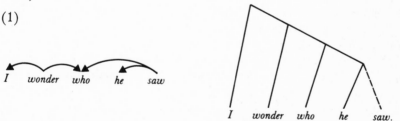

Similar comparisons could be made for a number of other constructions, in all of which the restricted word is a modifier of the restricting word in a dependency analysis, but quite remote from it in a phrase-structure analysis.

(c) Another example of phrase-structure getting in the way comes from predicatives, as analysed by Williams (1980). A predicative adjective defines a property of some entity, which is defined by some other word in the sentence, which we may refer to as the subject of the adjective. The adjective's subject may be the subject of the verb (e.g. *She seems nice*) or its object (e.g. *He made her angry*), but it cannot be a prepositional object (e.g. *John loaded the hay into the wagon green* is fine, but not **John loaded the wagon with hay green*). The relevant generalization is very easy to make in terms of dependency structure: the subject of a predicative adjective whose head is some verb V is some other modifier of V. In a phrase-structure analysis, on the other hand, it is more complicated: the subject of a predicative adjective P is either the noun-phrase which is sister of the verb-phrase containing P, or another noun-phrase which is sister of P itself. Moreover, this analysis does not explain why this particular range of noun-phrases should behave alike, since there is no other unifying factor which brings together the subject and the noun-phrases inside the verb-phrase.

(d) It has been claimed that experimental evidence points to the psychological reality of constituent structure, but Atkinson *et al.* (1982:250) comment before surveying this evidence: 'Historically, psycholinguists have paid little attention to a dependency approach to syntax, so the implications of the following discussion for such an approach are not clear.' Moreover, the available evidence is itself surprisingly inconclusive even in relation to a phrase-structure analysis, since it is not clear to which level of structure it is relevant – e.g. it could be indicative of semantic structure (Steedman forthcoming).

(e) One of the glories of phrase-structure grammar is the verb-phrase, which allows one to distinguish (among other things) among objects, subjects and peripheral (non-subcategorized) adverbials. Without phrase structure, there are no verb phrases, so none of these distinctions can be made – in that way. However, it is debatable whether these distinctions should be made in this particular way, as a matter of segmentation. The main difference is that subjects are introduced by a more general rule than those responsible for objects and other complements, and peripheral adverbials are introduced by a more general rule still. So we can achieve just the same distinctions, but more directly, by invoking the generality of the rules concerned. Verbs have three kinds of modifier: modifiers introduced by entries for specific verbs (complements), modifiers introduced by the entry for verbs in general, and then refined by the one for finite verbs in particular, and even further by the one for auxiliary verbs (subjects), and modifiers introduced by the entry for verbs in general (peripheral adverbials).

The order of elements will follow from these distinctions plus the general principle governing adjacency which we shall introduce in the next section.

A similar treatment is possible for another much-quoted piece of evidence for the bars in $\overline{X}$ syntax: the grammaticality difference between *a student of linguistics with long hair* and **a student with long hair of linguistics* (Radford 1981:98). This is said to show the need for a distinction between N (the node dominating *of linguistics*) and $\overline{N}$ (the one dominating *with long hair*), but once again the distinction will in any case be made by the different scopes of the rules responsible for the phrases concerned: *of linguistics* is permitted by the specific entry for *student* (*of* X defines the subject being studied), while *with long hair* is a phrase that could have been added to virtually any noun, to specify some property of the referent. As in the previous example, the general principle for adjacency will make sure that *of linguistics* is nearer to *student* than *with long hair* is.

(f) A related argument for $\overline{X}$ syntax is connected with the use of *one* as a dummy noun, the point being that *one* can combine with *with long hair*, but not with *of linguistics* (hence *one with long hair*, meaning 'a student with long hair', but not **one of linguistics* meaning 'a student of linguistics'). This is said to show that *one* can replace $\overline{N}$ but not just N (Radford 1981:98, Jackendoff 1977:58); but the facts could just as easily be taken to show that *of linguistics* is allowed, with that particular meaning, only after words whose strict subcategorization specifically permits such a phrase to occur, which means *student* can take it, but *one* cannot. In contrast, *with long hair* is the kind of phrase that can occur with any old noun, so it is just as good with *one* as it is with *student*.

It has often been pointed out that the existence of strict subcategorization information in the lexicon makes phrase-structure rules redundant (Heny 1977, Chomsky 1981:31, Starosta 1979; actually, this is true only for phrase-structure rules which introduce lexical categories). What I am in effect arguing is that the existence of strict subcategorization information in the lexicon also makes the distinction between X and $\overline{X}$ redundant (provided we have a theory which allows the grammar to exploit the information appropriately, as word grammar does).

In addition to the above arguments for $\overline{X}$ theory, it has been claimed that there is evidence for other constituency-based theories. For instance, I myself produced some arguments for higher nodes in my book on daughter-dependency grammar (1976a: Appendix A).

However, on further examination these arguments turned out to be very weak. I claimed there that gerunds could only be classified as both nouns and verbs if we had two separate nodes, one representing a noun-phrase, the other a verb making up the whole of this noun-phrase. But the same effect can probably be achieved by classifying gerunds both as verbs and as nouns, provided that we can prevent any of the general rules for noun-modifiers from applying to them. This is something I am not yet sure how to do, but the outlines of the analysis at least seem plausible. My other arguments were equally weak (see p. 187).

What I have tried to do is to show that a prima-facie case exists for my view that phrases, clauses and sentences need not be referred to in a grammar, and that it is now up to defenders of phrase-structure grammar to put their case. Even if they turn out to be right, I shall feel that the exercise has been worthwhile because it should have the effect of raising the level of argumentation about the need for constituent structure, which is generally very low at present (e.g. in introductory textbooks), because the dependency alternative is never considered. For the beginnings of a debate, see Hudson 1980c, Dahl 1980, Hudson 1980a, Hietaranta 1981 and Hudson 1981.

WORD-ORDER
Adjacency

Dependency structure is relevant to word-order in much the same ways as constituent structure: word-order tends to respect the integrity of the units defined by dependency structure (i.e. the units consisting of a head plus its modifiers), and it is with respect to these units that the rules for ordering words in relation to one another are stated. I am concerned here only with the first of these two facts, which involves the notion of 'adjacency' – a modifier tends to be adjacent to its head, in just the same way that the parts of a single phrase or clause tend to be adjacent, in constituent-structure terms. In other words, discontinuities are avoided unless specifically sanctioned.

The adjacency of heads and modifiers is covered by what I shall call the 'adjacency principle', which has been known to dependency theorists for some time. It was formulated by Robinson (1970) as follows:

(1)   *Adjacency principle*
    'If A depends directly on B [i.e. is a modifier of B], and some other

element C intervenes between them (in linear order of strings), then C depends directly on A or on B or on some other intervening element.'

The effect of this principle is to guarantee that a modifier is never separated from its head by anything other than (a) another modifier, together with its dependents or (b) its own dependents. These two possibilities are shown by the following pair of structures, in which the modifier concerned is *wine*, and its head is *bring*.

(2a)   (b)

Bring   all   my   important guests wine   bring   red   wine

Putting it more simply still, the principle bans the crossing of dependency lines. Like our other principles, this one too may be overridden by more specific requirements, but most constructions in English respect it, and I suspect that all languages will be found to respect it, if we bear in mind the dependency analysis of non-configurational languages which I suggested on pp. 81–2 (see in particular the dependency diagram (1) on p. 82).

We can break the adjacency principle down into two much simpler principles, called the 'simple-adjacency principle' and the 'priority-to-the-bottom principle'.

(3)   *Simple Adjacency Principle*
   A modifier must not be separated from its head by anything
   except other modifiers of the same head.
                 Priority to the Bottom Principle
   The adjacency requirements of a word A take priority over
   those of any other word which is higher than A in the same
   dependency chain.

Metaphorically speaking, when you are putting words together to make a sentence, and all you know is the dependency structure, then you start at the bottom end of each dependency chain, and work upwards; and if you do this, all you need pay attention to is the simple-adjacency principle.

What is the status of these principles – are they part of the grammar of English, or part of the structure of language, or part of the structure of thought in general? We can rule out the first possibility, on the assumption that very many languages are subject to the principles.

However, the principles do not seem to follow from the selective-inheritance principle (see p. 18), which is the only general principle that I have so far suggested for the exploitation of linguistic and non-linguistic knowledge. (The selective-inheritance principle does not apply because the dependency chain involves dependency, and not instantiation; a modifier is not an instance of its head, so there is no reason for its requirements to take priority over the latter's, as far as the selective-inheritance principle is concerned.) On the other hand, our dustbin example (see p. 39) showed that dependency relations are also found in non-linguistic knowledge, and it is clear that the simple-adjacency and priority-to-the-bottom principles apply here too. For example, if you know that the book is on the table, and that the coin is under the book, then you automatically assume that the coin is in between the book and the table, and not under the table. I take it, then, that these two principles are part of our general cognitive structure, and not specific to language. As such, they belong to the list of general principles which includes the selective-inheritance principle.

Although the selective-inheritance principle does not explain the above facts, it does interact with the simple-adjacency principle in an interesting way. As we have seen, it is normal for a word to be an instance of several different entities, such as a lexical item, an inflectional category, and a word class. For instance, the word *takes* is an instance of the lexical item *take*, the inflectional categories 's-verb', 'present', 'tensed' and 'finite' (see (3) on p. 47 for these categories), and the category 'verb'. Now each of these entities could be responsible for the presence of one or more modifiers on the word, and as we have already seen (p. 97) the adjacency requirements of an instance take priority over those of its model, as we might expect from the selective-inheritance principle (or at least its component principle, the priority-to-the-instance principle – see p. 16). In particular, the modifiers introduced by the lexical entry take priority, for adjacency, over those introduced by the entry for verbs.

Let us take an example: *John takes pills at night*. Here, *pills* must be nearer to *takes* than *at night* is, because *pills* is a lexically specified complement, and *at night* is not. (The distinction which I am making here is that between 'actants' and 'circonstants' made by Tesnière, and widely accepted by other dependency theorists; it also corresponds to the distinction between elements inside the verb phrase and those outside it, as I pointed out earlier.) Furthermore, the subject *John* has a different status from *pills* because it is allowed by the entry for verbs, and required by the entry for tensed verbs, rather than by the lexical entry for *take*; but there is no conflict between *John* and *pills* over adjacency because they are on different sides of the verb. The following diagram shows these relations between dependency, adjacency and instantiation. It can be seen that it is somewhat more complex than the dependency structures given so far in this chapter, because we have been disregarding the instantiation relations.

(4)

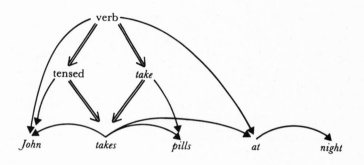

The effect of applying the principle of priority to the instance in cases like this is that dependency arrows originating at higher-level categories must not intersect one another.

Another application of this principle is that it may override the priority-to-the-bottom principle. This arises in cases of extraposition, such as the extraposed relative clause in *Anyone is wrong who disagrees with me*. Taking *who* as the head of the relative clause (along the same lines as the embedded interrogative clauses discussed earlier), it obviously does not comply with the simple-adjacency principle (as it would have done if it had not been extraposed). To account for such examples, we introduce a specific entry for extraposition, which overrides the general principle (being more specific), and adds another dependency line connecting the extraposed item to the verb. In effect, this allows us to pretend that the extraposed word is a modifier of the verb, and to treat it accordingly as far as its position is concerned. The diagram for the structure is as follows:

(5)

Anyone   is   wrong   who   disagrees   with   me.

Since this effect is to be achieved by a specific entry, I had better give
the entry.

(6)

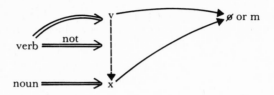

The extraposed item is represented here by *m* (for 'modifier'), and the
item from which it has been extraposed by *x*. (In the example sentence,
anyone is *x*, *is* is *v*, and *who* is *m*.) The dependency line pointing to *x* from
v goes straight down so as to avoid any implications of temporal order,
because *x* may come either before the verb (as in the example) or after
it (as in *I always think anyone wrong who disagrees with me*). This dependency
line is also dotted, in order to show that *x* is in the dependency chain
leading up to *v*, but need not be a modifier of *v* (e.g. *Very few of the people
are wrong who disagree with me*). The instantiation arrow with *not* written
on it shows that none of the words between *v* and *x* must be a verb –
hence the 'non-cyclicity' of extraposition shown by the ungrammaticality of examples like **That anyone is wrong is my firm conviction who
disagrees with me*.

I have discussed extraposition because it constitutes an exception to
the simple-adjacency principle, where the latter is overridden by an
entry which applies to an instance (verb) of the general category (word)
to which the former applies. There are other such exceptions, of course,
but I shall just mention one of them, which I consider problematic:
indirect objects. By this term I mean a noun, without preposition,
occurring between a verb and the latter's direct object, such as *Mary* in
the following: *I gave Mary a present*; *I bought Mary a present*; *I envied Mary
her present*. The first and last of these examples show lexically restricted
uses of the indirect object, so it is appropriate in these cases for the
indirect object to be next to the verb, whether before or after the direct
object (how to restrict this ordering is another matter, which is less of a
problem). But in the second example the indirect object is used in a way
that is quite generally available to all verbs that have certain semantic
properties (namely: 'It is possible to use the indirect object construction
when the process is one in which the direct object is something that is
produced, obtained or presented' – Young 1980:129). This being so,

the indirect object should be further from the verb than the (lexically selected) direct object, on the ground that there is no need for the lexical entry for a verb like *buy* to mention the indirect object at all. But in fact the order of elements is the same as in the other examples. This is a problem for word grammar, because it is not clear how we can explain this infringement of the simple-adjacency principle in combination with the priority-to-the-instance principle. But it is of course also a problem for phrase-structure grammar and transformational grammar, because the indirect object is within the verb-phrase, although it is not relevant to the strict subcategorization of the verb. Word grammar offers a number of possible lines of attack on the problem, but for the present it is best to identify the problem as one needing serious attention.

Temporal order

Once we have grouped words around their heads, by the principles that I have just explained, we have to consider the order in which they occur relative to the head and relative to one another. In order to talk about temporal order, we need some notation for saying 'A precedes B', since we cannot always exploit the left – right dimension on the page. (In particular we cannot do this if we are using the formulaic notation, but even if we are using the diagrammatic notation we sometimes face problems, such as when we want to leave the order of elements unspecified.) However, there is another area of language structure which raises the same problem: the semantics of time reference. We are concerned with the same relation in both cases, as we saw on p. 12, so we should use the same notation, and I shall adopt the convention, which is already widely used in temporal semantics, of representing points of time by digits whose value increases with time. Thus, 7 represents a later point in time than 4, and if we say '$x < y$', where x and y are points in time, then y follows x. (Please note the possible confusion here, arising from the use of '$<$' in historical linguistics; when a historical linguist writes '$x < y$', you verbalize it as 'x comes from y', where y exists earlier in time than x; but when you verbalize the same formula in word grammar, you should remember that '$<$' means 'is less than', as in mathematics.)

Without any real danger of confusion, we can now transfer this notation from points in time to events occurring at those points, namely uttered words; so we can let digits stand for the words in a sentence/utterance. This allows us to stop cheating in our notation, as

I have been doing so far in this chapter. I have been using the ordinary orthographic form to stand for each word in a sentence, but I also used this form to stand for the lexical item in the grammar, of which the word in the sentence is just an instance. Instances and their models are different entities (because they have different properties), so they must be kept separate in our notation if we are to avoid intolerable confusion. (The confusion becomes critical if there are two instances of the same word-model in a given sentence: if they both have the same name, how can we say different things about their heads and modifiers, their position in the sentence, their referents, and so on?) To solve this problem, then, we use digits for the words in the sentence, and show their temporal order by making the digits get larger with time. We can then reserve the orthographic forms for the lexical items in the grammar, of which the sentence words are instances. The dependency lines will then point to the digits, and not to the orthographic forms. (I have actually been preparing for this change by having the dependency lines will then point to the digits, and not to the orthographic forms. For instance:

(1)

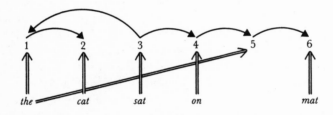

Armed with the new notation, we can state any ordering restriction with reference to these digits, using '<' to show which of two words comes first; and if we wish to say that one word comes immediately before another, we can represent the latter as n and the former as $n - 1$; or alternatively, as n and $n + 1$ respectively. (We shall see one of the apparently rather rare applications of the $n + 1$ notation to syntax in (7) below, but it is more useful in phonology, in that it allows us to refer to 'the next word' or 'the previous word' when dealing with things like the alternation between a and an in the English indefinite article.)

One of the most obvious attractions of a dependency-based grammar is in the field of word-order typology, where many generalizations can best be made in relation to dependency. This point was already recognized explicitly by Tesnière (1959:22), but it has more recently been made by other scholars such as Bartsch and Venneman (1972),

Dowty (1980) and Hawkins (1980). These scholars suggest that for many languages a single statement can be made about word-order, which is formulated in terms of the dependency categories 'modifier' and 'head' (though terminology differs somewhat from scholar to scholar) so that it applies to a wide range of constructions involving different word-classes. For example, one could say, quite simply, that in Japanese modifiers precede their heads, whereas in Welsh they follow them. Having stated these facts just once, for all constructions, there is then no need to add information about word-order in the rules dealing with the constructions concerned, and a very important generalization has been captured which would go unstated – even unnoticed – in a dependency-free grammar.

Such statements are very easy to formulate in word grammar, especially if we use the formulaic notation which is more neutral as to order than the diagrammatic notation. The relevant entry would be attached to the entity 'word' for the language concerned, and would cover any modifier that any word had; so for Japanese there would be an entry as follows:

(2)   modifier $_0^n$ (word): $\emptyset$ or m, m $<$ word

By the general principles for exploiting models, the name 'word' would be replaced by a number, so all we have to do in checking the word-order of a Japanese sentence is to make sure that the number standing for each word is lower than the number standing for its head. (The notation 'modifier ' is taken from generative phonology, and means 'any number (from 0 to n) of modifiers'.)

Of course, there are likely to be exceptions in most languages, and large-scale deviations in some. We have already seen that English is of the latter type (pp. 88 – 90), with a basic order of head before modifier, but the opposite order in compounds and those other patterns (e.g. adjective plus noun) which could, arguably, be taken as compounds. Another kind of deviation from the basic pattern may be produced by the influence of special structures, such as topicalization, but both kinds of deviation can be accommodated within a grammar that makes use of the selective-inheritance principle, because more particular word-order statements can override more general ones.

A particularly interesting discussion of deviations from the basic order is that of Hawkins (1980), from which a suggestive generalization seems to emerge: that some elements are more likely than others to be on the 'wrong' side of their heads, and that the likelihood of this being the case for a particular word-class is related to the size, and learnability, of the class. According to Hawkins, the most likely 'deviant' is the demonstrative, then the adjective, then the genitive, and finally the relative clause. Clearly, there are fewer demonstratives to learn than there are adjectives, so it would be easier for the whole class of demonstratives to be 'contaminated' by the odd lexical deviant than for this to happen to adjectives; and perhaps similar observations could be made about the other categories in the hierarchy.

We may assume, then, that some languages use the entry for 'word' to specify one order, and other languages use it to specify the other order. A third possibility is that a language might not say anything at all about the position of modifiers in its general entry for 'word', and this possibility is clearly realized in languages like Kalkatungu, which have completely free word-order (subject only to the requirements of adjacency). However, a language without a general order covering 'word' might well have more specific orderings for particular categories (e.g. one order for verbs and another for nouns). I do not know of such languages, but we might predict that they should exist, and if they do not, that will be an interesting discovery.

Dutch word-order

The topic of word-order in Dutch has been a popular talking-point since the paper by Bresnan *et al.* (1982) brought it to our attention. The problem is that the rules lead to crossed dependencies in some subordinate clauses. An example of such a sentence (actually, just the subordinate clause, since the main clause is irrelevant) is given in (3), with arcs linking verbs to their respective subjects.

(3)

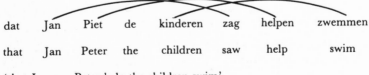

dat	Jan	Piet	de	kinderen	zag	helpen	zwemmen
that	Jan	Peter	the	children	saw	help	swim

'that Jan saw Peter help the children swim'.

Such constructions are interesting because they seem to be difficult to generate within the framework of phrase-structure grammar. This may or may not be so, but I can show that they are quite straightforward for word grammar. In the following analysis I shall have to make a few assumptions about Dutch which I cannot confirm, for lack of knowledge, but which seem reasonable.

All we need is four entries: one for each of *zag* and *helpen*, one for *dat*, and one for verbs in subordinate clauses.

(a) *dat*. This takes two obligatory modifiers, both of which follow it. The second is a tensed verb, the first is a word which is the subject of this verb, and therefore comes between the verb and *dat*. (I shall explain the labelling of subjects later.)

(4)

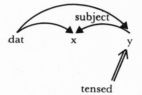

The dependency connection between *dat* and the subject is controversial, but some support for it comes from a West Flemish dialect in which the word corresponding to *dat* has two forms (*da* or *dan*) according to whether the subject is singular or plural (Haegeman 1983). The connection also helps to keep the subject before the object in embedded clauses, because of the effect of the adjacency principle keeping the subject (but not the object) next to *dat*.

(b) *zag*. This (or rather, the lexical item of which it is an instance) takes three modifiers: two nouns and an infinitive. One of the nouns is its own subject, and the other is taken as the subject of its infinitive. I shall not try to supply the semantic structure, but this would have a place for the referent of the first noun, but not for that of the second, which is semantically related only to its infinitive. It is important not to specify the positions of these modifiers in the lexical entry, so I shall use the formulaic notation:

(5)
        modifier(*zag*): a, model(a): noun
        subject(*zag*): a
        modifier(*zag*): b, model(b): noun
        modifier(*zag*): c, model(c): infinitive,
                    subject (c): b

This formula is compatible with the following structure, among others; and this structure is also compatible with the entry for *dat* in (4).

(6)

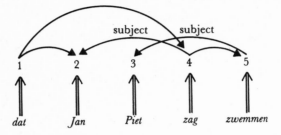

The only problem with (6) is that it infringes the adjacency principle, by separating *zwemmen* from its subject, *Piet*. So we now have to provide an entry which will override the adjacency principle in cases like this.

(c) *Verbs in subordinate clauses.* This is the entry we need, as it requires an infinitive which is a modifier of a subordinate verb to be the next word after that verb. It does not, however, allow any other of the subordinate verb's modifiers to follow it, so *Piet* must be separated from its head *zwemmen* by *zag* in (6). We can define 'subordinate verb' as any verb which has a head.

(7)   modifier $_0^1$ (x): x + 1, model(x): verb, head(x):y, model (y):word,
                     model(x + 1): infinitive
        modifier $_0^n$ (x): $\varnothing$ or b, b< x

In words, a verb (x) with a head may take an infinitive as its modifier, occurring as the next word in the sentence (x + 1); any other modifiers of such a verb must precede it. We have now justified the discontinuity in (6).

(d) *helpen.* The entry for *helpen* is just the same in all the relevant respects as that for *zag*, so there is no need to spell it out.

So what happens when we expand example (6), by replacing *zwemmen* by *helpen*, with *de kinderen* and *zwemmen* as its modifiers? Entry (7) requires the infinitive *helpen* to be the next word after *zag*, but it also requires *zwemmen* to be the next word after *helpen*, so the sentence must end in *zag helpen zwemmen*. There is no need to change anything at the front of (6), so the sentence must start with *dat Jan*. In.the space in the middle we have to fit *Piet* and *de kinderen*, depending respectively on *helpen* and *zwemmen*; but *zwemmen* depends on *helpen*, so the principle of priority to the bottom (see p. 00) requires us to give priority to the adjacency between *zwemmen* and *de kinderen*, and *Piet* is separated from its verb by *de kinderen*. So the correct word-order is the one shown in (3), and its dependency structure is as shown below. QED.

(8)

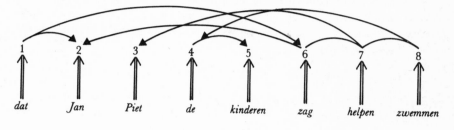

GRAMMATICAL RELATIONS
Dependency, instantiation and inherited variables

It is clear that we must be able to classify modifiers, because there are generalizations to be made about modifiers which are not just about the modifiers of single lexical items. Some such generalizations have to do with word-order, others have to do with case inflections (where available), others have to do with the semantic roles of the modifiers' referents, and so on. The question is, what kinds of groupings of modifiers are needed as a basis for these generalizations, and secondly, how should these groupings be reflected in the grammar. We shall see that word grammar allows two devices for expressing grammatical relations: inherited variables and explicit slot labels. Let us start with the former.

If the grammatical entry for some general word-type specifies a modifier, then all the instances of that word-type will automatically inherit that modifier, barring specific exclusions of it; but the rules for inheritance do not require the name of the modifier to be changed, so if it is called x as modifier of the word-type, it will be called x in the lexical entry as well. This means that all the different lexical entries which are instances of the same model word will inherit the same modifier from it, and will all have the same name for it (x). So if we want to make a generalization about all these modifiers, it is very easy to do so: we refer to x in the generalization, and write it down as part of the entry for the shared model.

Take the 'objects' of prepositions, for instance. Assuming that there is an entry for the category 'preposition', this will allow a modifier. Suppose we then want to make the generalizations about prepositional objects that they follow the preposition, and that they are nouns: we can impose these constraints on the modifier of the general word-type, and leave it to be inherited by all the instances. (Actually, of course, there would be no need to mention the word-order, because the order is the normal head-then-modifier.)

(1)   modifier (preposition): m, preposition $<$ m, model (m): noun

If some word is a 'regular' preposition, then it will inherit m, still labelled m to identify it with the modifier in (1), and with all the properties of m that are specified in (1). Now, suppose we have an irregular preposition, which is in fact a 'postposition' as far as order is concerned, but still only allows nouns as object (e.g. *ago*). We can still let it inherit m from (1), even though one of the constraints on m is different:

(2)   modifier (*ago*): m, m $<$ *ago*.

Since m in (2) is a variable, its properties can vary, but they will be inherited unchanged from (1) when they are not overridden, so there is no need to repeat the information about m being a noun.

Similarly, we could bring together all direct objects by having a direct object modifier in some general entry, and then leaving this to be inherited automatically by all instances of that category. That would imply, however, that we should divide verbs into those with and those without direct objects (i.e. into transitive and intransitive), and similarly for other modifier-types which some verbs have and others do not. In effect, this analysis would be tantamount to the use of arbitrary syntactic features for strict subcategorization, in preference to a direct statement of the strict subcategorization facts. (Examples of such arbitrary features are the traditional terms 'transitive' and 'intransitive', which Chomsky replaced in 1965; and the rule-numbers used for strict subcategorization in generalized phrase-structure grammar, explained in Gazdar and Pullum 1982.) The trouble with arbitrary features used in this way is that they are in one – one relation to some property, but they present this property indirectly, via another property; for instance, instead of saying '*take* needs an object,' we say '*take* is a transitive verb, and transitive verbs need an object, therefore *take* needs an object.'

An alternative way of handling such facts is to show the modifier concerned (in this case, the direct object) as optional for the general word-type, and then specify it as obligatory for those words where it is obligatory. Any generalizations about things like word-order and case inflection can be made in relation to the general entry, but the individual lexical entries can override this by making it more specific: instead of 'Ø or m', we have just 'm', which is more specific. Thus, whereas for verbs in general the entry would be 'modifier (verb): Ø or m', for *take* it would be 'modifier (*take*): m'.

It may seem that the converse situation, where the modifier is not allowed, should be equally easy to handle, but this is not in fact so. The link among all the direct objects is provided just by the variable-name (e.g. *m*) which stands for them all; but if we want to say that the direct object cannot occur, obviously we cannot use *m*, because we have to resolve the disjunction in favour of Ø, not *m*. So whereas 'modifier (*take*): m' makes it quite clear that the modifier concerned is the direct object (assuming that all the properties of direct objects have been assigned elsewhere to *m*), the corresponding proposition for (say) *sleep* would have to be 'modifier (*sleep*): Ø which could refer to any modifier, and is in no way relevant to the direct object *m*.

There are two solutions to the problem of showing that some modifier *m* is not possible with some word *w*:

(a) We might leave it to the lack of semantic correlate for *m* in the case of *w*; for example, *sleep* could be left to inherit the option of having an object from the entry for verbs, but be prevented from ever taking up this option by the fact that the object would always remain semantically unrelated to the rest of the sentence (the sentence would be 'semantically overloaded': Kac 1980, Cattell 1976). For example, *John slept an apple* would be excluded because it is uninterpretable: what is the connection between the apple and John's sleeping? In contrast, if the verb had been transitive, then its lexical entry would have told us how to integrate its object into its semantic structure, so this kind of problem would not arise.

(b) We might adopt the second device for showing grammatical relations, which I shall explain in the next subsection. This would require us to use a named slot, such as 'object', into which Ø could be put where no object was permitted. The entry for verbs in general would then contain 'object(verb): *∅* or m', and that for *sleep* 'object(*sleep*): *∅*'. The trouble with this solution is that it is the thin end of a big wedge, because there is a very large number of potential grammatical relations waiting for recognition in this way, and a host of problems of demarcation which are much better avoided.

On balance, then, I favour the first solution, provided it does not raise unforeseen difficulties. The matter deserves further study.

Subjects and non-subjects

The device of using explicit slot labels for showing grammatical relations is very powerful and, as I have just suggested, it needs to be used with care. (Hudson 1971 should be a warning to those who are not convinced of the dangers of letting slot labels proliferate in this area, since it uses no fewer than 86 'functions', which are equivalent to grammatical-relation slots.) I think, however, that a case can be made for one such labelled slot, namely 'subject', and I shall now present this case; and on pp. 124 – 30 below I shall introduce one more labelled slot, 'visitor'.

The main reason for needing 'subject' as a labelled slot is because it would otherwise be difficult to handle what I shall call 'subject-sharing' (a term which is meant to cover the transformationalist's subject-raising verbs and verbs of control, i.e. verbs like *seem* and *want*, and corresponding adjectives). For a large number of verbs we need to say that some modifier of the verb (say, its subject, but it could also be an object) is also the subject of an infinitive modifying the verb. We have already discussed such constructions in connection with 'modifier-sharing', on pp. 83 – 4, but it may be helpful to give another example of the structures we used for the Dutch verbs *zag* and *helpen* on p. 107). 'subject-to-object raising' verb, *believe* (whose structure is like the structures we used for the Dutch verbs *zag* and *helpen* on p.00).

(1)

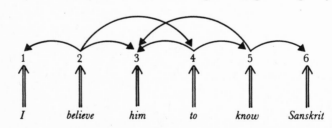

The main point about this structure is that *him* is taken as subject of *know* as well as object of *believe*. (The extra link between *him* and *to* is needed on the assumption that *to* is a verb, with its own subject; nothing else depends on whether or not this assumption is correct.)

Now, how can we formalize the requirement that the object of *believe* must also be taken as the subject of its dependent infinitive? The problem with using the first device (inherited variables) for picking out the subject of the infinitive is that the construction contains two subjects, that of *believe* and that of the infinitive, and there will be no way to distinguish them, because both will be represented by the same inherited variable. We need some different way of referring to 'subject' which will allow us to relate the subject to a particular verb, and for this purpose we use a labelled slot, 'subject'. The two subjects can then be referred to respectively as 'subject (*believe*)' and 'subject (x)', assuming that the infinitive is labelled x. (It cannot be labelled 'infinitive', because we are concerned here with a particular instance of the category 'infinitive', namely the infinitive used after *believe*.) It is now a simple matter to say that the subject of the infinitive must be the object of *believe*:

(2)   modifier (*believe*): m, model (m): noun
       modifier (*believe*): x, model (x): infinitive, subject (x): m

There are two possible objections to this kind of analysis, both of them analytical rather than theoretical. The first is that it is wrong to lump together verbs of control, such as *want* or *persuade*, with subject-raising verbs like *seem* and *believe*; after all, have transformational linguists not established to everyone's satisfaction that these two classes of verb are radically different, behind their apparent similarities? It is true that the two kinds of verb have been shown to be radically different – for example, the effects of passivizing the infinitive are quite different as between *believe* and *persuade*, as we all know – but it has not been established that these differences are syntactic, except within the rather special framework of assumptions on which transformational grammer is based. On the contrary, what is striking about the two classes of verbs is their similarity with regard to syntax, compared with their gross differences in meaning. (Such purportedly syntactic facts as the possibility of using *there* as subject of *seems* but not of *wants* can easily be explained semantically: *wants* requires its subject to fill a semantic slot, whereas *seems* does not.) So the analysis that I assume makes no syntactic distinction at all between the two kinds of verb, and leaves it entirely to the semantics to distinguish them, by relating the shared subject directly to verbs like *want*, but not to those like *seem*.

The other objection would be that the subject of the infinitive should be treated syntactically as zero, rather than identified with the subject or object of the superordinate verb. After all, did those discussions of 'Equi-NP deletion' not show that it was wrong to talk of syntactic, formal, identity between the deletable noun-phrase and the one with which it was supposed to be 'identical'? For example, *Everybody wants to win* means something different from *Everybody wants everybody to win*, so the latter cannot be an unreduced version of its underlying structure. However, all this objection amounts to is the observation that we shall have to make sure that the semantic structures for these two sentences are different. In particular, we shall need a structure in which the 'wanter' and the 'winner' are the same in the first sentence, and different in the second. But this is a matter of semantics, not syntax (see p. 202).

A more positive reason for the subject-sharing analysis, at the syntactic level, is based on data which are available in languages like Latin, but not in English. In Latin, an adjective used predicatively agrees in case with its subject, so if the subject is an accusative noun, because of its relation to a higher noun, then the predicative adjective must also be accusative:

(3)   *Brutus* (Nom.) *est fortis* (Nom.), 'Brutus is strong'
        Credo Brutum (Acc.) *esse fortem* (Acc.), 'I believe Brutus to be strong'

This shows that the subject of *esse*, 'to be', must be not just the referent 'Brutus', but the actual word *Brutum*, since it is only the latter that has a case. Moreover, this sharing is not restricted to subject-raising verbs like *credo*, but also applies to verbs of control, such as *velle*, 'to want'; so if the latter modifies *credo*, it transmits the shared subject *Brutum* down to *esse*, and the predicative adjective still needs to be accusative:

(4)   *Credo Brutum* (Acc.) *velle esse fortem* (Acc.), 'I believe Brutus to want to be strong'

(The data are similar to those which Lakoff (1970) uses as evidence for global rules, but the conclusion that I have drawn from them is radically different from his, since there is nothing in word grammar corresponding to the transformationalist's 'derivation'.) It seems clear that subject-sharing is part of Latin grammar, and I can think of no difference between Latin and English which might suggest that it was not part of English grammar too.

Let us assume, then, that a dependent infinitive shares its subject with the verb on which it depends, and that we cannot make this requirement apply to the relevant verbs without using a slot labelled 'subject'. This kind of analysis is not restricted to infinitives, of course, and it can also be applied not only to other inflectional classes of verb (e.g. all classes that are allowed after auxiliaries) but also to predicative adjectives. Indeed, the discussion of Latin rested on the assumption that predicative adjectives have subjects, and that they share their subjects with the copula verb. We can now extend the discussion to bring in pairs of adjectives like *eager* and *easy*, which have been so widely discussed in the transformational literature.

Adjectives like *eager* fit easily into the pattern already established: *eager* takes an infinitive as modifier, and this infinitive must have the same subject as *eager*; and the fact that *eager* itself, as a predicative adjective, must have the same subject as the copula verb is irrelevant to the entry for *eager*. So the dependency structure for *John is eager to please* is:

(5)

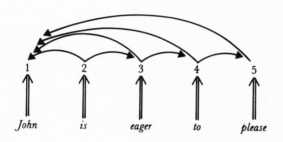

In contrast, adjectives like *easy* might seem to suggest that we need to be able to refer to the object of the infinitive, since it is this that the infinitive shares with *easy* (i.e. the object of the infinitive must be the same as the subject of *easy*). This seems to be so in examples like *John is easy to please*, where *John* is the object of *please*, and if it is generally so, then it would seem that we have reasons for recognizing 'object' as a slot too. This is the reason for bringing up the analysis of adjectives here. However, the facts are not really as I have just suggested, and the conclusion does not follow. All we need say about the modifier which the infinitive shares with *easy* is that it must not be the subject of the infinitive. For example, it could be object of a preposition (e.g. *This violin is easy to play on*), or it could belong to a further dependent infinitive (e.g. *Rice pudding is difficult to get children to eat*). So we still only need to refer to the subject, though in this case we use it negatively: 'not the subject'. The dependency structure for *John is easy to please* will be just the same as the one just given for *John is eager to please*, and the difference between them will lie just in the fact that *John* is marked as subject of *please* in one case, but not in the other.

As far as notation is concerned, then, we need a way of picking out subjects in a structural diagram, and the obvious solution is to write the word 'subject' on top of the dependency lines concerned. (Where this is difficult for lack of space, the letter 's' written by the arrow-head will suffice: ─s→.)

My conclusion is that subjects need special treatment, compared with all other grammatical relations, and that only subjects (and visitors) will be distinguished from other modifiers by means of a special slot, labelled 'subject'. This unique status for subjects seems appropriate in view of the rather special properties that subjects seem to have in most, or all, languages, though I recognize that there are problems in selecting a set of necessary and sufficient conditions for subjects in all languages (as shown by the papers in Li 1976). Whether or not all languages make use of such a slot, it is still an interesting fact that very many do seem to, and it would be good to know why this is so. Is the 'subject' slot just a particular manifestation, in language, of some more general category we use in conceptualization (such as our 'point of view', reflected in such differences as that between *John went to Mary* and *John came to Mary*, and others surveyed in Clark 1974)? Or is it restricted to language, but functionally explicable given the constraints on the speaker and hearer? Or is it unique to language, and functionally inexplicable? In this last eventuality, we may have to have recourse to genetic explanations, but a lot more research needs to be done before we are driven to that.

Deviant subjects in English, and passivization

I shall deal with the following descriptive topics in English grammar, to show how the subject slot can be exploited:

(a)   the normal pattern;
(b)   obligatory and impossible subjects;
(c)   dummy subjects;
(d)   inverted subjects;
(e)   passives.

(a) *The normal pattern.* The normal pattern is for the subject to be optional, and to precede the verb, so this is allowed for in the general entry for verbs. (In this discussion I shall concentrate on verbs, though we have just recognized that adjectives too can have subjects. There is a serious research problem for word grammar in the fact that nouns can also be used predicatively, so we have to find a general way for introducing subjects to predicatives, whether adjectives or nouns, and I assume that this will provide whatever we need to say about subjects of adjectives.)

(1)   modifier (verb): ∅ or s, s < verb, subject (verb): ∅ or s

In this entry we can also specify any general links there may be between subjects and semantic structure – for instance, we might include a list of the semantic roles typically available to subjects. This could be added as a disjunctive list of constraints on s, after either of the above propositions (e.g. actor (verb*): s* or controller (verb*): s* or . . .).

(b) *Obligatory and impossible subjects.* In some constructions the subject is obligatory, in others it is impossible, but these departures from the normal optionality of the subject can be imposed by entries for more specific types of verb (e.g. tensed verbs must have a subject) or by entries for contexts in which a verb can appear (e.g. adjectives like *easy* take infinitives which must not have a subject – Berman 1973). The existence of cases where the subject is impossible offers interesting confirmation of the decision to have a labelled slot for subjects, because we could not stop the subject from occurring by just not giving it any semantic correlate (as we can in other cases of impossible modifiers – see p. 111): there is always just the same semantic correlate for a missing subject as there is for an overt one. For example, the semantic structure for *John is easy to please* must contain some entity (however indefinite) as the 'pleaser', even though the pleaser cannot be defined by the subject of the infinitive. (As Berman argues, a *for*-phrase does not introduce a subject, but rather a noun-phrase from which the subject can be copied semantically.)

(c) *Dummy subjects.* The subject may be *it* or *there*, acting as 'place-holder' for the semantically significant would-be subject later in the sentence (e.g. *It was nice to see you; There's a fly in my soup*). We can accommodate such constructions by treating the would-be subject as a modifier of the dummy, and allowing the dummy to take its referent from the would-be subject. The subject and would-be subject can be separated by extraposing the latter in the way outlined on pp. 101 – 2.

(d) *Inverted subjects.* The normal position for the subject is before the verb, but if the latter is a tensed auxiliary, the subject may follow it. Three circumstances may lead to this inversion. If the sentence is interrogative in meaning, then we can treat the tensed auxiliary as a special subtype (an instance of 'auxiliary', which is an instance of 'verb') with its own requirements both for the position of the subject and also for the semantic structure:

(2)   model (interrogative): auxiliary and tensed
               subject (interrogative): s, interrogative < s
               referent (interrogative): . . .

If the inversion takes place in a subordinate clause, such as *Had I known you were away, then* . . . , it must involve one of just three verbs: *had, were* or *should*; so the entries for these three lexical items can contain particular instances with structures similar to the one in (2). The third possibility is that the inversion is triggered by the presence of an initial negative element (or *so*, or *only*). This is an instance of the requirements of the context overriding the normal patterns, and could be dealt with in a number of ways; for instance, the entry for the word *so* (as in *so did John*) could require its head (*did*) to come next, with the subject following; or another subtype of verb could be distinguished, called 'inverted', and we could use it in much the same way as 'interrogative'.

(e) *Passives*. It has been claimed that passivization is an operation that applies to lexical entries themselves (Bresnan 1978), but this cannot be so, in view of examples like *This paper has been written on one side of* (attested), *That bridge has been flown under* and *He's been cooked a lot of meals by her recently*. It seems most unlikely that any of the passive subjects would be mentioned in the lexical entries for the verbs *write*, *fly* and *cook*, so the basis for these sentences cannot have been the lexical entries themselves (as pointed out by Davison 1980). Instead, we must assume an abstract, hypothetical clause which was computed by the speaker before producing the passive clause. This is a complex notion, and needs a little discussion.

Passives are not the only constructions in which we have to construct a hypothetical parallel structure before we can analyse them (or generate them, in the technical sense). The same is true of 'verb-phrase anaphora' (e.g. how do we account for *there* in *Yes, there must be* said in reply to *There are many pleasures in my work*?), and even exophoric reference by pronouns (e.g. if referring to a pair of trousers, I must use *they/them*, not *it*, even though the plurality is a property of the word *trousers*, rather than of their referent (Tazmowski-De Ryck and Verluyten 1981); so I must have retrieved the word *trousers* before saying *they*). These examples show that the grammar of a language may require us to reconstruct 'underlying' structures as a basis for actual ones, but of course they lend no particular support to the transformational view, because the underlying structures are not recoverable. So there are linguistic precedents for using underlying (but not stored) structures in the generation of passives. Moreover, it would be odd if such constructions did not exist in language, because it is easy to think of similar things outside language. For example, you could recognize some object as an upside-down birthday cake with an ice-cream cone 'on top', although strictly speaking the cone would be *under* the cake; and you would presumably do this by taking the actual object as an inversion of a normalized, but not stored, concept.

In generating passives, then, we need to relate the passive verb, which I shall call 'passive', to its normalized reconstructed counterpart, called 'active'. (You will notice that neither of these terms appears in the network of inflectional classes on p. 47.) The entry for 'passive' links it, as an instance, to a lexical item X, and also to the inflectional category 'perfective' (whose other properties it overrides). The model for 'active' is the same lexical item, but since 'active' is an instance of this lexical item, not the lexical item itself, it can have a structure with any amount of detail in it, in addition to that already in the lexical item. So it can have various modifiers attached, and further modifiers for these modifiers, and so on. Now comes the main point of the passive entry: one of these modifiers other than the subject is made into the subject of 'passive'. Furthermore, 'passive' may (or may not) have a *by*-phrase modifying it and containing the subject of 'active'. Here is the entry:

(3) model (passive): perfective & X,   model (active): X,
                                             modifier (. . . active): m,
                                             subject (active): s

     subject (passive): m
     modifier (passive): Ø or *by*, modifier (*by*): s

This simple rule provides at least a good basis for a complete analysis of passives, in which the various constraints on passivization could be incorporated. I shall not try to develop it here, but note it as a topic for research.

The examples I have given all illustrate some kind of deviation involving the subject, which the labelled slot 'subject' helps us to deal with. There are very many other uses of the slot, such as in connection with reflexives and relative clauses; but this is not the point to discuss them.

VALENCY

General and lexical valency

'Valency' is the term used in dependency theory to refer to the particular demands of individual words for modifiers, and is exactly equivalent to the transformationalist's 'strict subcategorization'. (The term is based on its use in chemistry, to describe the bonding requirements of different elements). As I explained earlier, dependency theorists distinguish between modifiers which are referred to in relation to particular lexical items ('actants') and those which are not ('circonstants'), like the distinction made in other theories under other names (Matthews 1981:122). So in these terms, valency deals with actants, but not with circonstants. However, if we define valency in this way, we are left with no term for referring to the distribution of circonstants, so I shall use 'valency' in an extended meaning, to cover both kinds of modifier, and distinguish the two cases when necessary as 'lexical' and 'general' valency.

One of the advantages of taking a broader view of valency is that it encourages one to look for generalizations which cut across the boundary between lexical and general. For example, there seems to be a hierarchy of modifier-types, with those defined most formally at one end, and those defined most meaningfully at the other. The extreme of 'formality', in this sense, is achieved by a modifier whose pronunciation is fully specified and which has no independent meaning, such as the *up* of *give up*; then come restrictions on inflectional class (e.g. case), and on word class (e.g. 'noun'), with the lowest degree of formality achieved by modifiers on which no syntactic restrictions at all are placed. But at this zero degree of formality, there is likely to be the highest degree of semantic restriction (e.g. 'time expression'), and conversely as the formality increases, so the importance of semantic constraints decreases.

For example, in the sentence *I gave up tennis to concentrate on cricket*, there are three modifiers after *gave*. *Up* is totally constrained for pronunciation and word class, but empty of meaning; *tennis* is constrained for word class (it must be a noun) and roughly constrained for meaning (it must be some kind of activity or consumed object, and must be habitual); and *to concentrate on cricket* is completely unconstrained for phonology and syntax, but must be an expression of purpose.

Furthermore, the greatest degree of formality is found among the constraints imposed by particular lexical items on their modifiers (e.g. if *give* means 'desist from', one of its modifiers must be *up*), and the greatest degree of meaningfulness among the constraints imposed by general word-classes, so there will presumably be a general entry which allows an expression of purpose with virtually any word capable of being interpreted with it; but this entry will have nothing at all to say about the possible form that such an expression will have, leaving this to the entries for all the particular words which could help to build up an expression of purpose. If this link between the actant/circonstant distinction and the formal/meaningful hierarchy is a reality, it needs an explanation, but no doubt it would not be too hard to find a functional one (though I cannot at present see what it would be).

However, even if this link is a reality, it is only a tendency, because there are exceptions. For one thing, an actant can be defined in relation to its meaning only, which puts it at the 'wrong' end of the hierarchy from the one predicted. For example, the valency of the verb *put* includes an expression of place, on which there are no syntactic constraints (contrary to the impression given by most transformational treatments, where this expression would be specified as a prepositional phrase); thus, *I put it where I'd be able to find it again* is just as good as *I put it on the table*. Another example is the type of verb whose lexical valency requires it to have a predicative; it is well known (e.g. Williams 1980) that there are no syntactic constraints on predicatives, the only constraint being that they should express a property. Consequently they may be adjectives or noun-phrases or prepositional phrases or clauses (e.g. *He is tall/a linguist/in a good mood/as he always is*). A different kind of exception is provided by the indirect object, which we have already seen to be problematic from other points of view. Here the problem is that some indirect objects are circonstants, but they are formally constrained (they must be nouns), as in *He baked his students a cake*. It may be that the purported link between the two constraints is real, but more complex than I suggested above – sufficiently complex to be compatible with these examples. I shall leave this as another research topic.

Lexical constraints on modifiers

The following is a check-list of the various types of constraint that the entry for a lexical item may impose on its modifiers. The main conclusion, I think, is that it is hard to think of constraint-types which are not used, so it seems unlikely that we shall have to impose any general theoretical constraints on constraints.

(a) *Phonological/lexical constraints*

(i)   idioms – e.g. a modifier of *give*, meaning 'desist from', must be *up*;

(ii) collocations – e.g. a modifier of *need* which expresses the meaning 'high degree' must be *badly*;

(iii) empty linkers – e.g. a modifier of *ought* must be *to*, whose referent is the same as that of the infinitive which modifies it; a modifier of *rely* must be *on*, whose referent is the same as that of its modifier.

Morphological constraints

Most constraints on morphology are mediated by constraints on syntactic class, to the extent that this is reflected in morphology, but there are a few apparent examples of more directly morphological constraints. (However, even the one I am about to mention can be taken as an instance of a syntactic constraint, in view of the treatment given in the list of syntactic categories on p. 47.) The verb *try* can take *and* plus another verb (e.g. *Try and work harder!*), and I think on balance we should take the *and* as a modifier (an 'empty linker', perhaps), with the next verb as its modifier. This next verb must be in its root form, whether this counts as present tense (e.g. *We always try and get up early*; but not **He always tries and gets up early*) or the infinitive (e.g. *I will try and get up early*, but not **I have tried and got up early*) or the imperative (see the first example). But if the present tense form is not just the root, it is excluded (e.g. **We always try and are cheerful*).

(c) *Syntactic constraints*

(i)   position – e.g. *had*, *were* and *should* may have their subject after them, with the meaning 'if . . .' (see p. 118); any modifier of an indefinite pronoun must follow it (e.g. *somebody nice*);

(ii) optionality – e.g. the object of *devour* is obligatory, that of *eat* is optional, and no object at all is possible with *dine*, although these verbs are the same as far as the relevant parts of their semantic structures are concerned (Wasow 1976, quoted in Newmeyer 1980:123);

(iii)   model – i.e. any word-type, from the most general (e.g. noun) through subclasses (e.g. interrogative word) to specific inflectional classes; e.g. the object of *refute* must be a noun, that of *wonder* must be an interrogative word (see p. 195), and the modifier of auxiliary *have* must be a perfect participle; in German, the object of *folgen*, 'follow', must be in the dative case;

(iv)   modifier – e.g. the subject of an infinitive modifying *try* must be the same word as the subject of *try* (see the discussion of subject-sharing on pp. 112 – 16); any (?) modifier of the infinitive modifying *ready* may be the same as the subject of *ready* (e.g. *The cake is ready to eat; I am ready to go*).

(d) Semantic constraints

(i)   role – virtually all modifiers in the lexical valency of a word are given some semantic role in relation to that word's referent; e.g. the objects of *precede* and *follow* are given opposite semantic roles;

(ii)   reference – e.g. the referent of the reflexive pronoun which is the object of *behave* must be coreferential with the subject, and in fact is not assigned any separate role in the semantic structure; the referent of X in *crane X's neck* must be the same as that of the subject, but here it does have a distinct role in the semantic structure;

(iii)   model – e.g. the modifier of *covey* (linked by the 'empty linker' *of*) must refer to partridges; the subject of the German verb *essen* (in contrast with *fressen*, both meaning 'eat') must be a human being.

Lexical constraints on heads

Valency deals with restrictions imposed on modifiers, but there are also examples of restrictions that a lexical item imposes on its head. These are less common, apparently, so it is harder to find as wide a range of types as with modifiers. However, it may well be that further research will show that the range of possibilities is just the same in both cases. I have organized the discussion in the same way as before.

(a) *Phonological/lexical constraints.* In French, most verbs occur with *avoir*, 'have', as their head when used in the perfect participle, but a number of verbs are lexical exceptions and take *être*, 'be', instead. For example, *marcher*, 'walk', is regular, but *aller*, 'go', takes *être*.

(b) *Syntactic constraints*. The head of *enough* must precede it, whereas most modifying adverbs precede their heads; this is clearly a fact about *enough*, which must be reflected by a special constraint on its head, rather than a fact about heads which could be treated as a special constraint on the modifier. Similarly, a few French adjectives precede their heads, whereas most of them follow; and in German a few pronouns are followed by a 'prepositional' head, contrary to the normal pattern (e.g. *dar-in*, 'in it'). Apart from such positional constraints, there may be constraints on the model of the head; for example, unlike most adverbs, *very* cannot modify a verb.

(c) *Semantic constraints*. The head of *addled* must refer to an egg, and that of *fairly* must be a degree adverb. Such examples could be multiplied endlessly, and are well documented in the literature on lexical collocations.

I have shown so far that there are a good number of similarities not only between actants and circonstants, but also between modifiers and heads, as far as the restrictions are concerned which can be imposed. The conclusion is that the discussion could be satisfactorily conducted in relation to the term 'companion', which word grammar provides rather conveniently. If we consider the full range of properties that words can have, it is hard to find any types that are immune to restriction by a companion, but some constraints are certainly much more common than others, so it would be worthwhile to look for explanations for these differences.

UNBOUNDED DISPLACEMENT
Hopping down the dependency chain

My topic here is the treatment of constructions in which some modifier of a word A is moved away from A, and occurs earlier in the sentence than it otherwise would. The constructions concerned are well known: relative clauses and interrogative clauses, and sentences with a 'marked theme' (Halliday 1967), i.e. in which some element has been topicalized. In all these constructions, there is a word which would normally occur after its head, but which instead occurs before it (e.g. *What did you say?*), but this displaced word may also be separated from its head in a way that conflicts with the simple-adjacency principle (see p. 99). For example, in *What did you say he said?*, *what* is a modifier of *said*, but it is separated from *said* by the latter's head, *say*, and also by the head of *say*, which is *did*. Leaving the relations of *what* to these earlier words unspecified, the dependency diagram for this sentence is as follows:

(1)

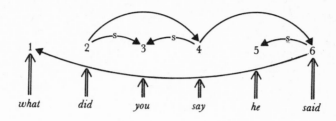

It will be seen that I have drawn the dependency arrow between *said* and *what* underneath the numbers, unlike the other dependency arrows; this will help to pick out the problematic dependencies.

The problem is how to give a unified treatment to these various constructions which will bring out the many similarities between them, and which will then generalize to various other constructions. For example, there are 'island' constraints which apply equally to relative clauses, wh-interrogatives and topicalized clauses, and prevent the displaced modifier from being displaced from inside a variety of constructions such as relative clauses (e.g. *What did you meet that man who said? *The thing which you met that man who said . . . . *That terrible thing you met the man who said*). However, there are a number of other constructions, such as comparative clauses, in which there is no displaced word as such but which are subject to the same constraints; for example, *He spent more than I thought he had in the bank* contrasts again with *He spent more than I know someone who has in the bank*.

Chomsky has attempted to unify these phenomena by considering them all as instances of wh-movement, with an underlying wh-word that can be deleted (1977). I shall produce an alternative account, which does not involve covert wh-words. Part of this account will be offered in the present subsection, where I shall show how to treat constructions where a word can be seen to be displaced. The rest of the story will have to wait till the next chapter, where we shall transfer the analysis into semantic structure (pp. 167 – 73).

The obvious place to look for the basis of our analysis is in the dependency structure, since this provides the links among the words in a sentence. What is the connection in structure (1) between *what* and

said? Let us simplify the structure somewhat, by missing out the
dependency links to the subjects:

(2)

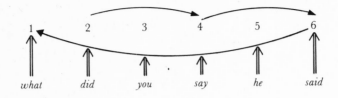

It is easy to see that the connection is provided by the dependency chain
from *did* to *said*, so once we have connected *what* to *did*, there will be a
continuous series of links between *what* and *said*, apart from the single
dependency line showing that *what* is a modifier of *said*. Having
established this chain of links, we can then work out a rule which says
'If a word A is linked to a later word B in the following way: . . . then
it may be a modifier of B whatever the requirements would normally be
for its position relative to B.'

In order to provide the missing link, between *what* and the top end of
the dependency chain, *did*, we can assume an extra companion-ship
relation between *what* and *did*, and we can call *what* a 'visitor' of *did*.
(This term seems suitable because *what* is only visiting *did* temporarily,
and will then visit *say*, and then *said*, before it finally comes to rest.) The
visitor relation is a clear instance of a dependency relation, as it is
asymmetrical: *did* provides the link between *what* and the rest of the
sentence, because it provides the point at which *what* can get access to
the dependency chain. Furthermore, when it reaches this chain, it will
travel down it, not up, as befits a modifier. Thus we can take a visitor
as a type of modifier.

What we need to provide in order to exploit these relations is a pair
of entries in the grammar, one to connect the displaced word, as visitor,
to the top of the dependency chain, and the other to allow it to pass
indefinitely far down the chain. Taking this second entry first, it will
have to say 'the visitor of one word may also be the visitor of this word's
modifier,' and allow this entry to apply recursively (indeed, it would be
hard to prevent it from applying recursively). The important point
about this informal formulation is that it raises the same problems as we
saw with subject-sharing: we need to refer to the same 'grammatical

relation' category in relation to two different words. The conclusion must therefore be the same as the one we reached in connection with subjects, namely that we need a labelled slot to hold visitors, and cannot identify them by means of inherited variables (see the discussion on pp. 112 – 13).

We are now ready to formulate the rule:

(3)   visitor $_0^n$ (word): $\emptyset$ or v,

$\{X(\text{word}): v, X \neq \text{visitor},$

$\text{or}[\text{visitor}(m): v, \text{modifier}(\text{word}): m, \text{word} < m,$

$\& \text{ not visitor}(m'): v, \text{modifier}(\text{word}): m']\}$

In words, a word may (or may not) have one or more visitors v, such that v either fills some other slot (X) in the structure of this word, or is taken over as visitor by just one postmodifier of the word. Thus, for each word in the chain, there is a choice between 'using' the visitor, as its own modifier, and passing it down the chain unused.

The other entry is responsible for connecting the displaced word to the dependency chain in the first place. This can be very simple, because we just need to allow the relevant class of words to have any number of visitors before them (any number, because of examples like *Tomorrow, what do you think I'm going to do?*). The relevant class of words is quite easy to define: it certainly includes tensed verbs, and may or may not include imperatives, according to one's reaction to sentences like *This one put over there* (which I have heard used). Assuming that such sentences should be generated, the relevant class is what I have called 'finite' in my classification of verbs (see p. 47). So the entry for linking visitors to their first 'host' in the dependency chain is:

(4)   visitor (finite): v, v < finite

This pair of entries completes the basis for the analysis. It will be seen that I have placed no restrictions at all on the visitor itself, except that it must precede the finite verb; all that is required of a visitor is that it should be compatible with some modifier slot later in the sentence. Otherwise, it will stay as nothing but a visitor, with no semantic connection to the rest of the sentence. For pragmatic reasons, the words of a sentence must all fit together into a single integrated semantic structure, so a sentence like *Bananas John met Mary* will be excluded pragmatically.

One final matter of notation: we can mark visitors in structural diagrams by writing *v* on the arrow pointing to them. Since subjects will normally be visitors as well, we can combine the two arrows into one, with both *s* and *v* on it. An example of a complete dependency diagram with visitors in it is the following:

(5)

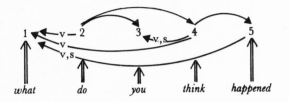

I have now extended the convention which I used earlier, by drawing all the arrows for visitors under the line of numbers.

It is interesting to consider the implications of this analysis for the position of the subject in English. We have seen that the subject is the only modifier (apart from those in compounds and putative compounds) that precedes its head, and we have also seen that it is the only modifier, apart from 'visitor', which needs explicit recognition as a named slot. It is possible that these facts are connected, and that the reason why subjects precede their heads is because this allows an extremely simple way of identifying the subject in the entry for verbs (or rather, in the entry responsible for the presence of visitors): that the subject must be a visitor. (We shall find interesting confirmation of this on p. 129.) Since visitors are already required to precede their heads, it automatically follows that the subject will do the same. And furthermore, of course, the typical pragmatic function of subjects is the same as that of many visitors, in their role as topic, so the connection between subjects and visitors is a natural one.

Some constraints on visiting

We must now consider some of the 'island' constraints on visiting. They seem to be of two types: those that follow automatically from the entries we have given, in connection with other facts about the grammar; and those that need to be stipulated, by adding extra conditions on the entries. We start with the first kind.

(a) *Automatic constraints*

    (i) Co-ordinate structures do not allow visitors to pass from conjunct to conjunct, because the relation between conjuncts is not dependency; so there is no reason to expect sentences like *What did John eat an apple and to be good. We shall see that the word-grammar treatment of co-ordinate structures allows conjuncts to share heads, however, so 'across the board' visiting is permitted, as in What did John cook and Mary eat?

(ii) So-called 'sentential subjects' cannot receive a visitor because that would mean that the visitor would be moving down a backwards dependency chain, which is not allowed by entry (3) above. For example, we can rule out *That sort of thing that he should say is surprising on the grounds that that sort of thing is a visitor of is, so the only chain it can pass down is the one going towards surprising, and not the one ending at say. We cannot attach that sort of thing directly to the next verb, should, because that would infringe the simple-adjacency principle (it would be separated from should by the latter's head, that).

(iii) A visiting subject cannot pass across that, as in *What do you think that happened?, although other kinds of visitors can (e.g. What do you think that he said?). This is because we must assume that the subject is a modifier not only of the tensed verb but also of that (compare the analysis of dat clauses in Dutch given on p. 107). Now, that can receive what as visitor from think, but then it must choose (so to speak) between using what for its own purposes, to provide the modifier it needs, and passing what on to happened as a visitor. It cannot do both, so what cannot satisfy the needs of that and those of happened at the same time. (It should be noticed that the situation here is different from that in cases like What do you expect to happen? because happened specifically requires its subject to be a visitor, according to the conclusion I suggested on p. 128; whereas the subject of to happen just needs to be the same as the object of expect, and need not be a visitor.)

(b) Stipulated constraints

(i) German and English have different constraints on visiting in that in German a visitor must not pass down onto a finite verb (Ebert 1973). For example, the literal translation of What do you think he said? is not grammatical (except in some south German dialects, I gather): *Was denkst du, (dass) er sagte? In contrast, there is no problem in transferring down onto infinitives (e.g. Was hofft er, zu tun?, 'What does he hope to do?'). This illustrates the arbitrary nature of some of the restrictions, and shows that we should need to add an extra condition on the equivalent of entry (3) in German, namely that the model for m (the modifier which receives the visitor) should be something other than 'finite' (or 'tensed', according to what the facts are).

(ii) Visitors cannot be received by a verb from a noun (this is the equivalent of the 'complex noun-phrase constraint'). For example, in *What do you dislike people who eat?*, the visitor *what* must 'hop' (using the terminology of Bresnan 1976) from *do* to *dislike*, then from *dislike* to *people*, and from *people* to *who*; but it cannot go from *who* to *eat* because the former is a type of noun, and the latter is a verb. For such cases, then, we need to restrict entry (3) by requiring m not to be a verb if 'word' is a noun: 'not = model (m): verb & model (word): noun3'. It is not clear at present how we can make this analysis apply to cases where the verb is introduced by *that*, coming between it and the noun (e.g. *What do you doubt the claim that he ate?*), but I think the general outlines are clear of the kind of analysis that is needed.

The analysis that I am offering has the advantage over other available analyses that it leads us to expect such special restrictions as these, given that all the relations concerned are relations between words, and we know that words can impose arbitrary syntactic restrictions on their companions (see the conclusion of the section on valency, p. 124). In contrast, other analyses link the visitor to its final head via phrasal and clausal nodes, which have no special connection with the words concerned. Moreover, the word-grammar analysis of visitors does not require any special apparatus at the theoretical level, since the visitor slot only exploits a possibility already provided for subjects (namely, the labelled slot for a type of modifier). It would be wrong to claim that this rather brief discussion has established the superiority of this treatment over all other available alternatives, but I hope to have shown that it compares favourably with others, and works well in its own terms.

4

Semantics

The status of 'semantic' structure

This chapter is about what I shall call 'semantic' structure, for lack of a better term, but, as I have already explained, I cannot accept the distinction which is often made between 'knowledge of the language' and 'knowledge of the world', so I shall make no attempt to distinguish my 'semantic' structures from some other kind of structure to be labelled 'pragmatic'. Having made this admission, I now drop the scare quotes round 'semantic', but I shall have to start by clarifying the status of semantic structure.

As I shall use the term, semantic structure is the structure which is assigned to a word, or word-string, and which has to do with the latter's referent. (The next subsection will explain why I assume that every word has a referent, so for the time being I shall simply take this for granted.) Since I am a linguist, I shall not be able to penetrate this structure much further than the point at which the structure is supplied more or less directly by the bits of the cognitive network which are closely connected to the words themselves, so in this sense the semantic structure is relatively 'linguistic', compared with some other information which would have to be derived by more complicated routes.

For example, take the sentence *Three couples came to dinner, but we only had enough meat for seven people.* The semantic structure for *three* and *couples* should show that three pairs of people came, and that for *but* should show (I assume) that there is some kind of incompatibility between the two clauses; but we must leave it to other parts of the cognitive structure associated with this sentence to show just what the nature of this incompatibility is. (Namely, three twos are six, plus the host couple of *we* makes eight, and all eight would normally be expected to eat the same food; moreover, meat is food.) I shall assume that my job as a linguist is done once I have given satisfactory definitions for the meanings of the words themselves, and my responsibility does not extend to covering the rules of multiplication and the etiquette of entertaining. On the other hand, I see no clear boundary between the 'linguistic' and 'non-linguistic' – for example, I can see no way of deciding whether or not it is the linguist's job to say that meat is food (see pp. 34 and 36).

I am well aware that my view on this matter is controversial, and that many linguists believe it is essential to make a clear distinction between semantic and pragmatic structures. However, I have not yet seen any convincing evidence either that it is possible to make this distinction on the basis of coherent general principles (compare for instance the inconclusive discussion in chapter 1 of Levinson 1983), or even that it is desirable to make it. Moreover, I take comfort from the fact that other linguists whose views I respect take similar positions – for instance, Jackendoff (1981) denies the assumption of 'autonomous semantics' that the inference processes which lead to semantic and pragmatic structures are different in kind, and Miller (1978) denies the difference between 'lexical information' about a word's meaning, and 'the general system of knowledge in which the concept that the word expresses is located'. More generally, according to Langacker 1982 'semantic structure is conventionalized conceptual structure,' and 'I think it very doubtful that linguistic semantics can ultimately be divorced from an overall characterization of human knowledge.' Such views seem to be becoming increasingly widespread among linguists as the serious study of semantics develops.

For the benefit of readers who are sceptical, here are some more specific arguments for the view that semantics is not autonomous in relation to general world-knowledge:

(a) Once one accepts the mentalist approach to language, then this approach must be extended to meanings as well as to the words that bear them, and we must see the object of our inquiry in both cases as the speaker/hearer's mental representations. Consequently, we cannot say that pragmatic structures are the mental structures which speaker/hearers construct in response to the semantic structures which somehow exist 'out there', in the language.

(b) Similarly, we cannot say that semantic structures are uniform across all speakers, because they are 'part of the language', in contrast with pragmatic structures which are idiosyncratic. After all, we know that plenty of clearly 'linguistic' things vary from speaker to speaker, such as pronunciations, so there is no reason to expect greater uniformity in meaning. On the contrary, in fact, I have already suggested (see p. 34) that uniformity is even less likely in meaning than in pronunciation, so we may expect to find words whose meanings would have no semantic component at all, by this definition, because there was no part of the meaning which was shared. For example, some people think that *inflammable* means 'unable to be ignited', and others think it means the opposite, so we should have to conclude that it had no semantic structure at all for anyone, which is surely nonsense.

(c) We cannot distinguish the semantic structures of words from structures found in our world-knowledge by pointing to formal properties shared by the former but not by the latter, because (so far as I am aware) no such formal differences have ever been found. For example, I know of no evidence that concepts which are tied to words are more (or less) clear than concepts which are not, and indeed linguists have often pointed out that there are 'lexical gaps', such as the word which does not exist, but would stand in the same relation to *tree* as *corpse* stands to *animal* (Chomsky 1965:170). The point about examples like this is that the uncoded concept is just as clear, as regards its structure, as the coded ones are.

(d) Nor can we reasonably tie semantic structure exclusively to syntactic structure, and exclude the whole of word-meaning from it, since this distinction is strictly irrelevant to the semantic structure as such. Moreover, it would prevent us from giving identical semantic structures to synonymous pairs such as *He didn't see either letter* and *He saw neither letter*, because two words in one (*didn't . . . either*) convey the same meaning as one word in the other (*neither*).

(e) It is hard to see how a speaker/hearer could learn the distinction between semantic and pragmatic structure, and where to locate it in particular cases. For example, suppose there was a difference between the semantic part of the dictionary entry for a word like *table*, and the encyclopaedic information about tables which is part of one's general knowledge: how could we find out which bits of information belonged in which compartment? Even consulting a dictionary and an encyclopaedia would not help much, since dictionary-makers have just the same problems as the linguist and as the ordinary language-learner.

At the very least, I think these observations show that it is by no means self-evident that the boundary between semantic and pragmatic structures is a reality. Furthermore, the most general theme of this book is that linguistic structures have the same formal structures as other types of cognitive structure, so the whole book can be taken as evidence that the semantics/pragmatics division is a priori unlikely to exist except by linguists' fiat. The onus seems to be clearly on supporters of the distinction to produce evidence for it, rather than on those of us who reject it to argue against it (Hudson, forthcoming).

To summarize the discussion so far, then, my semantic structures are those parts of cognitive structure which contain what we know about the referents of a word-string, and which are most closely-related to the words themselves. I assume no natural cut-off point between the semantic structure and the rest of our cognitive structure, such as the boundary implied by the semantics/pragmatics distinction, or the related distinctions such as dictionary/encyclopaedia. In this sense, then, I am advocating *non-autonomous* semantics: it is not autonomous in relation to other things *outside* language. However, when we consider its relations to words, it is *autonomous*, because a word is a different entity from its referent and the properties of the word are clearly distinct from those of its referent (see p. 9). For example, *John* (the word) is a noun, but John (its referent) is a boy. It makes no difference whether we say that this distinction leaves word-referents inside language or outside it, since this is just a matter of terminology (see p. 6). The main point is that the conceptual structure which I am calling semantic is distinct from the structure for the words which express it.

A number of consequences follow from this strict autonomy of semantic structures in relation to their linguistic coding.

(a) Semantic decomposition of lexical items is obligatory, because it is irrelevant to the semantic structure whether it is expressed by one word or by more than one. For example, we have already seen that *neither* expresses the same semantic structure as *not . . . either*, so we must 'unpack' the meaning of *neither* into a structure which at least shows its relation to *not* and *either*. Similarly, *hardly*, must be represented semantically as 'almost not', if we are to explain why *hardly* is treated like *not* and other negative words with regard to tag questions, *either/too*, and so on (compare *He can hardly/not/*really swim either, He can hardly/not/*really swim, can he* + falling intonation). The relevant rules must refer to '(almost) not' – i.e. a negative marker in the semantics, regardless of whether this is accompanied by 'almost'; it should be clear that they cannot refer simply to a semantic marker 'negative', because *hardly* is not negative (*He hardly touched her* implies that he *did* touch her).

These examples show that the semantic structure must not stop at the point where each word has a single entity assigned to it, as referent, but must go on to assign further entities related to this one. (For example, the structure for *hardly* must contain three referents: one for the basic proposition (e.g. 'he touched her'), another for the negation of this, and a third for a proposition which is nearly, but not quite, this negation.) The example with *neither* showed that the same semantic structure can be expressed by a single word as by a pair of words; and the one with *hardly* showed that rules may need to refer to just part of the semantic structure of a single word.

Similar points could have been made with reference to more 'lexical' types of word. For instance, I have already shown one of the benefits of giving the word *father* a semantic structure which refers to the child as well as to the father himself (see p. 80), in order to distinguish *fathers of many children* from *fathers with many children*. Similarly, we need to analyse the meaning of *thief* in such a way that we can refer to the action of stealing separately from the person who does the stealing, otherwise we cannot explain the ambiguity of examples like *good thief* (good person, or good at stealing). And we even need to recognize some reference to the function of a tool in order to explain why *good knife* is taken as referring to a knife which is good for cutting, whereas *good boy* refers to a boy who is good in his behaviour. Such examples could be multiplied easily, as there are very many types of modifier whose semantic structure relates to some *part* of the semantic structure of the head, which means that this part must be available to whatever rules relate the semantic structures of the two words to one another. (An example of a very general rule of this type is the one for compounds given on p. 51.)

(b) My semantic structures are quite different in status from Chomsky's logical form, since the latter is clearly located as a level of syntax (1981:29), along with S-structure and D-structure. Moreover, lexical decomposition is excluded from logical form, and reserved for the level of semantic structure which Chomsky envisages. Thus my semantic structures are just the same as Chomsky's. However, if we are to have a semantic structure, I can see no point in having a separate level of 'logical form' between it and the surface syntax, because any generalizations that need to be expressed in terms of logical form could presumably be expressed equally well in terms of semantic structure. Indeed, there is at least a strong implication in Chomsky's discussion that he sees logical form as part of semantic structure (which seems hard to reconcile with other claims about semantics and syntax), where he argues for including theta-roles in logical form on the grounds that 'these notions in fact enter into many different theories of semantic description' (1981:35).

Similar remarks apply to Bresnan's 'functional structure' (1978), and any other level of structure which is set up in such a way that it ties the semantics closely to syntactic structure. Given the view of semantics that I am advocating, there is no reason to assume in advance that semantic and syntactic structures must be in a simple relation to one another, and indeed it is easy to find examples of gross discrepancies between them, such as the following:

  (i)   complex semantic structures corresponding to just a single word (see the examples of lexical decomposition given above);
  (ii)   simple semantic structures corresponding to complex syntactic ones – i.e. some idioms;
  (iii) words without any independent semantic structure of their own (e.g. auxiliary *do*, the 'complementizer' *that*, lexically selected prepositions like *of* in *father of X*);
  (iv)   a number of syntactically distinct expressions all sharing the same semantic structure (e.g. *New Year follows Christmas = Christmas precedes New Year; He sought a solution = He looked for a solution = He had a look for a solution*).

In view of discrepancies like this, and the belief that any given semantic structure may be in one's head without being tied to any linguistic expression, we clearly need to make the absolute minimum of assumptions about the relations between syntactic and semantic structures.

(c) My semantic structures are also different from the structures of predicate calculus. Part of the reason for this difference is that predicate calculus is rather too closely tied to syntactic structure, in that it assumes a distinction between 'predicates' and their 'arguments', paralleling the distinction between verbs (or adjectives) and their subjects and other modifiers. If we abandon the assumption that semantic structure is closely related to syntactic structure, then there is no reason to expect verbs and nouns to be consistently and simply related to distinct parts of the semantic structure. Take a sentence like *John whistled*. The normal translation of this into predicate calculus notation would take John as an argument of a one-place predicate, 'whistle': *Whistle (John)*. Then if we added an object, such as *the Marseillaise*, this would be added to the list of arguments, along with John: *Whistle (John, the Marseillaise)*. But what reason is there, apart from the syntax, for distinguishing the statuses of these three elements in this way? Or even for saying that there are just three elements – what about the time when it happened, or the mouth and lips that John used, or the air-stream that was involved? I assume that all these three elements are essential to an act of whistling, just as much as the person and the tune, which happen to be linguistically expressed as separate items. In other words, if we did not know anything about the form of words used, but did know the meaning of the sentence, we might well arrive at quite a different representation of its meaning, such as a formalization of 'there was an event in which the actor was John, the mover was the air in John's lungs, the instrument was John's lips, the effect was a musical pattern, and the model for this pattern was the Marseillaise.' Roughly such a structure is in fact what would be generated in a word grammar. Similar analyses have apparently been suggested by Davidson, who according to Chomsky (1981:35) 'analyzes e.g. *John ran quickly* as: there is an event *e* which is a running event with John as agent, and *e* is quick'. Analyses along roughly these lines have also been suggested by other linguists, such as Van Langendonck (1982), who quotes Langacker 1978 and Hoard 1979 as precedents.

To summarize, semantic structure in word grammar is autonomous in relation to the words that express it in the sense that the only requirement of a semantic structure is that it should reflect the information conveyed by the string of words concerned (or more precisely, some part of this information), irrespective of the syntactic structure of the word-string itself. This principle distinguishes the semantic structures not only from the syntactically oriented logical form of transformational grammar and other similar kinds of structure, but also from the covertly syntactic structures of the predicate calculus. On the other hand, it must be possible to relate the semantic structure to the words in the string by assigning each part of it to some word, so that the contribution of each word is related directly to it. The examples in the following pages will all apply these principles, and show how it is possible to generate semantic structures with the necessary degree of autonomy, but one word at a time.

Referents

A word typically has not only an internal composition, but also a referent, which is a conceptual entity to which any semantic structure belonging to that word is attached. Not every word has a referent, the clearest cases of words without one being greetings like *hullo*: these are associated with particular types of utterance-event, but not with anything one could reasonably call a 'referent'. Apart from greetings, politeness formulae and so on, there are just a few words which have no referent, although they affect the semantic structure of the sentence; these include *and* and *or*, which we shall discuss in the next chapter. Virtually every word that makes a contribution to semantic structure, then, makes it via a referent, whether it is a noun, a pronoun, an adjective, a verb, a preposition, or whatever. In this section I shall try to justify this claim, and explore some of its consequences.

We start with a matter of terminology, where I have to point out that what I mean by 'referent' is not what this term means in the tradition going back to Ogden and Richards (Lyons 1977:98), namely an object in the world, outside the mind of the speaker/hearer, to which the word refers. Instead, I am using the term to denote de Saussure's 'concept' which is the signified part of a linguistic sign (1916/1959:66). Given that word grammar takes a mentalist view of the word and its properties, it would be inconsistent to take any other kind of approach to the word's meaning. At least some words have a mental entity as their meaning – for example, the pronoun *he* obviously refers in some sense to an entity, and this entity exists only in one's mind, because it need not correspond to anything at all in the real world (e.g. it may be a unicorn).

Of the obviously available words for referring to this mental entity, the word 'referent' seems the most suitable, in spite of its traditional links with the outside world. For instance, the term 'sense' is widely used just to refer to the properties picked out by common nouns and verbs (as when one talks of 'identity of sense anaphora', speaking of the use of expressions like *this one*). Of course, by using the word 'referent' in this way, we leave ourselves without a term for referring to whatever in the world may (or may not) correspond to the entity concerned. However, the connections between the real world and linguistic expressions are quite indirect and not of any particular importance to a linguistic theory, so it seems preferable to adopt the term 'referent' for an area where we do need it, rather than to leave it for use on a hypothetical occasion. What I mean by 'referent', then, is a mental entity (as defined earlier in this book) which is related directly to a mental representation of a word in the total network that constitutes our knowledge.

We now see that the claim that almost every word has a referent boils down to the claim that every word is matched in the semantic structure by a mental entity. This claim is harder to object to, given the vagueness of the notion 'mental entity', but it still amounts to the view that all kinds of words are significantly similar in their contributions to the semantic structure, in that they nearly all have an entity to match them – whereas we might imagine a situation where some were matched by a proposition rather than an entity. I can give a certain amount of empirical evidence that this claim is correct, or at least quite plausible.

(a) Virtually all types of words have meanings which can be referred back to by pronouns. If we take the meaning of a whole clause as being in fact the meaning of its principle verb (the dependency-based analysis), then the meaning of a verb can be referred to by *it*, *that* or *which*, as in *He put his hands in the stocks, which/but it/but that made him feel silly*. Ross has drawn our attention to similar facts about adjectives (1969), such as the possibility of sentences like *John was happy, which he hasn't been for years*, but similar possibilities exist for other kinds of predicatives such as prepositional phrases and noun-phrases (e.g. *John was in a good mood/was a happy man, which he hasn't been for years*). A degree adverb may be replaced by *that*, as in *that big*, and a prepositional phrase may be referred back to by *which*, or the pronouns for places and times, *there* and *then* (e.g. *We met behind the gymnasium, which is the usual place for duels*). Admittedly, it is hard to think of comparable examples involving some kinds of adverbial, but the general impression is that at least a very wide range of word-types have meanings which are suitable for identifying by means of a pronoun.

Now clearly the easiest way of defining the meanings of pronouns such as the ones quoted here is by saying that they have a referent which is the same as that of their antecedent, but that implies that their antecedent must itself have a referent, which is the point that I am trying to establish. It is also worth noting that the term 'referent' fits quite naturally into the discussion, with the mentalistic interpretation that I am giving it.

(b) If we take it as agreed that nouns have referents, then any word which has the same meaning as some noun must also have a referent. Rather conveniently, language provides ample means for providing noun synonyms for a wide range of non-nouns, through the various processes called 'nominalization'. For instance, the word *size* means not only the parameter on which size is measured, but also a degree of size above normal (e.g. *in a rugby player, size is more important than speed*). But this is precisely the meaning of *big*, so if *size* has a referent in both senses, *big* must have a referent too. Similarly, action nominalizations have the

same meanings as the corresponding non-tensed verbs, so the verb *act*
must have the same semantic structure as the noun *action*, including the
referent. And so on through the various word-types, most of which are
easy to match with nouns. In some cases, the relations between nouns
and non-nouns may be quite subtle. For example, take the adjective
linguistic, as in *a linguistic argument*. In the sense where this means 'to do
with language', we may in fact give it the same referent as the word
language itself, with the proviso that this referent should specify the
subject-matter of some entity such as an argument. Thus in words the
entry for this meaning of *linguistic* would be: 'the referent of *linguistic* is
language, where language is the subject-matter of the referent of the
head noun.'

(c) We shall see in the section on definiteness and mood (pp.
180 – 96) that there are clear parallels between the contrasts that apply
to nouns and those that apply to other kinds of words, notably verbs.
For example, we have interrogative pronouns (a subclass of nouns), but
we also have interrogative verbs (namely, those auxiliary verbs found,
with inverted subjects, in yes – no interrogative clauses). Assuming
that at least some of the parallels that I shall draw are reliable, it is clear
that we cannot show them in a grammar which assigns fundamentally
different semantic structures to nouns and to verbs.

(d) Similarly, it is well known that there are similarities between
the classification of verbs as events or states and the classification of
nouns as count or mass, with events treated as the equivalent of count
nouns, and states aligned with mass nouns. The similarity is easy to see
when we compare verbs with their nominalizations, since the 'action'
nominalization of an event is a count noun, and that of a state is a mass
noun (compare *death* with *hatred*, for instance). Moreover, we can push
the parallel even further, to show a similarity between the
singular/plural contrast in nouns, and the contrast between single
events and repeated events in verbs. For semantic structure, it is
irrelevant that one of these contrasts is realized by inflections, whereas
the other is not (e.g. *John visited Mary* is ambiguous between referring to
a single visit or to a series of visits). Once again, we can see the
similarity from the fact that different nominalizations, either singular or
plural, are possible (e.g. *John's visit to Mary*, versus *John's visits to Mary*).
In both cases, the semantic contrast should be shown in the same way
for verbs as for nouns, so if it is taken as a classification of referents in
the case of nouns, the same should be true of verbs; so verbs must have

referents. (See pp. 197 – 202 for an analysis which exploits these similarities in relation to the number distinction.)

We have already seen one of the consequences of the proposed analysis: that we cannot exploit the analyses developed within the predicate calculus, since these are based on the distinction between predicates (which do not have referents) and their arguments (which do have referents, or are referents). It may well be that the predicate calculus could be adapted to fit these new assumptions, but they lead more naturally to the type of semantic structure that I shall offer here, in which there is no clear parallel to the distinction between predicates and arguments.

Another consequence is that we have to be sure that our semantic structures show the relations among the various referents in a satisfactory way. For example, it is not enough simply to list the referents involved in a sentence such as *The goldfish died*: there is a goldfish *g*, and an event *e* of dying, in which the one that died was *g*. We also have to be able to show that the referent of the whole thing is the event *e*, in order to distinguish it from *the goldfish which died*, in which the referent is the goldfish *g*, and the event is just part of the definition of this goldfish. This kind of distinction is made naturally enough by using much the same kinds of structure in the semantics as we used in the syntax (naturally enough, because syntactic structures are much the same as other structures in our cognitive make-up, according to the arguments I have already offered). In one case, the referent of the verb *died* is subordinated to that of *the goldfish*, but not in the other.

A third consequence is that we must find a satisfactory account for the various fundamental differences that are found among referents. For example, there is an obvious difference between the goldfish and its dying, which we might describe by saying that one is an object, or more specifically an animal, while the other is an event; and objects and events are different fundamental categories, with different properties. To make distinctions such as these, we need to relate the referents, as instances, to different very general mental entities such as OBJECT and EVENT. Similarly, but much more specifically, we can distinguish the referents of *goldfish* and of *stickleback* by relating each, as instance, to a different mental entity (namely, GOLDFISH and STICKLE-BACK). I shall explain in the next subsection how such models can be exploited by the semantic structure.

Another kind of distinction is that between so-called 'referring' and 'non-referring' expressions, as exemplified by the two readings of *I'm looking for a student* (a particular student, or any old student?), and similarly the distinction between definite and indefinite. These distinctions seem to involve the relation between the referent concerned and the entities already known to the speaker and/or addressee, as we shall see on pp. 180 – 6.

I hope to be able to show that word grammar provides semantic structures in terms of which all the necessary distinctions can be made, but the general point that I should like to stress here is that I can see no justification for assigning referents only to nouns or pronouns, and not to other word classes. Having said this, though, I must recognize two important sources of the mismatch between syntactic and semantic structure which I discussed earlier in connection with the autonomy of semantic structure *vis-à-vis* syntactic structure:

(a) Not all of the entities in a semantic structure are referents, if we take seriously our definition of a referent as a semantic entity which is *directly* related to a word. For example, I take it that the semantic structure for *eat* is the same when used intransitively (e.g. *When shall we eat?*) as when it is used transitively, and specifically it must contain an entity which is consumed (i.e. the food), though the nature of this entity is left unspecified. (That is, it would be a contradiction to say *John ate at six, but he didn't eat anything*.) Consequently, the semantic structure for intransitive *eat* must contain an entity which is distinct from the referent of *eat* (because the latter refers to the event, not the food), and which is not associated with any other word in the sentence, so it cannot be a referent. (This is a similar point to the one I made on p. 134 about the need for semantic decomposition, in connection with examples like *hardly, neither, father* and *thief*.)

Of course, it could be objected that entities other than referents of words should not be counted as part of the semantic structure as such, but I have already argued that semantic structure is just one edge (so to speak) of general cognitive structure, and has no natural boundaries between it and the rest of one's knowledge of the world. In any case, the 'food' entity is linguistically expressed in *John ate at six* just as much as it is in *John ate an apple at six*, because it is part of the meaning of *ate*, and is certainly conveyed by the words themselves, rather than supplied by some kind of contextual calculation. So it is hard to see why one should restrict semantic structure so that it should not contain any entities other than referents.

The general point to be established is that there may be more entities in the semantic structure than there are words. Sometimes these extra entities correspond to optional syntactic modifiers, as in the case of *eat*, but sometimes not; so for example (as we have seen) *dine* cannot take an object, but its semantic structure must (presumably) be rather like that for *eat*, with an entity for the food eaten; and a verb like *cycle* or *ski* must make some kind of reference to the 'vehicle' concerned, although this cannot be expressed (except by a phrase like *on a brand-new three-wheeler*). Even where there is an optional modifier, as with *eat*, there are different ways of dealing with the situation in which the modifier is absent. In some verbs, the semantic entity is just left vague (e.g. *eat*), in others it is given a 'default' reading (e.g. with *drink* the default liquid is alcohol), and in others again it is left to be specified pragmatically (e.g. if *know* has no object, the thing known must be a contextually provided proposition). But wherever the entity 'comes from', in all these cases it will not correspond to a word, and therefore cannot be a referent.

(b) The converse situation is where there are more words than referents, because the sentence contains words which do not contribute any distinct meaning of their own. We have already mentioned some examples of words like this (see p. 136): complementizer *that*, auxiliary *do*, *of* in *father of X*. All these examples take a modifier, which is either obligatory or optional, and they may be analysed as having the same referent as this modifier. For example, instead of saying that auxiliary *do* has no meaning, we say that it has the same meaning as its modifying infinitive, whatever that is. One advantage of this analysis is that it allows us to give the same treatment to *do* as to *know*, mentioned in the last paragraph; if the modifier is absent, then the entity must be specified pragmatically by finding some contextually defined proposition. Moreover, it allows us to apply the usual semantic treatment of tense to *do*, because *do* (or *did*) will have a semantic structure, associated with its 'inherited' referent, with which the tense semantics can be integrated in the usual way.

In the analyses that follow, then, I shall assume that even a word like *do* has a referent. However, it is not at all surprising to find that some words 'borrow' their referents from other words; indeed this is precisely how many linguists would analyse the semantics of relative pronouns and reflexive pronouns, so we are simply exploiting this precedent. In doing so, of course, we are also decreasing the number of words that have no referent, so we can certainly maintain the original claim of this subsection, which is that a *typical* word has a referent, virtually regardless of its syntactic category.

It will be helpful to give a simple example to show how referents can be included in sentence structures, and in the grammar. It will be recalled that the diagrammatic notation for the connection between a word and its referent is a vertical line, and for any word whose name is x, the name for its referent is x^*. Thus if we took a five-word sentence such as *The cat chased a mouse* and showed nothing but the names of its words and their referents, the structure would be like this.

(1)

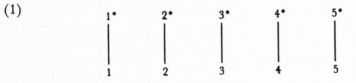

However, we can of course already do better than this, because each of the words is an instance of some stored word (and, in the case of *chased*, of an inflectional category). Each of these stored entities can be added to the structure, as model for one of the words; but it has itself a referent, which we can include in the picture so that we can make use of it in the next subsection. A further refinement that we can add is that the entries for *the* and *a* treat them as though they were empty words, in the sense defined above, although they add information not otherwise available about their referents; so their referents are required to be the same as those of their modifiers, *cat* and *mouse* respectively. (Recall that determiners are heads in this analysis – see pp. 90 – 2.) So by the time we have added all this extra information to the diagram, we get the following structure:

(2)

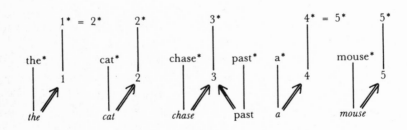

Because of the selective-inheritance principle, the referents of the words in the sentence (named 1* through 5*) inherit the properties of the referents of the models for these words (named the*, cat* and so on); and the referent of *chased* will inherit the properties of both chase* and past*. The question to which we now turn is what these properties are, and how they are defined in the grammar.

Models and other sources of semantic structure

There are two ways in which the grammar defines the properties of a referent (or, for that matter, of any other entity to which it refers in the semantic structure). It may define the properties concerned directly, in which case they are listed in the grammar; or it may define them indirectly, by causing them to be inherited from some model, without (necessarily) listing the properties of this model in the grammar. The two ways may combine in defining the semantic structure of a particular word, and I shall explain that the distinction between them is in any case more a matter of notation than of substance, but it will help to organize the following discussion if we take the distinction for granted.

The simplest proposition stating a property of a referent directly is the identity proposition which we have already seen, where an empty word is given the same referent as its modifier. This allows us, for example, to give *the* a referent, to which the properties of definiteness can be assigned, without adding an unwanted entity to the semantic structure. Thus, as far as the semantic structure is concerned, *the cat* defines just one entity, which is shown as a cat by the second word, and as definite by the first. Similarly, the auxiliary *do* is able to contribute information to the semantic structure about such matters as time and mood, which can combine with the information carried by the lexical verb in defining the properties of a single semantic entity.

On the other hand, a completely empty word like the complementizer *that*, or the infinitival *to*, can be part of the syntactic structure without adding anything at all to the semantic structure, since its referent is just the same as that of its modifier. It has been argued, notably by Bolinger (1971), that every word makes a distinct contribution to semantic structure, but there is no a-priori reason why this should be so. After all, to say that a word contributes nothing to the semantic structure is not the same thing as saying that it might as well not be there: it may well serve a useful function in signalling syntactic structure (e.g. *that*), or in some other way.

Other entries give more complex statements about referents and their relations to other semantic entities. Take the word *before*, for example. The referent is a time which is earlier than some other time, and in simple cases like *before Christmas*, this other time is the referent of the modifier of *before*. The formulaic statement for *before* would therefore include the following (plus other possibilities to allow for expressions like *before he left her*).

(1)   referent (*before*):before*, before* < m*
                         modifier (*before*): Ø or m

It will be recalled that I am using the symbol '<' to show ordering in time, so that 'before* < m*' means that the time referred to by *before* must precede the time referred to by its modifier (see p. 11).

In this example, the entry imposes a condition directly on the referent of the word concerned, but sometimes the condition is imposed on some other entity in the semantic structure, as in the case of the entry for past-tense verbs. Here the referent is the event or state defined by the verb, but the restriction is placed not directly on this, but rather on the time at which it took (or takes) place. (This basic temporal interpretation of past-tense verbs can be overridden contextually, e.g. by *if*, to give the 'unreal' interpretation which has no particular implications for time.) In other respects, the entry is similar to the one for *before*, except that it defines the time in relation to the deictic present, the time of the utterance-event, which I shall represent as NOW. (There will be more discussion of deixis in chapter 6.)

(2)   referent(past): past*
                         time (past*): t, t < NOW

Now consider the entry for *if*, in which we shall in fact ignore a number of complications such as the one just mentioned. Take a sentence like *if you read fast, you will finish this book today*. I assume that the dependency structure shows *if* as modifier of *will* and as head of *read*, but unlike most modifiers, it does not simply add an extra bit of information about the referent of its head, to make the latter more specific. On the contrary, the meaning of *You will finish this book today* is more specific than that of our example sentence, because the *if* clause allows for an extra possibility, namely that you will not in fact finish the book today (assuming that you do not read fast). Consequently, we have to add an entity to the semantic structure which corresponds to the combination of the *if*-clause with the rest of the main clause, but which coexists with a separate entity for the rest of the main clause minus the *if*-clause.

For our example sentence, this means that will*, the referent of *will*, must be taken in two different senses, i.e. as the name for two distinct semantic entities. On the one hand, we have the actual referent of *will*, as found in combination with *if*; this is the entity which would be taken as the referent of *will* in relation to superordinate parts of the semantic structure – for example, if the sentence were embedded in another, as a causal clause (e.g. *Don't worry, because if you read fast, you will finish this book today*). On the other hand, we have the referent of *will* as it would have been without the *if*-clause, which we might call will'*, where *will'* is a different instance of *will* from the one with which we are actually dealing – an instance like the actual one in every respect except that it lacks the *if*-clause. This abstract, hypothetical instance of *will* provides part of the semantic structure for the actual *will*, whose referent is taken as a disjunction between (not will'*) and (will'* & if*), where if* is of course the referent of the *if*-clause.

In other words, the semantic structure of *If you read fast you will finish this book today* shows that it is equivalent to 'either you won't finish this book today (not will'*) or you will finish this book today and also you read fast (will'* & if*)'. If we assume this analysis, then the entry for *if* is as follows:

(3)   referent(*if*): if*, if* = m*
    head(*if*): h, h = h',
            not modifier(h'): *if*,
                h* = {not h'* or (h'* & if*)}
    modifier(*if*): m

We shall see (p. 191) that this semantic structure is very similar to the one for yes–no interrogatives, which explains why *if* is also used to introduce embedded yes–no interrogatives. The presence of *not* also explains why forms like *any* and *ever* are possible in *if*-clauses as well as in straightforwardly negative ones (p. 208).

It can be seen from this example that the semantic effect of a word may be fairly remote from it in the semantic structure – in this case, the main effect of *if* is in the semantic structure of the verb on which it depends. We have already looked briefly at a construction in which the relation is even more remote between the word and the locus of its effect in semantic structure: in connection with the example *Fathers of few children have any fun* (p. 81). I showed there that negativity could be inherited by a head from its modifier, so that the negativity of *few* automatically extends to *of* because this is an empty word with the same referent as its modifier, *few*; then it is inherited by *fathers* from *of*, and ultimately by *have* from *fathers*. More research is needed before I can offer a formalization for negativity in word grammar, but the outlines of this particular part of the analysis are quite clear.

All the examples given so far have involved words or constructions which some linguists would call 'grammatical', as opposed to lexical or 'open-class' words, and this may have given the impression that it is only such words that can introduce semantic structure directly. This is not so, however. In particular, there are a fair number of adjectives and adverbs which would be 'lexical' by any criteria, but which have semantic structures somewhat similar to the one for *if*: they involve a structure which also contains a representation of the semantic structure that their head would have had if the word concerned had been absent. For example, *imitation diamonds* refers to an entity which is not diamonds, but is like diamonds in some respects; *a prospective student* refers to someone who is not yet a student, but would like to be one; *perhaps John will come* has a semantic structure which contains the structure for *John will come*, and marks this as only one possibility (the other being that John will not come); *unfortunately the goldfish died* contains the semantic structure for *the goldfish died*, with a comment on it; and so on.

All the words involved here – *imitation, prospective, perhaps, unfortunately* – will need entries with a semantic structure similar to the one for *if* given in (3), except for the specific spelling-out of h*. Consequently, we can simplify the grammar by defining the notion 'pseudo-head' once and for all, and then cross-referring to this general definition:

(4)   pseudo-head (word): h', h' = h,
                                    not modifier (h'): word
        head(word): h

The examples discussed above should make it clear what I mean by the entry for a word specifying semantic structure directly. We now turn to the other possibility where semantic structure is only specified indirectly, by inheritance from a model. This is presumably the 'normal' way to specify semantic structure, if we consider the vocabulary as a whole, and to the extent that we can assume that the models are known in advance of the words that exploit them, it must be relatively easy for learners to learn the meanings of such words. Examples of the kinds of word concerned are *cat, mouse, chase, balloon* and *pop*, where we can assume some cognitive entity which brings together knowledge of the typical cat, mouse, act of chasing, and so on. We can represent these entities by the ordinary English word written in upper-case letters: CAT, MOUSE, etc. Then all the grammar need do is to specify that the referent of the word concerned is an instance of such-and-such entity. By inheritance, any instance of that word will then be required to have a referent which is also an instance of the same entity. We can now expand the structure diagram for *The cat chased a mouse*, given on p. 144.

(5)

CAT   CHASE   MOUSE

1* = 2*   2*   3*   4* = 5*   5*

the*   cat*   chase*   past* a*   mouse*

1   2   3   4   5

the   *cat*   *chase*   past   a   *mouse*

One of the advantages for the linguist is that it is possible to leave the structure at that, without spelling out exactly what the properties of cats, mice and chasing are (or rather, what they are considered to be in the mind in question). These entities are independent of the words that express them, and indeed we may assume that many of them are at least partly supplied with properties before the word is learned; so it is not the linguist's business to say what these properties are. Unfortunately, there are important qualifications to this principle, which I shall discuss in the next subsection where we deal with semantic roles (p. 160 – 1); and other qualifications arise when we consider other parts of the grammar, such as the part that deals with definiteness (e.g. why can we follow a reference to a mouse by an otherwise unexplained reference to *the hole*, but not by one to *the bottle*?).

As I mentioned before, there is no clear division between the semantic structures that a word contributes directly, and those that it contributes via a model. For one thing, a particular bit of information could well be supplied in both ways, since we have already seen that information which can be inherited can also be stored, in order to save having to work it out on future occasions (see p. 27 in connection with regular inflections). For another, any bit of information which is specified directly could be presented as though it were inherited from a model. For example, we might even set up a general category for the referents of empty words, so that the referents of *that, the, do* and *to* were all instances of the same entity, and this entity would be defined as having no properties of its own beyond the property of being the same as the referent of a following modifier. It can be seen that there is a good deal of indeterminacy in the semantic structure, and it must be seen as a major research goal to try to work out to what extent the same indeterminacy exists in the minds of language learners.

Finally, I must give an example of a word in which the two methods of semantic specification combine. There are very many such words, and indeed we have already discussed two of them: the word *before*, and the word-type 'past'. In both cases, we have a semantic structure which includes an entity which is a time – namely, before* and t, in entries (1) and (2) respectively (see p. 146). These entries were both given in order to show how semantic structure can be specified directly, but we can now add to them the requirement that before* and t must be instances of the category TIME. This will not only prevent these entities from being given any interpretation other than a temporal one, but it will also make sure that '$<$' is taken temporally, and will allow another rule to identify the t of past tense and the referent of *before*, so that sentences like *He came in before tea-time* can be generated. (The time t which has to refer to some time before the present is also a time which preceded tea-time.)

Roles

So far, I have not tried to show how the bits of a semantic structure are connected up to one another, as they obviously must be. For example, in the structure for *The cat chased a mouse* given above, I left the referents of *(the) cat, (a) mouse* and *chased* unconnected. It should be obvious by now that the relation between referents that need to be connected up in this way is an example of the 'companion' relation which we have already studied as it exists between words in a word-string (and also, briefly, as it occurs between dustbins and houses, and other pairs of entities). Moreover, there is a very close connection, although not absolute isomorphism, between the companion relations of syntax and those of semantics, in that virtually every companion relation in syntax between two words A and B is matched by a companion relation between the referent of one of them and some part of the semantic structure of the other. (It seems never to be the case that a part of the semantic structure of one word is related directly to a part of the semantic structure of another word; at least one referent always seems to be involved in any semantic relation between a pair of words.)

However, as in the case of syntactic companion-ship, we must be able to assign companions in semantic structures to particular subtypes of companion-ship, in order to reflect the similarities and differences among companions. For example, we obviously have to be able to distinguish the relations of *the cat* and of *a mouse* to *chased* in *The cat chased a mouse*, but we also have to be able to show the similarity between these respective relations and those of the same referents in, say *The cat followed a mouse*. The general subdivisions of the 'companion' relation that we make use of in order to express these similarities and differences are what I shall call 'roles', following a well-established tradition which is matched by many other equally well-established traditions for naming the same concepts (e.g. 'role' is used by Lyons (1977:497), following Halliday (1970), but '(deep) case' is used by Fillmore (1968) and J.M. Anderson (1977), 'case relations' by Starosta (1978), 'semantic function' by Dik (1978), 'thematic relations' by Jackendoff (1972, 1976, following Gruber 1965) and 'theta-roles' by Chomsky (1981)).

The main reason why we need roles is so that we can bring out the similarities between entities involved in different semantic structures, rather than so that we can distinguish entities involved in the same one. This latter task can be done in many different ways without the use of roles – most obviously, by using different letters to name the variables concerned, as in predicate calculus. When it comes to bringing out the similarities between entities in different semantic structures, however, the options are more limited. If we used the letter-names for the variables in order to show the similarities, this would be equivalent to a set of roles with rather unhelpful names – if, for example, we always used x to represent the actor, and y to represent the affected entity; or if we showed the parallel between pairs like *follow* and *precede* by using x for the same element in both cases (e.g. for the follow-er). So far as I know, this possibility has never been exploited.

Another possibility, which is very widely adopted, is to identify semantic entities by referring to their syntactic realization. In the predicate calculus, for example, it is normal to present the arguments of a proposition as an ordered list, starting with the one which is realized by the syntactic subject. A similar practice is advocated by Bresnan (1978), in connection with her 'functional structure', in which the arguments are tied explicitly to the elements of syntactic structure. The objection to this solution is obvious: it is not in fact a solution to the problem in hand (Potts 1978). Our problem is how to show semantic similarities among entities, and not how to show their syntactic similarities; indeed, we have already solved the latter problem, simply by providing a syntactic structure linked explicitly to the semantic structure. There is no reason at all to pay any further attention to the syntactic structure, as I argued at length above in connection with the view that semantic structure is autonomous *vis-à-vis* syntactic structure (pp. 134 – 7).

A particular version of this possibility is also widely espoused by linguists, though perhaps less widely now than a decade ago when semantic studies were still gaining confidence. Many of the theories listed above involve role-type categories which are poised ambiguously between syntax and semantics, and are actually considered as part of syntactic structure, so that when they are exploited in the semantics, this is a case of the semantics exploiting syntactic structure. The problem is that often there is precious little syntactic justification (as such) for the categories concerned, even when such justification is set as a requirement of the theory (e.g. '[Lexicase] has placed the primary burden of identifying case relations on grammatical criteria' – Starosta 1982); and by leaning over backwards to fit the syntax, the categories fail to be semantically revealing. (Compare the explanation for the relative lack of support for Fillmore's 'case grammar' given in Newmeyer 1980:131.)

The only solution to the problem of showing semantic similarities among entities which seems worth developing is one in which the categories we refer to are genuinely semantic. This is not to say that they will be of no use in the grammar; on the contrary, they will be indispensable in a grammar, since they will give information which is not otherwise available, whereas the semi-syntactic categories criticized above are often simply duplicating information which is already available, in some other form, in the syntactic structure. One of the most obvious differences between a fully semantic approach and one based on syntax is that the former will include the internal semantic structure of single words, whereas syntactic structure leads one to take words as unanalysable units. Even an apparently simple sentence may turn out to have a very complex semantic structure, in which the relation between the semantic entities and syntactic structure is very indirect indeed. Later in this subsection we shall see that this is the case with our 'baby' example sentence, *The cat chased a mouse*.

Having established the general principle that roles should be established in such a way that they reflect the semantic facts, without regard to syntax, we now face the vast problem of deciding exactly what categories we actually need, and how they are related to one another. Most of the theories mentioned above include a list of role-categories, and for most of them the list is short (very short indeed in the case of J.M. Anderson 1977). But do we have any reason to expect the list to be short? It is true that it would be pleasant for us linguists if we could get by with a single-figure list of all-purpose categories, but it seems quite unreasonable to expect such simplicity. After all, by moving the analysis away from syntax, we have also moved it away from the relatively 'sheltered' domain of language, so what we are really concerned with is the set of relational categories which we use in cognition (regardless of how we express ourselves in language). Given the vastness and complexity of cognitive structure, it would be surprising if we could arrive at a short, simply structured list.

At the same time, there is every reason to expect some of the categories to be very generally applicable, partly because human beings have a capacity for generalizing, and partly because the world presents us with experiences that are already highly structured and that show considerable similarities from case to case. The most insightful discussion that I have read of these matters is Charniak 1981, which offers the basis for a solution which is highly compatible with the framework of word grammar. Moreover, this solution also fits well with the view that roles are tied to particular types of 'state of affairs', which is found in many of the theories mentioned earlier (notably, those of Halliday and Dik), and also theories based on Vendler 1967, such as Dowty 1979.

The proposal is that our knowledge of 'states of affairs' is organized hierarchically (just like our knowledge of other kinds of entity), with the most general type at the top of the hierarchy, and more particular types below it, and related to higher types as instances. Each type is treated as an entity which has other entities as companions, so that each type defines a particular range of companions, which are added to those which it inherits from more general types of which it is an instance. Furthermore, each of these companions is 'defined', in the sense that the entry for the type concerned imposes conditions on it, which will distinguish it from other companions. We can take each companion defined in this way as a distinct role, so that the range of roles available to a linguist is precisely the sum total of all the roles defined by all the entries for types of 'state of affairs'. We may assume that the total list will be very long indeed, because there are very many particular types – for example, I assume that the bottom of the hierarchy of 'states of affairs' consists of entities such as whistling, humming, and so on, each of which may contribute a distinctive set of companions.

On the other hand, the proposal also satisfies our other need, for a set of relatively general roles, because these would be provided by the more general types. I assume that notions like 'instrument' and 'purpose' would be defined in this way; indeed, since these words are part of the ordinary language which we have to analyse, we must be able to provide some kind of account of their ordinary meanings, and it seems reasonable to expect that this would require us to relate their meanings to general types of 'state of affairs', so we shall need to perform this kind of analysis whether or not we wish to use the categories concerned as semantic roles. It may well be, however, that the more general categories will include some for which we have no ordinary word, such as the categories referred to by technical terms like 'actor', 'agent' and 'patient'.

One of the reasons why it is so difficult to do the kind of analysis that I have just described is that it is common for a single entity to combine a number of different roles. For example, suppose we assume that one type of 'state of affairs' is what we could call an 'action', which involves an 'actor' – that is, some entity which (*inter alia*) provides energy for the action; and furthermore suppose we assume that 'action' is a model for a more particular type, called 'deed', in which there is some entity which is in control, called the 'controller'. Now, the entry for 'deed' will presumably have to show that the controller is normally the same entity as the actor, so in *John danced*, John will count not only as actor but also as controller. (Many of the theories mentioned earlier allow a single argument to fulfil more than one role, though this was not permitted in Fillmore's theory of case; so my suggestion is quite orthodox in principle.) The analytical problem, of course, is how to sort out when we have a single role which combines a number of distinct properties, and when we have two distinct roles which can combine with one another.

In view of this problem, and the sheer vastness of the analytical task, it would be premature for anyone to claim to have worked out an adequate set of roles, and I certainly have no coherent proposals to offer. However, I do want to make the discussion more concrete by giving examples of more complete semantic structures, so, with apologies, I shall include role names in my analyses without offering an adequate analysis into which they will fit.

One final general question is precisely how these roles should be shown in a formal analysis. Just as we found with syntactic companions, there are two ways in which we can identify roles: either by means of labelled slots, or by means of inherited variables (see pp. 109 – 13). For example, we might have a list of companions for each type, with each companion represented by a separate variable, and all the defining properties of each companion related to this variable. If some entity was an instance of some particular role defined in this way, it would automatically inherit all the defining properties, and all would be well. This would be the 'inherited variables' method. The alternative would involve slots with labels for the various roles, in addition to the apparatus just described.

Once again it is not easy to choose between the methods, but on balance is seems best to have labelled slots, such as 'instrument' and so on. One reason for this is that we seem to need to refer to roles in specifying the semantic structures for modifiers, as part of the valency statements for some verbs. For example, the infinitive which occurs with *try* must have a semantic structure in which the controller is the same entity as the subject of *try*. This would be hard to state if we could only refer to inherited variables, because we need to specify not only what the role is, but which verb the role is related to (the infinitive or *try*?). This argument is very similar to the one I used for including 'subject' and 'visitor' as named slots in syntax (see pp. 112 – 16 and 124 – 8). The other reason for including labelled slots is a practical one: it increases greatly the ease with which a reader can interpret the semantic structures that I shall give.

I should now like to offer a semantic analysis of *The cat chased a mouse*. We need not worry about the structure for *the cat* and *a mouse*, but can leave these as they are shown in (5) on p. 149, which means that their respective referents can be shown as 2* and 5*, and each of these referents has a model (CAT and MOUSE). We could add to this structure the propositions which distinguish definite and indefinite, but our main interest at the moment is in the connections between these noun referents and the verb.

Until one considers the meaning of *chase* carefully, it might seem that we need to add very little to the structure already given for *chased*. We have already shown that the referent of *chased*, which is 3*, is an instance of CHASE, combined with the referent of past tense, past*. We know from the entry for 'past' in (2) on p. 146 that the verb must have a time, *t*, which must precede NOW, so we could add that to the sentence structure, with 'time' as a labelled slot. As for the noun-referents, we might assume that they could be linked to the referent of *chased* by means of labelled slots such as 'actor' and 'goal', or some such. The result of this initial analysis would be (1):

(1)

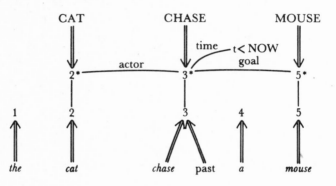

Such a simple analysis would be quite inadequate, however, if we accept that the semantic structure should show all the information which can be derived directly (or more or less directly) from the words. For example, are we to suppose that the mouse was inactive during the chase? Clearly not, as a chase implies two entities, both of which are moving. Following up this kind of observation, we find that the meaning of *A chased B* contains the following parts:

(a)   A moved fast (it would be a joke to say that a snail chased another snail);
(b)   B moved fast;
(c)   A followed B (A must not be moving away from B);
(d)   A's purpose was to catch B (though this purpose need not have been fulfilled).

In defining these parts, we have referred to a number of concepts which need further definition: 'move', 'fast', 'follow', and 'catch'. Of these, 'follow' also needs to be defined in relation to 'move', plus some other material (if A follows B, then A moves to place P at a time later than the time when B has already left place P, for a series of places of which P is only one); and 'move' can be taken as meaning 'vary one's place', where 'vary' means to be in various states at various times. Similarly, if A catches B, then A does something whose result is a change, from A not having B to A having B. This kind of conceptual analysis is common in cognitive science, and seems to exploit one's intuitions in much the same way, and with much the same degree of justification, as most other kinds of analysis in which we linguists engage.

The main point of this exercise is not so much to point out the hidden complexities of semantic structure, but rather to point out that the referents of *the cat* and *a mouse* are involved in many different ways in the meaning of *chased*. The cat is involved as a mover, a follower, and a would-be catcher; and B is involved as a mover, a follow-ee and a potential catch-ee. Each of these roles must be recognized by a separate mention of the referent concerned, filling a named slot which may vary from one proposition to another. In particular, the cat presumably fills two differently named slots in relation to the moving and in relation to the catching, because the latter involves it as a 'possessor' of the mouse, and this has nothing to do with movement – and vice versa. Similar remarks apply to the different roles of the mouse.

I assume that *chase* is involved in the following semantic hierarchy of models:

(2)

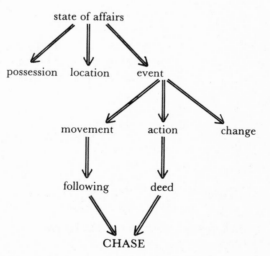

Each of the models contributes something different to the structure of CHASE (the model for the referent of the word *chase*), and although 'possession' and 'change' are not models for CHASE itself, they are models for one part of the structure of CHASE, namely the part that shows the chaser's purpose to be to catch (= become possessor of) the thing chased. In principle, the companions introduced by each of the models could be added to the diagram above, but this would make it too unwieldly so I shall lay the information out in a table, as in (3).

In a sense, the details of this analysis are not important, because we are concerned with the general principles of semantic analysis rather than with the pros and cons of particular analyses; however, if the reader cares to consider the details, it should be possible to understand the formalism on the basis of the previous discussion. (We shall apply this analysis to the structure of utterance-events too – see pp. 241 – 5.)

The only innovation in the notation is the use of subscripts to distinguish members of a list of similar entities, which allows the individual members to be linked to other entities, from other lists. For example, the structure for 'event' contains a list of times, each with a subscript, and assigns a distinct state to each of these times (thereby showing that an event must be 'dynamic', with changes through time). This is a convention that we shall use a good deal in semantic analysis, but it is hard to represent in the diagrammatic notation. For this reason, and because of the complexity of many of the structures, we shall have to make more use of the formulaic notation than we have in previous chapters.

On the basis of the semantic analysis given above, then, we can now give a semantic structure for the sentence *The cat chased a mouse*. We can simplify the structure by taking for granted the parts that we have already given:

(a)   the referents of *the cat* and *a mouse* are 2* and 5* respectively, and their models are CAT and MOUSE (see diagram (1), p. 156);

(b)   one model for *chased* is CHASE, which in turn has the models shown in diagram (2), on p. 157; the other model is 'past', which is shown in diagram (2), but we can include its semantic consequences in our structure.

So essentially we are concerned only with the semantic structure for *chased*, which is word 3; and all this structure will be associated with the referent of word 3, which is 3*. This structure is (4), p. 160.

(3)   entity (= X)   companion

---

state of affairs   time(X): t, model(t): TIME
possession   possessor(X): p, model(p): animate
                     possessed(X): q, model(q): object
location   located(X): a
                     place(X): l, model(l): PLACE
event   time(X): t, composition(t): t_1 . . . &
                                        t_n, model(t_i): TIME
                     $state_i$(X): x_i model(x): state of affairs
                     speed(X): n
movement   mover(X): m
                     $state_i$(X): x_i model(x): location,
                                        located(x): m,
                                        $place_i$(x): l_i
action   actor(X): b
change   time(X): t, composition(t): t_1 & t_2
                     $state_1$(X): not x_2
following   mover-2(X): c
                     $state_i$(X): x_i & y_i, model(y): location,
                                        located(y): c,
                                        $place_i$(y): k_i, k_h = l_i,
                                        h < i
deed   controller(X): b
                     purpose(X): d, model(d): change,
                                        $state_2$(d): e
                     $state_i$(X): not e, all i, $1 \leqslant i \leqslant n$
CHASE   speed(X): n, NORMAL-SPEED < n
                     mover(X): m
                     subject(X): m
                     actor(X): m
                     mover-2(X): o*, modifier(*chase*): o, *chase* < o
                     controller(X): m
                     purpose(X): d, $state_2$(d): e, model(e): possession,
                                        possessor(e): m,
                                        possessed(e): c*

(4)   model (3): *chase* & past
      model(3*): CHASE
      time(3*): t, t < NOW,
                    model(t): TIME,
                    composition(t): t_1 . . . & t_n, model(t_i): TIME
      speed (3*): n, NORMAL − SPEED < n
      actor(3*): 2*
      controller(3*): 2*
      mover(3*): 2*
      subject(3*): 2*
      purpose(3*): d, $state_2$(d): e, model(e): possession,
                                        possessor(e): 2*,
                                        possessed(e): 5*
      mover−2(3*): 5*
      $state_i$(3*): x_i & y_i, model(x): location,
                    located(x): 2*,
                    $place_i$(3x): x_i l_i, model(l): PLACE,
                    model(y): location,
                    located(y): 5*
                    $place_i$(y): k_i, k_h = l_i, h < i

To finish this discussion of roles, I should like to return to a remark
on p. 149, where I warned of important qualifications to the possibility
of abandoning semantic analysis at the point where we have identified
the semantic models. The problem should now be clear. Assuming that
we at least want our semantic structure to show the semantic
connections among the words in the sentence, we must link all the noun-
referents to the semantic structure of the verb on which they depend
(and similarly for other kinds of dependency patterns); but we cannot
do this until we know what roles these noun-referents play, and we
cannot know this until we have done a semantic analysis comparable in
detail to the one given above for *chased*. Indeed, we cannot even assume
that each noun-referent bears just a single role relation to the verb's
referent, which we could then simply leave unspecified, because each
noun-referent may be involved in more than one role (in the above
analysis, the referents of *the cat* and *a mouse* are mentioned six times and

three times respectively), and any of these connections could be with some entity other than the verb's referent itself (as with four of the nine connections in our example).

SEMANTICS AND SYNTAX
Subjects and predicatives

Having outlined the main principles of semantic analysis in word grammar, I want to comment on particular issues, starting with an explanation for something the reader may have noticed with some surprise in the semantic structures which I have just given, namely that the labelled role slots included one labelled 'subject'. As far as what I have already said is concerned, 'subject' is a category that is needed in syntax (see pp. 112 – 20), so what is it doing in a specifically semantic structure, associated with a referent?

The reason is simple: there are rules which refer to 'the subject', and which apply in the same way whether or not there is a syntactic subject, because they apply to the semantic entity which would have been realized by the syntactic subject, if the latter had been present. Take a simple example, the rule for verbs like *try* which says that their dependent infinitive must share their subject (I discussed rules like this on pp. 112 – 16). But what if *try* itself has no subject, as when it is an imperative? Does this leave the subject of the dependent infinitive free to be realized separately, or to be any old semantic entity? Clearly not, because imperative sentences like *Try John to come early!* or *Try to behave themselves* are just as bad as their equivalents among non-imperatives (e.g. *I tried John to come, *I tried to behave themselves).

Accordingly, we need an analysis which will anchor the subject of the dependent infinitive to that of *try* whether or not the latter is present in the syntactic structure. We cannot invoke a syntactic deep structure in which all subjects are present because transformations are not available in word grammar (and in any case, there are well-known problems for such analyses in the case of verbs like *try*, arising from sentences like *He tried to be needed by his family* where the deep-structure subject of the infinitive is in fact irrelevant). Instead, we can solve the problem by allowing the category 'subject' to appear either in syntactic structure, or in semantic structure. The rule for *try* can then require the semantic subject of its infinitive to be the same as its own semantic subject, as well as requiring the infinitive to share its syntactic subject, if it has one. Hence the need for 'subject' in semantic structure.

I should explain that this solution does not blur the distinction between semantic and syntactic structures, which I have claimed to be completely clear. This is because the semantic subject will always be recognizable as such, because it is always attached to a semantic entity (such as a referent), and not to a word; whereas the converse is true of the syntactic subject. Thus 'subject(*try*)' must refer to the syntactic subject of *try*, and 'subject(try*)' must refer to its semantic subject. So if we want to refer to the subject of *try*, without specifying the level, we must make this explicit by specifying 'subject(*try* or try*)'. On the other hand, this is somewhat clumsy, and makes the relation between *try* and try* look fortuitous, so we can introduce a mechanism for making the necessary generalization more directly, for any relevant word. The obvious mechanism is to allow a bracket round the asterisk, so 'X(*)', is to be taken as referring either to a word, or to its referent. We shall adopt this mechanism now, so the relevant part of the entry for *try* would be as follows:

(1)   modifier(*try*): $\emptyset$ or m,   model(m): *to*,

                          subject(m(*)): x, subject(*try*(*)): x

The definition for the new mechanism can be given in the entry for words in general, by the following addition:

(2)   referent (word): word*, word(*) = word or word*

An empirical objection to the proposed analysis is that the category 'subject' is a role when it is applied to semantic structure, but it does not satisfy our criterion for roles, which is that there should be a distinctive definition of the entities which it covers, and that this definition should refer to semantic factors, not to syntax (we established this principle in the discussion about the autonomy of semantics in relation to syntax, on pp. 134 – 7). In principle, this criterion is satisfied by all the roles I have introduced so far, even though I did not try to spell out conditions for all of them in the formal analysis. However, it is often claimed that there is no semantic property which is shared by all subjects and which distinguishes them from non-subjects – hence the widely held view, for example, that passivization makes no difference to meaning.

Although I have some sympathy with this objection, the assumption on which it rests may not in fact be valid, and it may be that 'subject' can be identified by properly semantic criteria which refer to notions such as 'point of view' (as I mentioned briefly earlier, on p. 000). For example, Allerton points out (1982:50) the difference between the sentence *The curtains matched the carpet* and *The carpet matched the curtains*, which (he claims) are not interchangeable even though the objective situations to which they refer must be the same. He suggests that the subject in each case is the 'foreground', being the focus of attention. Similarly, Dik (1978:87) observes that *John met Mary* refers to the same objective state of affairs as *Mary met John*, but presents it from John's point of view; so presumably *I met her* is a much more normal way of referring to a situation that could equally well have been expressed as *She met me*. Somewhat similar suggestions for giving a semantic status to 'subject' have been made by others too, such as Kac (1978:33), Small (1980:146) and Plank (1980).

Having now established that the category 'subject' is needed in both the syntactic and the semantic structures of verbs, we can continue the exploration in another direction, by asking whether 'subject' is relevant to the structures of any other kinds of word. We shall find clear evidence that it is relevant to a wide range of other types of word, and diminishingly clear evidence for an even wider range.

Take predicative adjectives. As we have already noted (see p. 115), adjectives like *eager* are similar to verbs like *try* in their effect on the subject of the dependent infinitive (though they also allow an overt subject introduced by *for*); so we have to require an infinitive depending on *eager* to share the latter's subject, unless it has an overt subject of its own. But how can we do this unless we include a subject in our analysis of *eager*? It is true we could sometimes make use of the subject of the copula verb on which *eager* depends, but this cannot be the solution for the lexical entry for *eager*, because adjectives used predicatively need not depend on a copula verb (e.g. *I found him eager to work hard*), or even on any verb at all (as in the *with* constructions discussed in McCawley 1983, like *With John eager to work hard, we made good progress*). The only conclusion seems to be that we must allow predicative adjectives themselves to have subjects.

This conclusion is supported by the parallel between sentences like *John is working* and *John is tired*. In the former, we showed on pp. 83 – 4 that we must recognize *John* as the shared subject of both *is* and *working*, so it seems consistent to do the same for the second sentence too, which means recognizing *John* (and John*, of course) as subject of *tired* (and tired*). More support comes from languages like French which have inflectional agreement between subjects and both (participial) verbs and adjectives, such as *Elle est partie/petite*, 'She has left/is small.' (Analyses in which subjects are connected to predicative adjectives have been suggested before, e.g. by Matthews (1981:92).)

This analysis of predicative adjectives naturally leads us to consider attributive adjectives. Clearly, if an attributive adjective has a subject, it must be provided by the adjective's head noun, so what evidence can we find for a subject relation between, say, *legal* and *argument* in the expression *a legal argument?* The main piece of evidence is that the relation between an attributive adjective and its head is generally the same, semantically speaking, as the relation between the same adjective and its subject noun when used predicatively. For example, *a legal argument* presents just the same ambiguity (argument which is legitimate, or argument about the law) as does *This argument is legal*. If the possible semantic relations were defined separately for the predicative and attributive uses (referring respectively to the subject and the head), then we should not expect so much consistency between the two uses. But we should expect it if the relations were given a single common definition which could be generalized to both uses; and since we already accept that 'subject' is used in relation to predicative uses, it follows that it should also apply to attributive uses. Thus for *legal* we need just one mention of each of its two meanings, each one referring to the subject.

A further piece of evidence for taking the head of an attributive adjective as its subject is that verbs are commonly used as attributives, in the form of a participle, but the head noun always has the semantic role normally reserved for the subject of the verb concerned (allowing for the effects of passivization), so it would be reasonable to say that in an expression like *man-eating tiger, tiger* is the subject of *man-eating*. But it also seems reasonable to generalize this analysis to other attributives, such as *carnivorous* in *carnivorous tiger*, especially when these are virtually synonymous with attributive participles.

An interesting consequence of adopting this analysis would be that 'subject' would become neutral as to the direction of dependency, because the subject of an attributive adjective will be its head, whereas that of a predicative adjective (and, of course, a verb) is its modifier. The consequence raises no serious problems, because the 'companion' relation is itself symmetrical, so 'subject' can appear as a subclass of 'companion', rather than as a subclass of 'modifier', as I have implied so far. Indeed, we may welcome the consequence, as an explanation for the uncertainty that has existed among dependency theorists as to the dependency status of the subject (e.g. Heringer 1970 treats subject and verb as interdependent). We could even see here the basis for an explanation for the observation of Keenan and Comrie (1977) that subjects are much more 'accessible' for relativization than any other modifiers of the verb; this could be due to the fact that relativizing a subject makes the verb of the relative clause into a modifier of what is in a sense its own subject, the antecedent. Structurally, this reversal of the usual relation between verb and subject is anticipated in the relation between attributive adjectives and their subjects, whereas no such precedents exist for other modifiers.

Leaving attributive adjectives on one side, how else could we generalize from predicative adjectives? Clearly, to other predicatives, be they prepositional phrases (e.g. *in a hurry*), noun-phrases (e.g. *a good swimmer*) or whatever. But how can we introduce 'subject' into these structures? We might assume that what we have seen so far shows that the entries for verbs and adjectives both need to allow for a subject, and we might consider the possibility of using this as evidence for a super-category to cover both verbs and adjectives (as suggested by Jackendoff 1977, for example). The predicative use of other word-classes, however, casts doubt on this analysis, and seems to suggest a radical alternative: that every word-class be permitted to have a subject, both in syntax and in semantics. We then have two alternatives to decide between. On the one hand, we could treat the subject as simply optional for all word-classes except verbs and adjectives, and make sure that the option could never be taken up by other word-classes except when used predicatively. On the other, we might consider making the subject obligatory for all word-classes, and then find some way of accommodating it in the analysis of non-predicative nouns, prepositions and the like.

On the whole, my preference is for the radical solution, with an obligatory semantic subject for all word-classes, plus an optional syntactic subject under various conditions. The question is, what is the semantic subject of (say) *cat*? My proposal follows the suggestive analysis of Bach 1968, in which the underlying structure (corresponding, in this case, to my semantic structure) for every noun contains a referential variable (my referent) as antecedent to a relative clause in which the noun is used predicatively; so the structure for *cat* would be 'x, such that x is a cat'. Thus the subject of *cat*, in my terms, is the referent of *cat*, and the entity of which this referent is subject is one which we have not needed in our analyses so far, namely the property of having CAT as a model. We could then explain the ambiguity of sentences like *John is a grammarian*, which can be taken either as giving a property of John, or as identifying him; so in one case, the subject of the property of having GRAMMARIAN as a model is John, while in the other it is the referent of the noun *grammarian* itself, and *is* tells us that this referent is the same entity as John. Not surprisingly, there is precious little difference between these two interpretations, but the two possibilities are easier to distinguish in examples like *That hut is the principal's office* (equative) and *That hut is a draughty hole* (descriptive).

These speculations suggest a number of research programmes, and until more of their implications have been explored, I shall avoid building them into my analyses. The main points that I feel fairly sure about are, firstly, that we must recognize 'subject' in semantic structure, and, secondly, that we must allow subjects not only for verbs, but also for adjectives. I shall assume that the subject slot is obligatory in the semantic structure of all verbs and adjectives (though we may have to allow some verbs exceptionally to have no subject, such as the 'weather' verbs); and I shall also assume that the syntactic subject is obligatory under some circumstances (e.g. if a verb is tensed), impossible under others (e.g. if a verb is an infinitive and is dependent on an adjective like *easy*), and otherwise optional.

I should like to finish this subsection on subjects with some general observations on the part which the category 'subject' plays in grammars. It is helpful, I think, to think of the subject as a 'lexical anchor', to which other semantic roles can be bound in order to link them to their syntactic realization. This allows the relations between the syntactic realization (i.e. the syntactic subject) and the corresponding semantic role(s) to be defined in two (or even three) steps, rather than directly. The first step is to link the roles to the semantic subject, which is done in the lexical entries for the words concerned. (Some of the links may also be stated at a more general level – for example, the 'actor' is presumably always, or at least usually, the same entity as the subject.) Having defined the normal alignment of other roles with the subject, we now have the possibility of tampering temporarily with them, by passivization (and other similar 'subject-changing' operations). This has the effect of realigning the subject and other roles, but it leaves the relation of semantic subject to syntax unaffected (though in English at least it affects other parts of the syntax, notably the inflectional type of the verb). Now comes the third step: relating the semantic subject to its syntactic subject, if there is one. At this point, there are numerous complexities, such as the possibility of the subject being in a number of different positions, or being entirely absent.

The functional advantage of having a stable category (subject) which is part of the structure of every verb is that this can act as a barrier between the two kinds of complexities, so that the complexities of the semantics, to do with semantic roles, can be kept separate from those of the syntax, where it is a matter of position, presence, inflectional case, and so on. Putting it another way, this arrangement allows great flexibility at both levels. If, in contrast, each semantic role had to be related directly to its syntactic realization, then the latter would need to be kept simple, thereby reducing the flexibility actually found in syntax. Alternatively, we might find flexibility in syntactic realization, but with the flexibility permitted by each verb having to be learned separately (rather like the situation we find with indirect objects, where *give* has to be distinguished from *donate*). In this system, we should expect complex interactions between the semantics and the syntax – so that, for example, we might find actors occurring in more syntactic positions than possessors. Interestingly, what we actually find in language (at least, in English), is the exact opposite of this: so far as I know, there is hardly any interaction between the semantic and syntactic structures involving subjects, so virtually the same range of syntactic options is available to every subject, irrespective of the other semantic roles with which it combines. There may be some interaction (e.g. imperative syntax may be restricted to identifiable semantic roles), but at least there is sufficient independence of syntax and semantics to suggest that the 'boundary' function of subjects is actually exploited by English (or, more accurately, by English speakers).

Visitors

On pp. 112, 128 I argued that 'subject' and 'visitor' were the only two grammatical relations that need to be made explicit in syntactic structure by means of labelled slots, and I pointed out various other syntactic similarities between subjects and visitors, such as the fact that they are both primarily associated with verbs, and both of them precede the verb, in contrast with other modifiers. In view of these similarities, it is worth asking whether visitors are also like subjects in needing to be marked in the semantics as well. We shall see that they are.

The reason for including 'visitor' in the semantic structure as well as in the syntax is very similar to the reasons for doing this with subjects: that there are visitors which are present in the semantics, but not in the syntax. These visitors occur in the constructions for which Chomsky (1977) postulates wh-movement followed by deletion of the moved wh-word (with the exception of topicalization) – i.e. constructions which involve a 'trigger' (e.g. *than*), and a gap separated from the trigger by an unbounded amount of structure, but no word next to the trigger suitable for filling the gap. For example, in *John bought more potatoes than Mary had said that she needed*, the trigger is *than*, the gap is after *needed* (which lacks an object), and the trigger and gap are separated by two clause boundaries (or three verbs, according to how you measure structural distance). But there is no word in this sentence which has been displaced from the gap, in contrast with the examples which we discussed in the syntactic account of visitors (see pp. 000 – 00). However, as Chomsky points out, the constraints on the relation between the trigger and the gap in these cases are just the same as those on the relation between displaced words and their gaps in constructions like wh-interrogatives and topicalization (e.g. both are subject to the 'complex noun-phrase constraint', or its equivalent, and all the other constraints discussed on pp. 124 – 30). Consequently, we should look for an analysis of these constructions which will bring out the similarities to the constructions which we have already handled in terms of visitors.

The outlines of the analysis are simple, though the details of a complete treatment of comparative clauses are too complex for us to present them all here. In essence, we allow *than* to be modified by a tensed verb, and also to supply a visitor for this verb; but this visitor only exists at the level of semantic structure, because there is no word corresponding to it, so the gap is filled semantically, not syntactically. Once the verb after *than* has its visitor, the rule for passing visitors down the dependency chain comes into force (see rule (3) on p. 127), and all the usual constraints apply, as desired. But of course all this is only possible provided that we accept semantic visitors as well as syntactic ones, which is the main point that I am trying to establish.

Let us take a simpler example: *John bought more potatoes than Mary wanted*. What is missing after *than* is a reference to some quantity of potatoes, which could be taken as object of *wanted*, and this information must of course be deduced from the previous words, specifically *more potatoes*. The quantity of potatoes that Mary wanted is of course different from (and, specifically, less than) the quantity that John bought, but in other respects what is understood and what is expressed by these words are the same. In the syntactic structure, *potatoes* is head of *than*, so we can refer to it as *h*, and its referent as h*; so what we need to reconstruct in this case, and more generally in similar constructions, is a semantic entity which is like h* except in that its structure contains a degree which is different from the degree contained in the structure of h*. The semantic structure of *more potatoes* shows already that this latter degree, which we can call *d*, is greater than some other degree; so the *than*-clause supplies the other degree. To simplify the analysis, we can assume that the referent of *than* is itself the degree concerned, copied 'up' from the reconstructed semantic structure in its modifier, so the standard of comparison is than*. So what the semantic structure shows is that the degree *d* is greater than the referent of *than*, than*. (I assume that the notion 'degree' is a coherent one, and suitable not only for the analysis of comparatives, but also for the semantic structure of degree words in general; this view has been disputed (e.g. Klein 1980), but I have not yet seen any reasons for abandoning it.)

A similar but somewhat simpler analysis is needed for examples like *John bought more potatoes than that* (or *This string is longer than two inches*), where the degree is expressed explicitly by the modifier of *than*, *that*. The degree is the referent of *that*, so if we treat *than* as an empty word, it will inherit its referent from its modifier in the usual way, and the referent of *than* will itself be the degree of comparison, as in the analysis of the more complex examples given above. We can start by giving an entry for the simpler use of *than*:

(1)   head(*than*): h, degree(. . . h*): d, than* $<$ d
             modifier(*than*): m, model(m): noun, m* = than*

This entry shows that the head of *than* must contain some degree in its semantic structure, that *than* itself refers to a degree which is less than the first one, and that the degree of *than* may be derived from its modifier.

We can now build on this entry to formalize the analysis introduced earlier for the cases where *than* is followed by a clause. The main point is that the entry will have to load a semantic visitor into the structure of the following verb, and this visitor will be defined as having the same semantic structure as the head of *than*, except for the different degrees. We can call the visitor *v*, so all we need to add to entry (1) is that the modifier may be a tensed verb, and if so, then this verb must have a semantic visitor with the properties just defined. The result is the combined entry in (2), in which the first two lines are the same as (1):

(2)   head(*than*): h, degree(. . . h*): d, than* < d
        modifier(*than*): m, model(m): noun, m* = than*,
                            or model(m): tensed, visitor(m*): v, v = h*,
                                        degree(. . . v): than*

This entry seems to cover two of the main types of comparative constructions in a satisfying revealing way, and it could be shown to provide the basis for an entry for the other main type, exemplified by *John bought more potatoes than Mary*. To the extent that the analysis is satisfactory, it shows the need for semantic visitors, because these play a crucial part in the analysis.

Similar arguments could have been produced on the basis of constructions introduced by *before, after* and *since*. We have already seen how the semantics of *before* can be analysed when it is followed by a time expression like *Christmas* (see p. 145). This entry was rather similar to the first one given above for *than*, in that it involved a comparison, between times rather than degrees. I repeat it here for convenience, with a couple of minor additions which were irrelevant earlier.

(3)   referent(*before*): before*, before* < m*, model(before*): TIME
        modifier(*before*): Ø or m, model(m): noun, model(m*): TIME

The kind of construction which is relevant to the present discussion is exemplified by a sentence like *You mustn't go out before your mother told you you could finish your practice*. Here, *before* refers to a time before some other time, *t*, which is the time such that your mother told you you could finish your practice at *t*. Once again, we have a 'trigger' (*before*) which permits a gap (after *finish*) any distance down the dependency chain, subject to all the usual constraints on visitors. So we need an analysis which involves the visitor mechanism, in order to capitalize on these similarities to the syntactic visitor constructions; but we can only produce such an analysis if we can have visitors in the semantics as well as in the syntax. Provided we make this assumption, then a small expansion of the existing entry for *before* is all that we need:

(4)   referent(*before*): before*, before* < m*, model(before*): TIME
        modifier(*before*): Ø or m, model(m): noun, model(m*): TIME
                            or model(m): tensed, visitor(m*): t,
                            model(t): TIME, before* < t

Once we have established the need for visitors in the semantics, another possibility emerges: that the semantic visitor may not always be the same as the referent of the syntactic visitor. So far as I know, this possibility of a mismatch is never exploited for the subject, but it may be that visitors do exploit it specifically in the case of restrictive relative clauses, as I shall now explain.

Consider first a relative clause construction in which there is no mismatch between the syntax and semantics of the visitor, namely where there is a relative pronoun. For example, *the student who likes linguistics* has a dependency structure in which *who* modifies *student*, and then is in turn modified by *likes*; and the entry for relative pronouns requires *who* to be loaded as a visitor onto the following verb. Here there is no reason for distinguishing the semantic visitor of *likes* from the referent of *who*, but the question is, what is the referent of *who*?

In some sense, of course, the referent of *who* is linked to that of its antecedent *student*, but we have to be able to distinguish between the 'defining' and 'non-defining' interpretations, and it is the non-defining interpretation which seems to require straightforward identity between the referent of *student* (which, it will be recalled, is the same as that of *the* − (see p. 144)) and that of *who*. In contrast, the 'defining' inter-pretation, as its name implies, helps to define the referent of student, and could be paraphrased as 'the x such that x is a student and x likes linguistics'. Moreover, the defining interpretation may well be associated with a distinct mental entity: the student-who-likes-linguistics, who/which is an instance of the category 'student'. For example, this must be so if one could then go on to specify other concomitant properties, as in *The student who likes linguistics is typically female, with a frustrated desire to be a scientist . . . .* Considerations such as these suggest that the referent of the relative pronoun in a defining relative clause should be the same entity as the *model* for the antecedent's referent, rather than the antecedent's referent itself; the latter can be reserved to provide the referent for non-restrictive interpretations.

Now we return to the main topic in hand, the kind of restrictive relative clause in which there is a mismatch between syntactic and semantic visitors. This possibility seems to be realized in relative clauses that have no relative pronoun at all. (For simplicity, I shall ignore the relative *that*; to the extent that this is simply an empty marker of a clause boundary, it would be easy to bring into the analysis, but there is some evidence that it is sometimes taken as a relative pronoun − e.g. in some Scots varieties, *that's* may be used as a possessive (Romaine 1980), and *that* is sometimes used to introduce non-restrictive relative clauses (Quirk *et al.* 1972:872).

Let us assume that the semantic structures for *the book which he wrote* and for *the book he wrote* are at least very similar, and that the analysis for the one with *which* gives *which* the same referent as the model for book* (according to the discussion in the previous paragraphs). On this assumption, both of the relative clauses must have a semantic visitor attached to the verb *wrote*, and in both cases this semantic visitor should be the entity which acts as model for the referent of *book*.

Now the question arises as to the *syntactic* visitor of *wrote* in the case where there is no relative pronoun, *the book he wrote*. There seem to be two possibilities, without a great deal to choose between them. One is to assume there is no syntactic visitor at all, and to give an analysis similar to the ones given above for comparatives and *before*. The other is to assume that the antecedent itself, *book*, is the visitor as well as the head. On balance, the second analysis seems preferable, because it gives *book* a similar analysis not only to *which* (as head and visitor of *wrote*), but also to *what* in a 'headless' relative clause. The significance of the so-called headless constructions (e.g. *what he wrote*) is that *what* is antecedent, head and visitor all rolled into one; and it is in this respect just like *book* in my proposed analysis for *the book he wrote*.

The analysis of relative clauses still needs research in order to follow up the implications of the various analyses I have suggested, but it seems that we should take seriously the possibility of treating the antecedent noun as the syntactic visitor of the 'relative verb', where there is no relative pronoun. But if we do adopt this analysis, we shall have found an example of the mismatch between syntax and semantics in question here, because the syntactic visitor of *wrote* in *the book be wrote* is *book*, but its semantic counterpart is not the referent of *book*, book*, but the model for book*, BOOK. This mismatch can of course be specified directly by the entry responsible for such relative clauses, so it is just a matter of theoretical interest, rather than of theoretical worry. The entry concerned is part of the entry for nouns, and is as follows:

(5)   modifier(noun): $\emptyset$ or m, model (m): tensed,
                     visitor(m): noun,
                     visitor(m*): x, model(noun*): x

For all their apparent complexity, I think the constructions discussed in this subsection permit surprisingly simple analyses provided we allow visitors to occur in semantic structure as well as in syntactic structure. I know of no other grammatical relation, apart from 'subject', that requires this dual status, so I conclude that 'subject' and 'visitor' constitute a very natural class, at least as far as English is concerned.

Anaphoric dependence

This term was introduced by Evans (1980) to refer to the kind of anaphora in which the referent of a pronoun is necessarily derived directly from some co-occurring noun-phrase, in contrast with the cases of anaphora in which a pronoun and a noun-phrase are assigned referents independently, but both happen to refer to the same entity. It is a fortunate term from the present point of view, because it reflects not only the semantic dependency just described, but also the fact that the syntactic dependency structure is highly relevant to the rules responsible for this kind of anaphora.

However, I should admit from the start that the range of phenomena that I shall apply the term to are rather different from Evans's range. For me, it is more restricted, and covers just reflexive, reciprocal and relative pronouns, because these seem to me to be the only pronouns that satisfy his criteria. In contrast, most of Evans's discussion focuses on personal pronouns when used with non-specific antecedents (e.g. *they* in *No-one said they liked it*), which Evans claims have special constraints on their relations to their antecedents. I find his evidence uncompelling, however; for example, a pronoun may have a non-specific antecedent in a different sentence, as in the following exchange between A and B:

A: Nobody came early.
B: Just as well too – they'd have had a surprise if they had.

Consequently, I shall leave the discussion of all personal pronouns till the subsection on definiteness.

The easiest type of 'anaphorically dependent' pronoun to deal with is the set of relative pronouns, which we started to consider in the last subsection. The relevance of dependency relations is very straight-forward here: a relative pronoun depends anaphorically on the noun which is its head – i.e. the word on which it depends anaphorically is also the word on which it depends syntactically. As we saw in the earlier discussion, the anaphoric dependence is simple in the case of a non-defining relative, because the relative pronoun has the same referent as the noun on which it depends; but when given the defining interpretation, the pronoun's referent is the same as the model for the noun's referent. It is worth comparing the very simple syntactic relation between pronoun and antecedent in this dependency analysis, with the much more complex relation between them in a constituent-structure analysis; in the latter case, the antecedent is at best an 'aunt' of the pronoun, and in many currently popular analyses, it would be a 'great-aunt', or worse.

Reflexive pronouns are much more complicated, but again it is easy to see the relevance of syntactic dependency. It is worth starting the discussion by asking why a language should benefit from having reflexive pronouns (not that every language does have them – many languages achieve roughly similar effects by means of verbal inflections, for instance). One plausible explanation is that they help to fill a communication gap produced by a restriction on ordinary definite noun-phrases (including personal pronouns). This restriction allows the hearer always to simplify somewhat the task of resolving ambiguities, by ruling out the possibility of coreference between two 'sister' noun-phrases or pronouns, even if their forms would otherwise allow them to be coreferential. For example, we can discount the possibility that in *He saw him*, *he* and *him* refer to the same person, because *he* and *him* are 'sisters' (both modify the same word, *saw*). This reduction in the number of possible interpretations is helpful for the hearer, but it does raise the problem for the speaker of how to express the message in which the subject and object are in fact the same person. Presumably it was to solve this communication problem that our ancestors developed the reflexive pronoun, which is also helpful to the hearer because it reduces ambiguity by eliminating the other interpretation (where the subject and object have different interpretations). (We shall see in the subsection on definiteness – pp. 180 – 6 – that the restriction on coreference is in fact somewhat more complex than this, but the above account is sufficient for our purposes.)

Once the device of reflexive pronouns is available for filling the communication gap left by the ban on coreference, it would not be surprising if it were extended to cover other cases, since reflexive pronouns always have the attraction of allowing fewer interpretations than ordinary personal pronouns. Since reflexive pronouns are a type of noun, we could in principle extend their use until they could occur in any position available to nouns, and in a variety of relations to their 'antecedent', but each such extension would require a separate entry in the grammar which would specify it as permissible. The result will be a grammar with a number of different entries controlling the use of reflexives, but making up for this extra learning task by the flexibility that it offers the speaker and hearer. We can expect considerable differences from language to language not only in the devices by which they cope with the communication gap (assuming they have one – some languages may not have this ban on coreference), but also on how far they extend the devices beyond their basic gap-filling purpose.

All this preamble is a preparation for the rather chaotic state of affairs in English with regard to reflexive pronouns. Reflexives are by no means restricted to cases where the reflexive and its antecedent are sisters (e.g. *John hurt himself*; in all the examples I shall use *John* as the antecedent and *himself* as the reflexive). The reflexive need not be a syntactic sister of the antecedent (e.g. *John has a large collection of pictures of himself*), nor need the antecedent 'c-command' the reflexive – that is, in dependency terms, the antecedent need not be a modifier of a word in the dependency chain leading down to the reflexive (e.g. *the collection which they gave John of pictures of himself*, taken from the discussion in Stockwell *et al.* 1968:226). Indeed, I believe it is even possible to concoct examples in which the antecedent is supplied pragmatically, contrary to the claims of most discussions (e.g. Hankamer and Sag 1976). For example, imagine the following exchange between A and B:

A: I hate the stories that John always tells about Mary.
B: Well, I prefer them to the stories about himself.

Any account of reflexives should try to cover the full range (and no doubt there are other possibilities of which I am not aware, and which may be beyond the present range of my grammar); but at the same time of course it must not overgenerate, and we have to impose whatever restrictions are necessary – such as the one which rules out **Mary told John that a picture of himself is hanging in the post office*, and **John says that they've put a picture of himself in the post office*, while allowing *John says that a picture of himself is hanging in the post office*.

Most of the problems are familiar from the literature on reflexives, but so far as I know it has not yet proved possible to give a unitary account of them all. What I have is not really a unitary account either, since it consists of three separate bits, but I make no apology for this, because I do not believe the phenomena are 'unitary' either, so the search for a unitary explanation is a wild-goose chase. On the other hand, I think my account is no less unitary than the facts it describes, and compares well with other treatments.

The three bits of the grammar correspond to three distinct ranges of construction in which reflexive pronouns are found, so we can explain their analyses one at a time, starting with the 'basic' one.

(a) The primary construction is the one in which the antecedent and the reflexive pronoun are 'clause-mates', in transformational terms. More precisely, the antecedent is either a modifier of the nearest verb above the reflexive in the dependency chain, or else a semantic entity directly related to the referent of this verb. The first possibility is illustrated by *John has a large collection of pictures of himself*. The dependency structure for this sentence is given below, and shows clearly how *John* is linked 'upwards' to *has*, by a single link, and then 'down' from *has* through a number of links to *himself*.

(1)

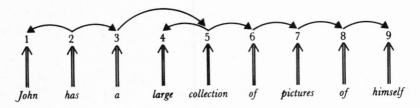

The other possibility has to be included because the antecedent need not be overtly expressed; it is sufficient if it is in the semantic structure. Hence the possibility of reflexives in imperative clauses, for example (e.g. *Wash yourself!*), or in gerundive clauses (e.g. *Having a large collection of pictures of himself is a bit weird, don't you think?*). Notice that in this last example the antecedent must in fact be reconstructed pragmatically; but notice also that this would still be necessary even if there were no reflexive pronoun present, because the gerund *having* needs a subject entity in its semantic structure, and where this is not provided by the syntax, it must be reconstructed pragmatically. Thus it makes no difference where the semantic antecedent came from (so to speak), as far as the reflexive pronoun is concerned.

There are two main constraints on this use of reflexives. The first is that the antecedent should be related *directly* to the verb which links it to the reflexive (i.e. to *has* in the above example). The antecedent must be the whole of one modifier of this verb, if it is overt; so it must not be part of a co-ordinate string of words which jointly constitute a modifier (hence **John and Mary saw himself*), nor may it be a dependent of the modifier (hence **John's mother saw himself*, and **The picture of John surprised himself*). Similarly, an 'understood', semantic, antecedent must be related directly to the verb's referent, and it is not sufficient for it to be part of the semantic structure (say) of an understood subject: *Not having seen himself for a long time, John's mother was very pleased.*

This constraint is very similar to the claim in transformational analyses that the antecedent must 'c-command' the reflexive, but the semantic provision allows it to deal with a range of constructions that should be ruled out by a c-command constraint. These are examples such as *They spoke to John about himself*, where *John* is not related directly to *spoke* at the syntactic level (in phrase-structure terms, it is a 'niece', and in dependency terms it is a modifier of a modifier), but is directly related to its referent in the semantic structure, since *to* is an empty preposition, so its referent is just the same as that of *John*. Thus *John* satisfies the semantic part of my criterion, though not the syntactic part, so we see another reason for locating the criterion for antecedents at both levels. Furthermore, it is now very easy, and natural, to do this in word grammar, since we allowed ourselves the new mechanism for making entries neutral as to level (see p. 162); so if we represent the antecedent as *a* in the entry for reflexives, then we can give a very simple formulation indeed to the requirement that the antecedent must be directly related at either level to the verb: 'X (verb(*)): a(*)'. (In words, the (referent of) the antecedent must fill some slot labelled X whose 'owner' is (the referent of) the verb.)

The second constraint on this kind of reflexive construction is that the verb to which the antecedent is directly related must be the only verb in the dependency chain leading to the reflexive pronoun. This rules out examples like *John said that they have put a picture of himself in the post office*, or even *John thought she liked himself*. On the other hand, since there is no other constraint on the dependency chain down to the pronoun, there is no upper limit to the number of links in the chain, so we could (in theory) produce recursive strings like *John designed the pattern on the cover of the most expensive edition of the collection of pictures of himself*. The constraint does not exclude sentences like *John has been trying to draw a picture of himself*, contrary to what might perhaps be expected at first sight, because (according to the analysis on pp. 112 – 16) the verbs all share the same subject, both syntactically and semantically, so *John* is in fact the subject of *trying*, the verb which is nearest to *himself* in the dependency chain, and the condition is satisfied.

We are now ready to formulate the entry. I shall present this as applying to the word-class 'reflexive', so a separate entry (which need not concern us here) will specify that *himself* is an instance of this category, and define the semantic conditions on its referent.

(2)   referent (reflexive): reflexive*, a* = reflexive*
               head (. . . reflexive): h, model (h): verb,
                              X (h(*) : a,
                              not {head (. . . x . . . reflexive): h,
                              model (x): verb}

In words, a reflexive has the same referent as its antecedent (*a*), and depends (directly or indirectly) on a verb (*h*), to which the antecedent is directly related at the semantic or syntactic level, and which is not separated (dependency-wise) from the reflexive by any other verb (*x*).

(b) The second reflexive construction has the effect of extending the dependency chain that can lead down to the reflexive pronoun, by providing one condition under which there may be an intervening verb: namely, if the antecedent is the subject of its verb, and the reflexive pronoun depends on the subject of the intervening verb. This lets in sentences like *John said that a picture of himself is hanging in the post office*, in which *John* is subject of *said*, and *himself* depends on the subject of the intervening verb *is*. On the other hand, as we have seen, if either of these subject-based requirements is infringed, the sentence is ungrammatical: **They told John that a picture of himself is hanging in the post office.* **John said that they've put a picture of himself in the post office.* It is interesting to speculate about the reason for the existence of this special provision, and for this particular combination of constraints, but the main point is that it seems extremely unlikely that it would be possible to subsume these types of sentence under the same entry as the basic construction, without making specific provision precisely for this particular construction. The constraints on the two constructions are quite different: in the basic one, it is not necessary for the antecedent to be subject, nor is it possible for the reflexive to depend on the subject.

The only problem in formulating the necessary entry is how to allow this entry to override the one for the basic construction, which specifically forbids the pronoun to be separated from the antecedent by an extra verb. The solution I shall adopt is to include the necessary details in the entry for verbs, rather than in the one for reflexives, so that the properties of the verb on which the reflexive and antecedent depend will be able to override the entry for reflexive pronouns themselves, by virtue of the principle of 'priority to the instance' (p. 16). Accordingly, we shall need the following entry:

(3) modifier (. . . yx . . . verb): Ø or p, model (p): reflexive,
                    subject (verb(*)): a(*), a* = reflexive*

$$\text{model (x): verb,}$$
$$\text{subject(x): y}$$

In words, a verb may or may not have a reflexive depending on it, separated from it (dependency-wise) by two words, x and y, of which x is a verb and y is that verb's subject; but if this is so, then the antecedent of the reflexive must be the first verb's subject (syntactically or semantically).

(c) The third construction extends the possibility of using a reflexive pronoun into constructions that provide no verb for the antecedent to use as a point of access to the dependency chain that leads to the reflexive. The antecedent and reflexive must still be linked in the dependency structure, and (naturally enough, in view of their semantic identity) neither can depend on the other, so they must be linked through a word on which they both depend – which we can call the 'pivot'. The pivot is the word which had to be a verb in the first two types of construction, but in this construction it must not be a verb, and I shall assume that it must be a noun (simply because I cannot think of any relevant constructions involving other word-classes).

The constraints on the antecedent are much less restrictive than in the other constructions; so we find examples like *the picture they gave John of himself*, where *John* is extremely distantly related to the pivot word, *picture*. In this construction, however, there seems to be a constraint preventing the antecedent from being separated from the pivot by another noun, as witness **John's mother's picture of himself* and **a picture by a girl who admired John of himself*, where *John* is separated from *picture* by *mother* and *girl*. Moreover, we have the constraint found in the first construction which bans another verb between the reflexive and the pivot (e.g. **John's explanation of why people trusted himself*). The entry needed to capture these constraints is the following:

(4) modifier (. . . noun): $\emptyset$ or p, model (p): reflexive,
$$\text{X (. . . noun (*)): a(*), a*}$$
$$= \text{reflexive*}$$
$$\text{not \{modifier (. . . x . . . noun):}$$
$$\text{a, model (x): noun\}}$$

The analysis formalized in these entries is certainly not complete. For instance, we probably need to allow the second and third entries to interact, in order to explain examples like *John's claim that a picture of himself is hanging in the post office*; and we need to produce some account of the badness of examples like **John bought Mary's picture of himself*, in contrast with *John bought a picture of himself*. A number of possibilities suggest themselves for these extensions, but it is sufficient for the present to have shown, as I hope I have, that the dependency structure of the sentence is quite crucial to the analysis of reflexives.

Lastly, we have reciprocal pronouns (*each other* and *one another*). These are very similar to reflexive pronouns in their distribution, to the extent that they could be subsumed under a common word-type, so that all the above entries would apply equally to them. The main difference between them and reflexives seems to be that a reciprocal can be the subject of a subordinate clause (e.g. *They don't know what each other are doing*), especially if the latter is a wh-interrogative. It may be that this will require a special entry, but if so, the conclusion is quite reasonable, since speakers differ on whether they accept such sentences as well formed. Apart from this syntactic difference, there is little to say about the syntax of reciprocals, but their semantic structure is different from that of reflexives in an interesting way, in that a reciprocal pronoun requires coreference with its antecedent in one sense, but in another sense it requires distinct reference. We shall be able to deal with the semantics of reciprocals better in the section on quantifiers (see p. 202).

KNOWN AND UNKNOWN
Definiteness

This section will deal with two areas of semantic structure which relate to the state of knowledge of speaker and addressee, namely definiteness (this subsection) and mood (the next). However, it may not be obvious that either of these areas has anything to do with the participants' state of knowledge, less still that they have anything to do with one another, so I should admit from the start that the analyses which I shall formalize in terms of word grammar are quite controversial.

Before we get into the semantics of definiteness, however, we need to consider the syntax. I take it that 'definite' is a word-type, of which some nouns are instances, and others are not. The ones that are instances are: proper nouns, various pronouns (personal, reflexive and reciprocal, and relative) and the determiners *the, this/these* and *that/those*. (I have deliberately avoided discussion of genitives in this book wherever I have been able to, so I also omit them from this list, although they clearly have a strong definite element.) Thus whatever we arrive at as the semantic structure for definites needs to be stated only once, in connection with the referent for the noun-type 'definite'.

In contrast, there seems to be no reason to treat 'indefinite' as a word-type to match 'definite', as what we might call indefinite nouns are simply nouns that lack the semantic and syntactic properties of being definite. (The best syntactic 'test' for definiteness that I know of is the possibility of occurring after the partitive *of*, as in *half of them* (Postal 1966, McNamer 1975); but even this is restricted in its usefulness, as it fails to apply to various obviously definite words like *he/him* and the reflexives.) The traditional 'indefinite article' is simply a marker of countability, which occurs to prevent a countable noun from occurring without some kind of determiner; it even occurs in predicative positions, from which all other determiners are (virtually) excluded (compare *He is a doctor, They are doctors, *They are some doctors*). Words like *some* and *every* clearly have specific semantic structures, but there is no need to assume that they have anything in common to justify a general word-type 'indefinite'.

Returning to definites, we have already seen the mechanism by which the determiners are used to mark a neutral noun as definite (see pp. 144 – 5). Take an expression like *the cat*. Here *cat* is neutral, but *the* has the same referent, and *the* is syntactically definite, so its definite meaning attaches to the referent of *cat* too. In contrast, *George* is syntactically definite, so it has the semantics of definiteness which it inherits from the category 'definite', and does not need a determiner.

So what should be our semantic analysis for definite nouns? I take it for granted that we cannot leave it simply as a semantic marker 'definite', so we must provide a structure which will relate definiteness to other parts of our cognitive structure. Two main traditions of analysis seem to coexist in the treatment of definiteness. One tradition says that a definite noun has a referent which exhausts the set defined by the head noun plus its modifiers (e.g. Hawkins 1976, Chomsky 1974, Rivero 1975). This tradition has problems with straightforward examples like *the cat* used to refer to a particular set (e.g. *a cat and a dog were running around in the garden, and the cat* . . .), and it is often suggested that for such cases there is an underlying relative clause which defines the particular entity in question (e.g. Vendler 1967). In contrast, according to this tradition, indefinites are taken to have referents which specifically do not exhaust the set defined in this way, but here again problems arise, with examples like *a man I met for the first time in the pub last night*, which could well refer to the only person in the world who satisfied this description.

The other tradition is the one I shall follow. This is the one which relates the meaning of definite nouns to the existing knowledge of the addressee, so that *the cat* has a referent which is already known, in contrast with *a cat*, which the addressee must assume they do not already know (e.g. Dahl 1976, Comrie 1981:128). An attraction of this interpretation is that it is easy to give a functional, even a procedural, explanation of definiteness. When a noun is used, the hearer needs to know what to do with its referent. One possibility is to add its referent as a new entity to the existing stock of knowledge, and the other is to look for an existing entity in this stock, and identify the referent of the noun with this. This choice would be forced on the addressee whether the grammar contained the category 'definite' or not, so the overt marking of some nouns as definite can be taken as a way of helping the addressee to make the choice.

According to this analysis, the difference between *the man I met for the first time in the pub last night* and its indefinite equivalent (quoted above) is that the definite phrase assumes that the addressee already knows that such a man exists, but it does not assume any more than this; in particular, the addressee need not 'know' this man in the ordinary sense in which some people can claim to know (e.g.) Chomsky, and others cannot, even though they know *of* him. All that is required is that there should be some entity stored in the addressee's mind, even if only one fact is known about this entity (e.g. that it is the x such that I met x for the first time in the pub last night). Thus as soon as you (the addressee) know of the event (e.g. the event in which I met someone for the first time in the pub last night), you also know of its participants (e.g. the someone that I met), even if you know nothing else about them. So if I then want to tell you something about any of these participants, I must use a definite noun to refer to them. Conversely, if I use an indefinite noun, then I am telling you that you do not already have any mental representation of its referent, so the phrase *a man I met for the first time in the pub last night* could only be used if you did not know that I met someone for the first time in the pub last night.

As with most other parts of semantic structure, we can exploit this one too in order to convey information which we are pretending is already known; for example, if I say to you *Have you seen the letter I got from the Queen?*, I am pretending to assume that you already knew that I got a letter from the Queen, but I may well know full well that you do not yet know this, and wish to remedy the situation. Another important source of complication is that we exploit general knowledge, and choose between definite and indefinite according to whether we think the addressee ought already to know, or be able to work out, that the entity concerned exists. For example, it would be normal to refer to one's old Latin teacher as *the man who taught me Latin* (assuming that there was only one such person, and that the person was male), rather than *a man who taught me Latin*; and this would be normal even if we were talking to a relative stranger who knew nothing of our school days. In contrast, it would be less normal to say *the man who taught me Sanskrit*, under the same circumstances, and decidedly odd to say *the man who taught me Aztec*. The differences here are clearly due to the fact that we expect people (of a certain age and class) to have been taught Latin at school, but not Sanskrit, less still Aztec. So when I say *the man who taught me Latin*, I am not assuming that you already know that I (in particular) learned Latin but rather that you know enough to be able to work out that I probably did, so that my definite noun counts as an invitation to you to provide yourself with a mental representation of this fact, without implying that you are learning something new in the process.

Examples of this kind, showing that the choice between definite and indefinite is closely tied up with general knowledge, could be multiplied endlessly, and are well known (e.g. Hawkins 1978). Just to give one more instance, we can follow a reference to a house by a definite noun referring to its chimney-pot, provided we believe that houses typically have chimney-pots; but we could scarcely do the same for a rocket-launcher that happened to be built into the roof of the house, because this is not part of our normal expectations about houses. For word grammar, such connections between linguistic entities and general knowledge are very easy to formalize, because they are both part of the same giant network of knowledge; and it is equally easy to refer formally to particular knowledge (restricted to particular knowers, or to particular times), for the same reason.

Assuming, then, that definiteness is related to knowledge, we can work out the analysis in more detail. I have already suggested that indefinites are simply the unmarked category, in other words there are 'nouns' and 'definite nouns', and what we have been calling indefinites are simply nouns that are not definite, and that therefore have all the 'normal' properties for nouns. In view of the analysis of definite nouns just outlined, we must have a contrasting interpretation for indefinites, and it seems reasonable to assume a general ban on coreference, so that when we assign a referent to a noun, we must assume that it is *not* the same as any entity that we already know. The function of definite nouns is then to override this ban, with the effects described above.

I have assumed for simplicity so far in the discussion that the only knowledge which is relevant is the addressee's, but we need to specify also that the entity concerned is already known to the speaker. Although it may seem obvious that this must be so, we need to be able to distinguish definite nouns from another class in which the speaker does *not* already know the entity, namely interrogative pronouns (an observation which anticipates the analysis of mood which I shall offer in the next subsection). For example, if I say *Who did you meet in the pub last night?*, I am recognizing that you do know the person concerned, but telling you (or at least implying) that I do not. (Actually, of course, I do already know the entity, but I know nothing more about it than what is contained in the interrogative clause; so what you know, and I do not, is another entity, with extra properties, with which we can identify the referent of *who*.) Accordingly, the analysis of definites needs to show that the referent is already known to both speaker and addressee.

What we have established so far is that nouns in general are subject to a general ban on coreference, which is overridden if the noun is definite by the requirement that the referent must be the same as some entity which is already known to both speaker and addressee. The ban on coreference can be formalized quite easily, by adding 'not x = noun*' to the entry for nouns, meaning 'there is no x such that x is the same as the referent of the noun concerned.' For the overriding requirement of definite nouns, however, we need to refer to what the speaker and addressee already know, which is more difficult to formalize. Let us take the entities 'speaker' and 'addressee' for granted, as part of the cognitive structure of any person; we shall discuss them further in the section on the structure of utterance-events (pp. 241 – 5). Let us furthermore assume a cognitive structure corresponding to the verb *know*, in terms of which people can represent to themselves facts about what is known to different people (e.g. I can represent to myself the fact that my mother knows where I was born but our local postmaster does not). The cognitive structure for 'know' would have to include at least three entities, a knower, an item of knowledge, and a time. What we need to say about a definite noun, then, is that its referent is part of the knowledge in two instances of knowing, namely those where the knower is the speaker and the addressee respectively, and where the time is just before the word concerned was uttered.

This relatively informal account has prepared us for formalizing the entry for definite nouns, so here it is:

(1) referent(definite): definite*, knowledge(p): . . . & definite*,
                                                knower(p): speaker
                                                time(p) t_1, $t_1 <$ NOW
                                      knowledge(q): . . . & definite*,
                                                knower(q): addressee,
                                                time(q):t_1

In words, the referent of a definite noun is part of the knowledge known to the speaker at some time before the utterance-event, and likewise for the addressee. Of course, it goes without saying that a more complete formal representation could have been given of all the relevant bits of the cognitive structure which this extract presupposes, such as the bits dealing with knowledge and the time NOW.

One final point about definite nouns is that their ability to override the general ban on coreference is limited, as we have already noted in connection with reflexives (see p. 174). Specifically, the referent of a definite noun must not be the same as any other entity directly related to the same head. As usual, it makes no difference whether this other entity is syntactically realized or not, since it is the semantic structure that is relevant. This restriction is why *John saw him* requires us to take *him* as referring to someone other than John, in contrast with *John discussed some pictures of him* where *John* can be coreferential (and therefore synonymous with *John discussed some pictures of himself*). In *John saw him*, the referent of *him* is directly related to the referent of *saw*, and so is the referent of *John*, and consequently they must not be coreferential; but in the other sentence the referent of *him* is only indirectly related to that of *discussed*, and coreference between *him* and *John* is permitted. The restriction also explains why *John looked about him* allows coreference while *John talked about him* does not (a well-known pair). In the first sentence, the referent of *him* is only indirectly related to the referent of *looked*, via the place defined by the phrase *about him* (this place is obviously distinct in reference from the person John); but in the second sentence, there is a direct link between the referents of *him* and *talked*, namely the 'subject-matter' relation (whose directness is shown in the syntax when the verb is *discuss*). To formalize the restriction, we add an extra condition on definite*, in (1): 'not definite* = a, X (h*): a, head (definite): h'.

This ban on 'sister coreference' may not be part of the grammar of every language. In particular, it seems likely that it must be absent from 'non-configurational languages', such as Kalkatungu (see p. 81 – 2). The reason is that in such languages some fellow-modifiers of the same verb must be taken as coreferential, because they help to define the same semantic entity (e.g. the words for 'this' and 'dog' are both related directly to the verb, as its modifiers, in the syntactic structure; but in the semantic structure they are in the same relation as English, with a common referent).

To summarize the various constraints and devices that I have discussed, I have suggested the following:

(a) a general constraint on coreference of nouns, which is overridden, when necessary, by the use of a definite noun;

(b) A constraint on coreference between a definite noun and any other entity directly related to the same head in the semantic structure; this constraint may be overridden by the use of a reflexive pronoun, but the distribution of the latter is more generous than is needed just to plug this particular communication gap, so ordinary definite nouns (including pronouns) are not in complementary distribution with reflexives.

Mood

I shall discuss the semantic structures for the various syntactic clause-types based on 'mood' – declarative, imperative, interrogative and exclamative, in that order. Since the theory of semantics which I am developing here is not tied to the truth-conditional approach, there is no reason to doubt that the distinctions with which we shall be concerned are suitable for inclusion in the semantic structure, but since I have also argued that the only clear boundary of semantic structure is the one dividing it from syntactic structure, it makes no difference whether we call the mood structures 'semantic' or not. The main point is that they are part of the knowledge-structure which is associated with a string of words, and which is derived almost exclusively from the words in the string.

Unfortunately, I shall have nothing to say about intonation, an omission which is particularly regrettable in this case, because of the obvious connection between intonation and the semantics of mood. My suspicion is that the semantic contribution of intonation will turn out to be fairly independent of the contributions of the words, so I comfort myself with the hope that this suspicion is correct, and that the conclusions I draw below would not be affected very radically if I was able to take account of intonation.

In each case, I shall consider only main clauses to start with, as these are free of possible influence from the linguistic context. However, I shall discuss subordinate clauses briefly, in order to show how the default structures may be overridden by the influence of linguistic context.

(a) *Declaratives*. I take it that 'declarative', as applied to a constituency-free analysis like mine, means just the same as 'tensed', in the absence of any overriding mood category. All the semantic structures which we shall discuss below are (of course) part of the structure of whichever word the rest of the words in the clause depend on, and in a declarative clause that means the tensed verb. (The possibility of assigning mood structure to single words makes it unnecessary to assume clause nodes, *pace* my earlier arguments in Hudson 1976a, 44, 205.)

When we use a declarative, we imply that we believe the content of it ourselves, and are presenting it as a true statement. This implication may be overridden by the non-linguistic context, it is true; for example, we may tell a joke, or take part in a make-believe game, but there are ways of making this clear to our addressee, and if we do not make it clear, then it is fair to accuse us of being misleading. In contrast, there is no such implication when we use a non-finite verb-form, unless this is imposed by the linguistic context (compare *He tried to do it* and *He managed to do it*; the second implies that we believe he did it, but the first does not). Thus I think we must make it clear that the content of a declarative clause is something the speaker believes to be true. Of course, the distinction between knowledge and belief is irrelevant here because it depends on objective truth (you can only know things that are true, but you can believe anything), so what we are really saying is that the content of a declarative is assumed to be part of the speaker's cognitive structure. This is what I called the speaker's 'knowledge' in the previous subsection, and I shall go on using this term in the same rather general way here.

This claim is not meant to imply that everything in one's knowledge is labelled as being part of one's knowledge; that would lead to an infinite regress, and in any case there is no reason to believe it is true.

One part of my personal knowledge is the proposition 'My name is Dick Hudson', and I assume that this is stored without any epistemological trappings; but in contrast, when I say the sentence *My name is Dick Hudson*, the semantic structure must contain the proposition that this content is part of my knowledge. Epistemological labelling in one's mind is possible, of course; for example I know that the little boy next door used to think my name was Gake, so I know the proposition 'My name is Gake', but it has a very different status from the correct proposition, because it is stored only as what the little boy next door used to think. So when I am quoting this false proposition, I have to give it along with all the epistemological information, otherwise my hearers will think I am offering it as the truth.

As far as the formalization is concerned, there is no great problem now that we have a way of referring to the speaker's knowledge (see p. 185). If the referent of a tensed verb is tensed*, then we simply add to the entry a requirement to the effect that tensed* should be part of the speaker's knowledge as of the moment of utterance. Thus:

(1)   referent (tensed): tensed*, knowledge (p): . . . & tensed*

We can in fact leave the entry at that, relying on the fact that p is already defined in the grammar (by entry (1) on p. 185) as the speaker's present state of knowledge.

It is very easy to generalize this entry to subordinate uses of tensed verbs, in order to distinguish between 'factive' and 'non-factive' constructions (Kiparsky and Kiparsky 1971). Any dependent tensed verb is introduced by some entry, associated with its head, and the entry concerned may or may not override the entry for tensed verbs just given. Thus the entry for *believe* does override it, but that for *know* does not (in spite of the examples of contextual overriding in Wilson 1975); in other words, 'opaque' contexts suppress the requirement that the proposition is part of the speaker's knowledge. Such distinctions need to be made in areas of syntax other than verb complements; for example, restrictive relatives do suppress the presupposition that the speaker believes the content, but non-restrictive ones do not. The details remain to be worked out, but at least it should be possible to use the entry in (1) as the basis for other constructions. Moreover, it is worth pointing out that the way in which (1) is formalized will be helpful for other constructions because it does not impose an extra layer of structure (showing the speaker's beliefs) between the referent of the verb and its context; thus for both *believe* and *know* the complement is simply the referent of the tensed verb following it, with the distinction made by the presence or absence of the presupposition about this referent. In this respect, my analysis is very different from the 'performative' analyses of generative semantics (e.g. Ross 1970).

Since we are coupling the discussion of mood with that of definiteness in this section, it is interesting to ask if there is any place for similar semantic structures among nouns. The answer is not self-evident, but it may well be that there is a parallel in the kind of noun introduced by *a certain*. It is hard to be sure what this expression means, but I think it may mean that the speaker knows the referent, and the addressee may or may not know it. For example, if I say *I've got a complaint to make about a certain person*, I think I am leaving open the possibility that you know the referent of *person* already. If this is so, then the semantic structures for *a certain person* and for a declarative clause are similar in both containing an entity known to the speaker, and maybe also to the addressee. In contrast, if I simply say *I saw a cat*, then you must assume that you do not already know the cat concerned; and if I say *Some cat has made a mess in our garden*, then neither of us knows the cat.

(b) *Imperatives*. The word on which the whole of an imperative clause depends is an imperative verb (see the network of inflectional classes in (3) on p. 47), so once again the mood semantics can be located in the semantic structure of this verb. In this case, the semantic structure has nothing to do with the state of knowledge of the participants, but it is worth including an analysis in this subsection for completeness. To come straight to the conclusion, the best analysis I can think of is one in which the referent of the imperative verb defines the purpose of the speech-event. For instance, imagine I say to you *Hurry up!* The referent of *hurry* is a state of affairs which could have been expressed by *You will hurry up*, but unlike this declarative sentence the imperative does not imply that I believe you will hurry up. Instead, my reason for saying the sentence is to get you to hurry up, so my purpose in making the utterance is that you should hurry up – that is, the content of the verb itself, but defining a (possibly unrealized) future state of affairs. Similarly, if I say *Let's hurry up!*, my purpose is to get both of us to hurry up, so it can be defined simply as the content of the clause, 'We shall hurry up.'

This analysis was made possible by the decision to make no crucial distinction between sentence and utterance (see pp. 21 – 3), since the structure of the word-string itself can now refer to the purpose of uttering it. However, we have already had plenty of examples where the semantic structure has to refer to other properties of the utterance-event, namely the speaker, the addressee and the time. It should be clear that an utterance-event is an instance of the kind of state-of-affairs that has a purpose (i.e. a 'deed', according to the analysis in (3) on p. 159), so we are not adding this slot specially for the sake of imperatives; all we are doing is allowing the form of words to restrict the filler of the slot.

(c) *Interrogatives.* With interrogatives we come back to the state of knowledge of the participants. In contrast with declaratives and imperatives, the word on which the rest of an interrogative clause depends is not necessarily a verb. Specifically, it is a verb in yes–no and alternative interrogatives (e.g. *Is it raining?* and *Was the baby a boy or a girl?*, respectively), but it is an interrogative pronoun in a wh-interrogative. Of these three types of interrogative, the most tricky to analyse are alternative interrogatives, so we can leave them till last.

Let us start with yes–no interrogatives. If I say to you, *Is it raining?*, it seems reasonable to assume that I believe you know whether it is raining, but that I do not know whether it is raining; so whatever the answer is, and however we represent it formally, I shall assume that it is part of the addressee's knowledge, but not part of the speaker's. (I defended this view in more detail in Hudson 1975.) What is it that I assume you know, when I say *Is it raining?* I cannot assume that you know that it is raining, because I do not myself know whether this is true. Rather, I assume that you know one or the other of two propositions: 'it is raining' or 'it is not raining.' This assumption is easy to represent formally. We let x stand for the knowledge that the addressee is assumed to have, and then define x as either verb* or not verb*, where 'verb' stands for the interrogative verb.

Before giving the entry concerned, we need to pay some attention to the classification of the words concerned. I said earlier that the word which carries the semantic structure for a yes–no interrogative construction is the verb on which the whole clause depends, but only certain kinds of verbs are possible in this position: namely, tensed auxiliary verbs whose subject is inverted. I propose to recognize such verbs as a general word-type, called 'interrogative verb', and to include the instantiation relation shown in (2) in the grammar of English. I have included in this diagram information which anticipates discussion in later paragraphs, but what we are concerned with at the moment is just the left-hand side of the diagram, where 'verb' is connected, via 'auxiliary', 'tensed' and 'operator', to 'interrogative

(2)

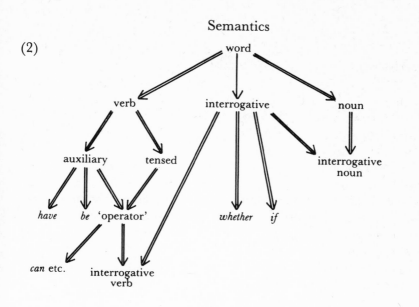

verb'. According to this analysis, an interrogative verb is an instance of 'operator' (a term used e.g. in Quirk *et al.* 1972 to refer to all tensed auxiliaries, be they modals or not); but what is not shown above is that the subject of an interrogative verb must follow the verb. This can be imposed in the entry for such verbs, and the special order will automatically override the normal one by the selective-inheritance principle. We can take this much syntactic analysis for granted.

The entry in which we can specify the semantic structure for yes–no interrogatives, then, is the one for 'interrogative verb' (actually, we shall be able to improve on this shortly). The entry needed is this:

(3)   referent (interrogative verb): x,
           knowledge (q): . . . & x,
    x = interrogative verb* or not interrogative verb*

In this entry I am exploiting the variable q which we defined in entry (1) on p. 185 (for definite nouns); q is the instance of knowing in which the knower is the addressee and the time is just before the moment of utterance.

Before leaving yes–no interrogatives, it is worth pointing out the similarity between this semantic structure and the one for *if* (entry (3) on p. 147). An *if*-clause has the effect of leaving it uncertain whether the referent of the main verb is true or false, so again we have a variable defined as 'either *a* or not *a*'. There are other obvious parallels between *if*-clauses and yes–no interrogatives, which all confirm the similarity in the semantic analysis: both kinds of clause allow words like *any* and *ever* (because of the *not* present in both semantic structures); *if* can introduce a subordinate yes–no interrogative (and *whether* can introduce a special kind of conditional, as in *I'm going whether you come or not*); inversion of the subject can mark a subordinate operator as conditional (e.g. *Had I come earlier, I'd have seen him*); and so on.

We now turn to wh-interrogatives. If I say to you *What happened?*, I am again assuming that you have some knowledge which I lack (or at least, which I may lack), and again I have to represent this knowledge as a variable in my mind, precisely because I do not necessarily know what it is. So we can transfer the first line of the entry for interrogative verbs directly into the entry for wh-words, using x again to stand for the variable in question. What then are the possibilities for x in *What happened?* First, it must be a non-human entity (because the word is *what*, not *who*), so we can require it to be an instance of THING. And secondly, of course, it must have happened – i.e. it must be the entity which is linked in your mind with the particular event of happening to which I am referring. This second requirement need not be spelled out in the entry, though, because *what* is already linked semantically to *happened*, so its referent (x) already fills the 'happener' slot. Thus all we need to specify for the semantic structure of *what*, in its entry, is that its referent is the unknown x, and that the model for x is THING. (Similarly, the models for the other interrogative pronouns will be PERSON, TIME, PLACE, and so on.)

Once again, we have to deal with a couple of syntactic points before we can give the entry for interrogative pronouns (which I have called 'interrogative noun' in the network of (2), because pronouns are a type of noun, and there is no need to recognize 'pronoun' as a unitary category, so far as I can see). We have to allow for clauses with multiple interrogative nouns, such as *Who said what to who?*, as well as for the cases where there is just one initial interrogative noun. We also need to allow an initial wh-word to stand on its own, without a clause after it, because the rest of the clause is in fact optional (e.g. *Somebody must have done it, but who?*). We can kill two birds with one stone, by allowing interrogative nouns to have an optional modifier, namely the verb on which the rest of the clause depends. Thus, in *Who said what to who?*, the first *who* has taken up this option, but the *what* and second *who* have not. For wh-words which have no such modifier, there is no need to say anything more, because they occur in their 'usual' position (i.e. as though they were ordinary nouns), and their semantic structure is just the one specified for interrogative nouns, as explained above.

An initial wh-word is syntactically special, however, partly because it may be in the wrong position (given its grammatical relations), partly because it always reverses the usual dependency relations between verbs and their modifiers (as witness the optionality of the verb illustrated above), and partly because it may trigger inversion of the subject, as in *What did you say?* Starting at the end of this list, we deal with the inversion by requiring the modifying verb to be, specifically, an interrogative verb, then the inversion requirements on interrogative verbs will automatically apply. However, if the wh-word is the subject this requirement does not apply (for obvious functional reasons), so the entry will say that either the wh-word is subject, or the modifier is an interrogative verb. The unusual dependency relation between wh-word and verb is partly dealt with already, by the part of the entry which introduces the verb as modifier of the wh-word, but we also have to show that the wh-word is a modifier of the verb as well as being its head. This is easy to do now that we have the visitor slot, because we simply load the wh-word into the verb's visitor slot, and let the machinery for transferring visitors ensure that it ends up as the modifier of some word down the dependency chain. Finally, the fact that the wh-word is out of its 'normal' position is covered by the requirement that the modifier should follow the wh-word, though this requirement need not actually be stated, because all modifiers are assumed to follow their heads in English.

After this excursion into syntax, we are ready to formalize the entry for interrogative nouns:

(4) referent (interrogative noun): x,
    modifier (interrogativenoun): Ø or m,

                                    visitor (m): interrogative noun,
                                    {subject (m): interrogative noun
                                    or model (m): interrogative verb}

The semantic part of this entry is extremely simple. This is partly because we can exploit the definition of x given in the entry for interrogative verbs (entry (3), p. 191), partly because the models for x will be specified in the entries for individual wh-words. For example, here is the entry for *what*:

(5)   model (what): interrogative noun, model (x): THING
        composition (what): /w/ + /o/ + /t/

As far as I can see, there is no need for any more information than this in the entries for individual wh-words.

One last detail, about subordinate clauses. If a wh-word introduces a subordinate clause, there is no subject-inversion. We can capture this fact in the formal entry for interrogative nouns by making the presence of an interrogative verb conditional on there being no head for the wh-word: we add 'head (interrogative noun): h or {O & (subject (m): interrogative noun or model (m): interrogative verb)}.

There is no need to point out how close this analysis has brought us to the analysis of definite nouns given above, since we have been dealing with nouns again here, and this classification of nouns has related their referents to the state of knowledge of the addressee.

Lastly, we have alternative interrogatives. These combine the syntax of yes–no interrogatives (specifically, an interrogative verb or *if/whether*, which introduce a subordinate yes–no interrogative) with the presence of a disjunction (containing *or*), and the intonation pattern typical of wh-interrogatives. We already have the basis for a satisfactory analysis, because once again we assume that the addressee knows x, where x is defined by the rest of the clause. So for example, in *Was the baby a boy or a girl?*, we are (as it were) saying, 'I know you know x,' where x is either 'The baby was a boy' or 'The baby was a girl.' The connection with yes–no interrogatives is clear, because both of them define x as one of a set of alternative propositions.

However, there are two problems that prevent me from offering an immediate formal analysis. The first is that I have not yet introduced the apparatus for 'unpacking' the semantic structure of a single verb into a string of propositions, each associated with a different dependent of the verb; and this apparatus is needed if we are to take the semantic structure of *Was the baby a boy or a girl?* as containing two propositions both associated with the same word, *was*. This apparatus will be introduced in the next section, and developed further in the chapter on co-ordinate structures. The second problem is that I do not at present see how to give a unified analysis for examples like the one just quoted and those like *Was the baby a girl or did she have yet another boy?* In one case, there is a single interrogative verb, but in the other there are two, and the question is whether it is possible to give a simple account which will cover both cases. (Similar problems arise in subordinate constructions, where *whether* may occur either once or more than once, and where a given occurrence of *whether* may also have either one or several verbs depending on it: *I asked whether it was a boy or a girl; I asked whether it was a girl or (whether) she had yet another boy.*) Accordingly, I shall leave alternative interrogatives as an area needing research.

Having discussed the three types of interrogative construction, we can now unify their analysis even more. This is necessary, because there are certain verbs whose valency requires them to have an interrogative as modifier. We have already given an example of such a verb (see p. 123): *wonder*. How should we define the modifier that *wonder* allows? We might consider a semantic definition, in which we cross-refer to the x of the entries for interrogative verbs and nouns given above, but this would suggest that the constraint was purely semantic, and that if we could find an alternative way to express the same semantic structure, that would do. There is an alternative, namely an ordinary definite noun, as in *I asked the time* (synonymous with *I asked what the time is*). But although this alternative is permissible with some verbs (e.g. *ask*), it is not permissible with *wonder*: so *I wonder what the time is* contrasts with **I wonder the time*. This shows that the constraint on the valency of *wonder* must be syntactic, and not just semantic.

Assuming, then, that we need to define the complement of *wonder* in relation to its syntax, how are we to do this? The modifier can be either an interrogative noun or *whether/if* (in each case modified by a verb, in the first case optionally, and in the second obligatorily). At present we have no way of referring to these two types of word together, so we can now group them together under the single category 'interrogative word'. However, there is obviously a very close link between *whether/if* and interrogative verbs, because they both have the same semantic structure (for yes–no interrogatives or alternative interrogatives), and they are in complementary distribution (interrogative verbs occur only without a head, except for cases mentioned specifically, whereas *whether/if* occurs only with a head). So we should also include interrogative verbs under the category 'interrogative', and we arrive at precisely the structure shown in the diagram in (2) on p. 191.

This allows us to say simply that *wonder* takes an interrogative (word) as its optional modifier, and the fact that this cannot be an interrogative verb will be covered automatically by the fact that the entry for such verbs explicitly requires them to have no head. It also allows us to improve on the analysis given above in one respect: we can define the element x, and its relation to the addressee's knowledge, in the entry for 'interrogative', and leave it to the entries for particular types of interrogative word to spell out the definition of x as appropriate.

(d) *Exclamatives.* I shall assume that 'exclamative' covers the following types of clause: those introduced by *what* (e.g. *What big eyes you have!*) or *how* (e.g. *How hard it is to avoid mistakes!*) or by an inverted operator, which in Britain contains *n't* (e.g. *Isn't she pretty!*), but apparently not so in the United States (e.g. *Is she pretty!*). The semantic structure for exclamatives is somewhat complex, because it must contain some reference to a 'degree', and involves a comment on the 'highness' of this degree, even if it is buried deeply in the semantic structure, far from any syntactic realization; for example, *Didn't she run!* is easy to take as an exclamative, because we can take it as referring to her speed, but it is harder to take *Didn't she open the door!* in this way, because there is no obvious parameter we could be commenting on. I have no analysis to offer for this part of the semantic structure, nor do I want to offer a syntactic analysis (though this could quite easily be designed to exploit the analysis of interrogatives given above).

The main point on which I want to comment is the epistemological status of the clause's content. This is interesting for our present purposes because it offers an example of a direct parallel to definite nouns. If I say to you *Isn't she pretty!*, then I must take it for granted that you agree, so I assume that the proposition expressed, complete with its comment on the degree, is already part of your knowledge. But since it is also part of mine, that makes the semantic structure just the same as that for definite nouns, whose referent is known to both speaker and addressee (see p. 184). (As I suggested in Hudson 1975, such exclamatives are different from the ones introduced by *what* or *how*, whose status seems more like that of declaratives in that their content may or may not already be known to the addressee.)

These brief comments on exclamatives completes our discussion of mood, in which I have tried to show that the semantics of mood is similar to the semantics of definiteness, and that in both cases one of the most important parts of the analysis is the reference to the current state of knowledge of the speaker and/or addressee. It will be helpful if I end with a table summarizing the analyses with regard to this particular question. The table allows for all the theoretical possibilities in regard to the speaker's and addressee's knowledges, taken independently of one another. For each knower, and each potentially known entity, there are three possibilities: it is known (+), it is not known (−), or it may or may not be known (shown by a blank). It will be seen that according to the table not all these possibilities are exploited; in particular, I could think of no kind of expression for referring to an entity which the addressee does know and the speaker definitely does not (interrogatives leave open the possibility that the speaker already knows the answer, as in rhetorical questions and examples like *Oh, are you back already?*), nor could I think of a way of using a verb to refer to an entity which is not known either to the speaker or to the addressee. It is possible that these gaps are due to oversight on my part, but if not they call for an explanation; either way, they need more research. The numbers in the table refer to the relevant pages.

(6)

in speaker's knowledge?	in addressee's knowledge?	nouns	verbs
+	+	definite (184)	exclamatives with inversion (196)
+		*a certain . . .* (189)	declaratives (186) wh-exclamatives (196)
	+	interrogative nouns (192)	interrogative verbs (190)
+	−	specific indefinites (182, 189)	*now* + declarative?
−	+	−	−
−	−	*some . . .* (189)	−

QUANTIFIERS
Plural nouns and 'plural' verbs

This section considers the semantic structures that are associated with such things as plural nouns and words like *every* and *no*. Once again we shall be able to demonstrate the importance of dependency structure in assigning semantic interpretations. We start with a discussion of the semantic effects of plural nouns.

Take a sentence like *The cats scattered*. This clearly refers to just one event, because scattering can only be done by a collection of individuals acting together. Consequently, the semantic structure for *scattered* must provide just one entity as its referent. In contrast, the sentence *The cats died* can be taken to refer to a number of distinct events, in each of which one cat died; and as we have already seen (p. 140) nominalizations provide evidence for this claim, because it is possible to use a plural noun to refer to the same events. Thus we can imagine a discourse in which *The cats died* is followed by *Their deaths upset us a lot*. Of course, I am not claiming that this interpretation is the only one possible; indeed, I think it would be possible to use *their death* to present what happened as a single event involving all the cats. It is all a matter of mental representations, and for the same objective reality there is often more than one way of conceptualizing it. The main point is that some utterances require a semantic structure for a single verb which represents its referent as a number of distinct events.

There was a time in the history of linguistics when linguists were suggesting that the deep structure of a sentence like *John and Mary died* contained a pair of sentences, *John died* and *Mary died*; and one of the arguments for this analysis was that it was true to the semantics, in view of facts such as those just quoted. However, it is easy to see that these facts have nothing at all to do with the presence of a co-ordinate structure such as *John and Mary*; rather, they are related to the presence of an expression which refers to a set of entities, whether this is a plural noun (e.g. *the cats*) or a co-ordinate structure (e.g. *John and Mary*) – or even a collective noun like *family* (e.g. *the deaths of her family shook her*). Hudson 1970 argues the case.

In order to cope with examples like those suggested above, we need to allow the plurality of the dependent noun to 'travel' up the dependency chain and be reflected in the semantic structure of the word on which it depends – the nominalization or the verb, as the case may be. So in our example *The cats died*, we have to recognize a difference between the referent of *the cats* and the entity which fills the subject slot; the former is a set, but the latter is an individual, showing that only one cat was involved in each event of dying. At the same time, the referent of the noun influences the referent of the verb by making it into a set, instead of an individual.

Having outlined the analysis informally, we now turn to the

formalization. First we need a formal representation for the referents of plural nouns, but we have already provided one, as an incidental part of the elementary examples in the first two chapters – in particular, in (2) on p. 46. According to this analysis, the referent of a plural noun, plural*, is a set whose composition can be represented very simply, by a series of dots (standing for an indefinitely long series) and a variable, x. This x is then linked to the same semantic model as the referent of the noun when singular (i.e. the unmarked referent of the noun); so if the plural is *cats*, its referent is represented both as (say) cats*, and also as '. . . & x', where x, like cat*, is an instance of CAT.

A number of alternative structures are imaginable, and no doubt several have been suggested in print, but this one seems to be free of the problems which beset the others that I have considered, at least. For example, we might consider a pair of contrasting features 'set' and 'individual', which would combine with the 'lexical' part of the noun's semantic representation; thus cats* would be broken down into 'set' and 'CAT', in contrast with 'individual' and 'CAT' for cat*. But this implies that the set is a cat, which is nonsense; the only cat-like thing about the set is its individual members, and the set as such has none of the characteristics of a typical cat (a tail, whiskers, and so on).

Now one of the important attractions of this analysis of plural nouns is that we can add subscripts to the variable x, to allow us to refer to members individually. This device is one we have used already, to allow us to link the different time-stages of an event to the different states existing at these times (see (3), p. 159), but of course it is familiar in logic. When we want to refer to the members of the list without distinguishing them by means of subscripts, we can still do so; for example we can still use plain x in saying that each x must have the same model as the referent of the unmarked noun. But when we want to distinguish the members, we can also do so; and if we want some proposition to apply, individually, to all the members of such a list, we can refer to the individual member as x_i, and add a condition 'all i'. To link some other list of entities pairwise to this list, we then use the same subscript, i, in relation to the other list. (Conversely, if we have two lists in the same entry and we do *not* want to link them, then we must use different subscripts for them; but by convention I shall assume, as I have up till now, that variables in *different* entries are independent of one another unless explicitly identified.)

We now have the basis for our formalization. What we need to do is to allow any kind of word (verb or noun) to have a list of referents each tied to a member of a list contained elsewhere in the semantic structure. For example, in *The cats died* the referent of *died* consists of a list of entities, each of which is linked to a different member of the set defined by *the cats*; and we can say that the list of cats 'determines' the list of events, in a fairly obvious sense. The determining list is the one which depends syntactically on the other, as *the cats* depends on *died*, but the determining list need not be expressed overtly; for example, I could say to a group of people *Tell me your names*, intending each of them to perform a distinct action. Because of this, we must define the relation in terms of 'semantic dependency', rather than ordinary syntactic dependency: A depends semantically on B if there is some slot in which B is the 'possessor' and A the filler. We can express semantic dependency formally as 'X(B): A', as indeed we have in several previous formalizations.

More specifically, the determining list must be *directly* related to the determined one (i.e. A must fill a proposition in which B is the possessor). It is not enough for the two semantic entities to be indirectly related; for instance, we cannot take *I saw a man who had five cats* to refer to five different events of seeing. On the other hand, since the rule applies to any kind of word, it can apply recursively, so that a list which is determined by another list may itself act as determining list in relation to a third, higher, list. For example, *He sat under three trees* can refer to three distinct acts of sitting, because *under three trees* can refer to distinct places, one per tree, and there can therefore be three acts of sitting, one per place. Similarly, it is easy to take *the fathers of three children* as referring to three separate children, but virtually impossible to do the same for *the fathers with three children*; we have already compared these two constructions (see p. 147) and seen that the first but not the second allows negativity to 'travel' up the dependency chain, so it should be easy to see how the explanation given there generalizes to this similar pair of examples.

The entry for linking lists is the following:

(1)   referent (word): word*, word* = a or $\{\ldots \& b_n\}$, all i, $1 \leqslant i \leqslant n$,
$$X(b_i): c_i, d = \ldots \& c_n$$

This entry is reasonably simple, but somewhat abstract, so it may be helpful to explain it in relation to *The cats died*. The word to which the entry applies is *died*, whose referent is a list of entities '$\ldots \& b_n$' (though it could have been taken as just one entity, *a*). This list is tied, through the subscript i, to the list of entities defined by *the cats*, whose referent is d and consists of a list of entities ' . . . & c_n', where each c stands for a cat. Each cat is linked semantically to an event of dying via the subject slot (shown as '$X(b_i)$: c_i' in the entry), and all the cats are involved because the entry says 'all i'.

There is no limit to the number of times that this entry can apply to the same word, so if a word has more than one plural modifier, its referents may be determined by all of them in combination. This is a possible interpretation of *The four cats chased the three mice*, with a separate chasing event for each combination of a cat and a mouse, giving twelve events altogether. The representation generated by the entry does not require the speaker/hearer to construct a separate mental entity for each of these combinations, of course, let alone to calculate the number of such entities; if this were so, it would take much longer to process *The four hundred cats chased the three hundred mice* (and infinitely long to process *An infinite number of numbers follow the infinite set of odd numbers*!). Instead, I assume we use the equivalent of my row of dots in our minds, and leave the semantic structure with the dots in it.

A problem would seem to arise in sentences like *The four candidates answered three questions*. What if the candidates each answered a different set of questions? If we assume that *three questions* has a referent, which we can call q, then we cannot represent this interpretation of the sentence, because we need to allow the referent to vary from one candidate to another. However, an easy solution to the problem is at hand. We may allow the referent of *three questions* to vary by getting the list-linking rule to work in reverse, with the head determining the referent of the modifier rather than the other way round. As applied to *The four candidates answered three questions*, this will mean that the list of four candidates determines the list of four events of answering, which in turn determines a list of four referents for *three questions* (each of which, incidentally, is a list of three questions). All we need do in order to achieve this effect is to add 'or $X(c_i)$: b_i' to the entry in (1).

Why do we not find a comparable interpretation for *The four candidates answered the three questions*, in which different candidates answered different questions? Obviously, because *the three questions* is definite, and we have already linked the referent of a definite noun to another entity, in one's knowledge, so the option of having a variable referent is ruled out by the more specific demands of the entry for 'definite'.

Moreover, since the rule which permits a variable referent is only an option, which may or may not be applied, if we have a sentence like *Four candidates answered three questions*, we find the well-known multiple ambiguity: a single set of four candidates answering a single set of three questions, or a single set of four candidates each answering a different set of three questions, or a different set of four candidates answering each of a single set of three questions. But notice that we have been able to generate distinct semantic representations without invoking the traditional apparatus of the quantificational calculus, with its quantifiers and brackets, and the only piece of apparatus needed to do this is the entry in (1), with the simple addition mentioned above.

As can be seen, the analysis proposed here explains a lot of things which have previously been explained either in terms of abstract deep structures, or in terms of semantic structures based on the predicate calculus and quantificational calculus (or in terms of both these constructs). We are now almost ready to explain why *Everybody wanted to win* means something different from *Everybody wanted everybody to win*, a problem mentioned earlier (see p. 114). As we shall see in the next subsection, words like *everybody* allow an interpretation in which there is a separate state-of-affairs entity for each referent of the noun accompanying *every*, so *Everybody wanted an ice-cream* can indicate a separate state of wanting per person. Similarly, then, *Everybody wanted to win* indicates a separate state of wanting per person, but the entry for *want* requires the subject of the infinitive to be coreferential with the subject of *want*, for each state of wanting; so this sentence could be paraphrased as 'For each person x, x wanted x to win.' In contrast, *Everybody wanted everybody to win* is not subject to the requirement of coreference between the two subjects, so the range of people covered by the subject of *win* is the full range of people referred to by *everybody*, and this full range is covered for each of the individual wanters. Hence the difference between the two sentences.

Some quantifiers and other words

This subsection will be devoted to a number of individual words, some of which are (sometimes) called 'quantifiers', though nothing at all hangs on this classification as far as my analysis is concerned. What they all have in common with each other (and also with many other words which I shall not discuss) is that their semantic contribution is relevant to the structures discussed in the previous subsection. The words I shall discuss are: *every, each, each other, all* and *any*.

(a) *Every*. As I have just mentioned, *every* has the effect of requiring its head to have a multiple referent. For instance, *Every cat caught a mouse* allows just one interpretation of the relation between the cats and catching-events, in which the events are in a one–one relation to the cats. This effect is very easy to formalize, because we are treating determiners as heads, not modifiers, of the following nouns (see p. 90 – 2), so *every* is directly related, as modifier, to *caught*.

What is at first sight curious about *every* is that it refers to a set of entities, but takes a singular noun and a singular verb. We can capture this fact, and explain it, as follows. *Every cat* is different from *all cats* in that *every cat* offers an individual to the rest of the sentence (as referent of *every*), whereas *all cats* offers a set: but *every cat* is like *all cats* in that it contains a set as part of its semantic structure. The connection between the individual and the set is that the individual is a subscripted variable which stands for all members of the set, taken one at a time. So if the set consists of . . . & x_n, where n stands for the total number in the set, the individual referent of *every* can be shown as x_i, for all i, where i is any subscript up to n. Now we can bring in the referent of the noun following *every*. The connection between this and the structure established so far is that it helps to identify the membership of the set, because each member is a referent of the noun. Thus, if we call the noun *m* (for modifier), its referent is m^*, and we can replace x in the above by m^*; so the referent of *every* is m^*_i, and the membership of the list is . . . & m^*_n. In other words, the semantic structure of *every cat* contains the following elements:

(i) $every^* = cat^*_i$;
(ii) $s = \ldots \& cat^*_n$ (where   *s*   stands   for   'set').

I said above that *every* has the effect of requiring its head to have a multiple referent, so this ought presumably to be made explicit in the entry, by linking the multiple referent of the head to the set in the semantic structure of *every*. The entry below seems to do this, and to reflect the rest of our analysis:

(1)   referent(*every*): $every^*$, $every^* = m^*_i$ all i, $1 \leqslant i \leqslant n$,
$$s = \ldots \& m^*_i$$

model(*every*): noun
modifier(*every*): m, model(m): noun
head(*every*): h, $h^* = \ldots \& x^i$, all i

To make the entry complete, we should need to take account of the possibility of expressions like *every five minutes*. The entries for compounds like *everybody* will presumably be based on this one, with the suppression of the entry for a modifier, and the addition of a model (PERSON, THING, etc.) for m*. However, an individual interpretation is not in fact obligatory for *everybody*, because examples like *Everybody scattered* are possible; so this alternative needs to be allowed for, possibly building on the entry for *all*.

(b) *Each*. *Each* is very much like *every* in its semantic effects, but there are two differences. One is that *each* assumes a known (i.e. 'definite') set, in contrast with the presumably unknown set of *every*; so *He looked each way before crossing the road* is much more natural than *He looked every way before crossing the road*, because we all know the set of possible ways to look: left and right. It is easy to build this requirement into the entry for *each*, by requiring that the set (called *s* in the entry for *every*) should be part of the speaker's and addressee's knowledge, just like the referent of a definite noun (see p. 182).

The other difference is syntactic rather than semantic, in that *each* can 'float' (to use the established transformational term) away from the noun to which it is related. For instance, alongside *Each cat has caught a mouse*, we find *The cats have each caught a mouse*. Transformational grammarians tended to assume that this relation was the result of a transformation, 'quantifier-float', but there are fundamental problems in making such a transformation work satisfactorily. What is the underlying structure of *Tabs and Spot have each caught a mouse*? And how do we·explain why *each* is possible in a position which is otherwise reserved for adverbs (e.g. *quickly* is permitted there, but *fast* is not: *He quickly/*fast got up*)? The solution I have to offer is to recognize *each* as an instance of two separate syntactic word-types, noun (like *every*) and adverb (like *quickly*, but more restricted in its distribution).

The semantic analysis offered above explains why an adverb could achieve the same semantic effect as a determiner. What the determiner does is to take a set of entities and relate its members individually to the state of affairs defined by the verb. But we can achieve the same effect by just using a plural noun and exploiting the option discussed in the first subsection, of giving the head a multiple referent. The trouble is that this is just an option, so if we want to make it clear that we have taken up the option, we use an adverb as marker: *each*. (There is another adverb, *respectively*, which is used in a similar way to impose a particular type of multiple interpretation on the verb, as in *Tabs and Spot have respectively caught a mouse and a bird*, or preferably . . . *a mouse and a bird respectively*.)

The entry for the noun and adverb uses of *each* is as follows:

(2) model (*each*): {*every*, knowledge (p): . . . & s,
                        knowledge (q): . . . & s,
                        modifier (*each*): Ø or m}
        or {*every* & adverb, modifier (*each*): Ø,
                head (*each*): h, *each* = h − 1 or h + 1,
                        model (h): verb,
                        subject (h*): s}

This entry exploits the option offered by word grammar of taking one word as a model of another; in this case, we take *every* as a model for *each* (just as *cat* is a model for *cats*). So all we need to specify is the respects in which it differs from *every*. The first three lines cover the determiner use of *each*, where it presupposes a definite set (and, unlike *every*, need not have a following noun). The bottom four lines cover the adverb use, in which I assume there cannot be a modifier (but this may need to be revised in the face of examples like *They have each of them caught a mouse*); the second and third lines up from the bottom say that *each* must have a verb as head, and must be next to it; and the bottom line says that it is the subject of this verb that defines the set *s*.

At least two facts about *each* are not covered by this entry, and count as outstanding problems for research. One is that *each* can be used in a third position as well, attached as a postmodifier after a late noun, in which case the set need not be defined by the subject (e.g. *I have given a bowl of food each to the cats*); there is some discussion of this construction in Hudson 1970. The other problem is that *each* is different from *every* in not allowing *almost* (Jackendoff 1977:165) or *not* (Hogg 1977:138). This difference shows *every* to be more like *all* than *each* is, and I cannot explain why this should be. The best I can suggest is that *each* cannot take any premodifiers, but *every* and *all* are free to take premodifiers.

(c) *Each other*. This is one of the two reciprocal pronouns (along with *one another*) and I know of no difference between the two, either in semantics or in syntax. This immediately makes transformational analyses look less attractive that assume an underlying structure for reciprocals which contain, specifically, *each* and *other* (e.g. *The cats chased one another* would have to be derived from *Each cat chased the other*). On the other hand, there is a clear similarity between the semantic effects of either reciprocal pronoun and the effects of *each* and of *other*, so the analysis ought to bring out these connections, as well as the connections with reflexive pronouns which I discussed on p. 180. The reciprocal pronouns are like *each* in that they force the word on which they depend to have a multiple referent; they are like reflexives in that their semantic structure contains an entity (a list) which is the same as one contained in the structure of their antecedent; and they are like *other* in requiring the multiple referent of the head to be a list of entities each linked to a pair of members from the first list, such that the members are always different.

The entry below seems to express these links (provided that we assume that the semantic structure for the word *other* will contain $\neq$, meaning 'is not the same as').

(3) model (reciprocal): reflexive

referent (reciprocal): reciprocal*, reciprocal* $= x_j$, all j, $1 \leqslant j \leqslant n$

$$a = x_i, \text{ all i, } 1 \leqslant i \leqslant n$$

$$s = \ldots \& x_n$$

head (. . . reciprocal): h, X(. . . a): h*, h* $= \ldots y_{i,j}$, $i \neq j$

In words, reciprocal pronouns are like reflexives, except in the following respects. The referent of a reciprocal is some member, x_j, from a set of entities s, which also provides a member, x_i, to act as antecedent (as defined in the entries for reflexives). The referent of the reciprocal ranges over all the members of this set, and so does the antecedent. Now, the word on which both the reciprocal and its antecedent depend (h) has a multiple referent, consisting of a set of entities $y_{i,j}$, linked to the variables x_i and x_j in such a way that x_i and x_j are always different.

(d) *All*. Unlike the words treated so far, *all* has no effect on the semantic structure of its head, and in particular it does not impose a multiple referent; so *All the cats scattered* is fine, as is also *The deaths of all the cats upset us* (illustrating a single and multiple referent respectively). Its present relevance is that its semantic structure makes reference to a set, and of course it also contains the element 'all' which we have used in the previous formalizations.

One problem is that *all* can be used with a mass noun, such as *all the milk*, and it is not clear how we can generalize the entry so that it will apply equally to a set and to a mass. However, it is possible that we can use the same representation in both cases, and treat a mass as a set of entities, each of which is an instance of the mass, and which are infinite in number (i.e. n = infinity). For the present I shall have to leave this problem unsolved.

The question is, what is the difference in meaning between pairs of sentences like *The cats are asleep* and *All the cats are asleep*? The immediate answer is of course that there is very little difference, but the presence of *all* seems to rule out a certain vagueness. So if we have twelve cats, and I say *The cats are asleep*, it is possible that I have only checked the majority of the cats, and have assumed that the rest are asleep too; in other words, I am allowing for some deviation in this respect between the state of affairs defined in my sentence, and the actual state of the world. (According to the general theory outlined on pp. 14 – 21, this is a perfectly legitimate form of behaviour, so it would be unfair to accuse me of lying or misleading, in spite of the Gricean maxim of quality: Don't say what you are not sure of.) However, if I add *all*, then I am committing myself to a closer fit between my utterance and the actual state of the world. The contribution of *all* is thus similar to the contribution of words like *exactly* (compare *It is ten o'clock* and *It is exactly ten o'clock*). In both cases, we must give different semantic structures according to whether or not the qualifying word (*all, exactly*) is present, but it is debatable whether the differences concerned affect the truth conditions as such. (As I have already pointed out, this need not worry us at all, since the notion of 'truth condition' plays no part in this semantic theory.)

The way in which I propose to handle the qualification or assurance which is due to the presence of *all* is by adding a double negative to the semantic structure. Thus, if we were dealing with *exactly*, we should be saying that *exactly* X means 'X*, and not not X*'. Even if this is tautologous, it provides additional cognitive structure for processing, and seems to have the effect that we want, namely to rule out some kinds of deviation between instance and model. (It may be that we ought to add a general theoretical constraint on the matching process, that a proposition 'not X' is less infringeable than a positively stated proposition.) As far as *all* is concerned, the double negative applies to the membership of the set concerned, and says that whatever is true of the set must not be untrue of the set when it is taken to include any one of its members. So *All the cats are asleep* has a semantic structure like that for *The cats are asleep*, except that it shows that the subject of *are* is the set of cats in question, and it is not the case that the subject excludes

any one of the members of this set. The entry for *all* is as follows:
follows:

(4)   referent (*all*) all* , all* = m*, m* = . . . & x_n
      modifier (*all*): Ø or me, model(m): noun
      head (*all*): h, X(h*): all*, not x_i, not X(h*): . . . & x_i, $1 \leqslant i \leqslant n$

According to this entry, the modifier of *all* defines a set (m*) whose
members are a list of x's, and its head defines some proposition (labelled
'X') which is true of the set m*, and there is no member of the list, x_i,
such that this proposition is not true of this member.

So far I have used 'all' in the formalizations as an unanalysed
primitive, along with 'not', '&' and 'or', but the above entry suggests
that we could link this element to an explanation in terms of double
negatives. In terms of cognitive structure, this does not mean that we
should have 'not . . . not . . .' *instead* of 'all', but only that we can link
it to more primitive concepts, in just the same way that we retain the
entity 'chase' even after we have linked it to its component concepts.
Exactly how this analysis of the concept 'all' is related to the entry for
the word *all* is a question I shall leave open.

(e) *Any*. One of the attractions of the semantic analyses proposed
here, and in particular of the representations for sets, is that they allow
a satisfactory solution to the long-standing problem of how to analyse
any (for discussion, see for example McCawley 1981:98, Hogg 1977:47,
Seuren 1969). We have discussed a number of semantic structures in
which a set is referred to as ' . . . & x_n', but a set need not involve the
'and' relation (represented by the primitive '&'). The other possibility
is a disjunctive set, whose members are linked by 'or' (which I use for
representing the primitive of exclusive disjunction). So we might well
wonder whether this possibility was used in the internal semantic
structures of words (apart from the word *or* itself), and it comes as no
surprise to find that it is, in the structure of *any* (and other related words,
as we shall see below).

Suppose I say *Any student could solve this problem*. What I am claiming
is that *x* could solve this problem, where *x* is a student selected arbitrarily
from the total set of all students. It is different from the rather similar
Every student could solve this problem because it is limited to just one
hypothetical occurrence of solving the problem; so the difference can be
made clearer by adding an expression like *for the first time: Any student
could solve this problem for the first time* (or *Any student could be the first to solve
this problem*) is fine but **Every student could solve this problem for the first time*

is contradictory, because once one student has solved the problem, no one else can be the first to solve it. On the other hand, *every student* is also like *any student* in that it leaves the whole range of students open for supplying the referent.

It is easy to explain this relation between *any* and *every* in the light of my remarks about disjunctive sets. The referent of *any* is a member of a disjunctive set: any* = . . . or x_n; whereas the referent of *every* is a variable standing for each individual member of a conjunctive set: every* = x_i, all i, s = . . . & x_n (see the entry for *every*, which is (1) on p. 203). Thus, if we imagine a set with a limited membership – say, the set of people in my family, labelled respectively G, L, A and D – then the referent of *any*, as applied to this set, is a disjunctive set containing all the same members; so the referent of *any of my family* is 'G or L or A or D'. Similarly, if we imagine a set with unlistable membership, such as the set of students, we can take an abstract representation of its membership (. . . or s_n), and this gives the referent of *any* as applied to the set in question (i.e. the referent of *any student*).

The entry to generate the structures we need is this:

(5) referent (*any*): any*, any* = . . . or x_n, all i, $1 \leqslant i \leqslant n$,
$$s = . . . \& x_n, x = m^*$$
modifier (*any*): $\emptyset$ or m

In this entry, the difference from *every* lies in the disjunctive set, as I have just explained, but the similarity to *every* is shown by the conjunctive set with which the disjunctive one is matched, pairwise. The individual members of the set are defined by the following noun (the modifier of *any*), whose referent is m*. One of the benefits of this analysis is that it does not restrict the number of the noun modifier, so we expect both *any student* and also *any students*. In the latter case, the referent of the modifier, *students*, is itself a set, so the set from which *any* selects is a set of sets of students. (Similarly, we find expressions like *any two students*, which are allowed by this entry.)

We can now consider the range of words to which this analysis will apply. The examples we have considered so far have all been what we might call 'positive' examples of *any* (i.e. where it occurs in a positive sentence). One of the most discussed problems in the analysis of *any* is how to relate this use of *any* to its other use, in negative sentences (e.g. *I haven't seen any students*). The problem disappears when we accept the disjunctive analysis, because both uses can be given exactly the same semantic analysis. That is, to return to our simpler example, *He doesn't know any of my family* means 'He doesn't know G or L or A or D' – which is, of course, a possible paraphrase for anyone who knows who the members of my family are. The disjunctive structure is possible in negative contexts because, logically, 'not . . . (A or B)' is equivalent to '(not . . . A) & (not . . . B)'. So *I haven't seen any students* means 'I haven't seen . . . or s_n, where the dots and s_n stand for the total set of students. On the other hand, this meaning does not fit with a positive context in which an individual event is reported, such as **I've seen any students*, for just the same reason as it is odd to say **I've seen John or Bill or . . . .* Since the event has already taken place, it is too late to offer a free choice, though I can leave the addressee in the dark about the identity of the individuals concerned (by using *a student* or *some students*).

We have already seen how we can explain the occurrence of 'negative' *any* in other, apparently non-negative, contexts; in particular, we have provided explanations relating to *if* (see p. 147) and to yes – no interrogatives (see p. 192), both of which allow *any* in clauses which would not otherwise accept it (e.g. *If you see any students . . . , Have you seen any students?*, compared with **You have seen any students*). The explanation which I gave was that the semantic structures for these constructions contained 'not', although no negation was present in the syntax; and of course we now understand why this 'not' permits *any* to occur.

Any is not the only word which has this kind of semantic structure, containing a disjunction; nor is it the only word which occurs in negative contexts but not in their positive equivalents. On the one hand there are the 'indefinite pronouns' *anybody, anything, anywhere* and *anyhow*, all of which contain *any-*. Then there is *ever*, which fills the gap left by the absence of **anywhen* to parallel *anywhere* in this list. And lastly, we have *either*, which is like *any* but restricted to a definite set (like *each*) with just two members (like *both* and *neither*). For all these words, it is very easy to build on the structure for *any* given above.

I hope I have shown in this chapter that the types of structure which word grammar allows us to use in syntax and morphology are also suitable for semantic analysis. Since we have also seen a good number of points where general knowledge and context-specific knowledge are mixed up with what we might call 'semantic structure', the discussion of semantics will have helped to reinforce my general claim that the structure of language is very much like other kinds of cognitive structure.

5

Co-ordinate Stuctures

OVERVIEW
Introduction

The main purpose of this chapter is to explore one area of English grammar in some depth, in order to show how a coherent account of it can be given in terms of word grammar. I selected co-ordinate structures as a testing ground for the theory for two reasons: I have been interested in it for nearly two decades now (ever since I wrote the relevant chapter of Huddleston *et al.* (1968), in fact), and it is sufficiently challenging to test any theory to its limits. The analysis which I now have to offer covers all the well-known patterns – so-called phrasal and sentential co-ordination, reduced conjuncts ('conjunction reduction'), gapping, right-node raising, and layered structures. I leave the reader to decide how satisfactory the analysis is, but I think it compares favourably with other available analyses in all respects – explicitness, elegance, consistency with other parts of the grammar and compatibility with the facts. There are a few minor points which I have not tried to cover for fear of making the grammar too big and hard to grasp, but I shall note these points during the discussion.

Another reason for including a chapter on co-ordinate structures is that such structures are particularly important in the theory of dependency structures because they are *not* dependency structures. Tesnière distinguished the two kinds of structure (1959:80), and so far as I know the distinction has been generally accepted since then. I shall accept it too, though I recognize that the point could be disputed – it could for example be objected that in a co-ordinate structure like *John and Mary* there is a head, namely *and*, with the other two words as its modifiers. Even if this case could be supported by strong evidence, there will still be a good number of properties which distinguish co-ordinate structures from (other) dependency structures, so for simplicity I shall simply assume that they are not dependency structures, and leave it to others to prove the contrary.

However, even if co-ordinate structures as such are not dependency structures, I shall be able to show that dependency structures are crucial to a complete analysis of some types of co-ordinate structures. For example, the 'gap' in a pattern like *John invited Mary and Bill, Ø Sue* must be taken to include the head of the first conjunct and all but two of its dependents. Consequently, the chapter will show extra evidence for the value of dependency analysis, and will do so in an area of grammar where such evidence is least to be expected because it has traditionally been assumed not to involve dependency structures at all.

Overview of phenomena and terminology

John and Mary is an instance of a *co-ordinate structure*, consisting of two *conjuncts* (*John, Mary*) and a *conjunction* (*and*). Co-ordinate structures may be complete orthographic sentences (*John sang and Mary danced*), or parts of such sentences (*John sang and Mary danced*, but Bill just watched; *John and Mary* danced). Indeed, co-ordinate structures are traditionally considered to be truly endocentric, which means that they can occur in any environment where their conjuncts could occur. One consequence of this is that a co-ordinate structure may itself act as one conjunct in a larger co-ordinate structure, which is then said to be '*layered*', in that its analysis requires us to recognize two separate layers of co-ordinate structuring; we have already had an example of this, where *but Bill just watched* is co-ordinated with *John sang and Mary danced*. We can show this layering by means of brackets, as follows:

([{John sang} and {Mary danced}] but {Bill just watched})

It will be seen that the brackets enclose not only co-ordinate structures but also conjuncts which are not themselves co-ordinate structures. They anticipate the analysis of the next few sections, in which we shall recognize both co-ordinate structures and their conjuncts as constituents. The different shaped brackets all have the same status and significance – they are meant simply to make it easier to pair off the left and right brackets.

I shall assume that the following words are conjunctions: *and, or, but, nor* and *then*. Later sections will discuss the difference between them, but they all have in common that they can conjoin clauses with shared subjects, a property which no other words seem to share. For example, in *John came in and went out again, John* is shared by both clauses *John came in* and *John . . . went out again*. Instead of *and* we could have, for example, *then* (*John came in then went out again*), but not *so*, even if we change the content of the example to make it more plausible (e.g. **John came in late so missed the fun*). I am aware that other properties of conjunctions are shared with words not on my list – for example, *so* is similar in being obligatorily initial in its clause, and in not requiring a conjunction, in contrast with words like *next*. However, I think we need to recognize that one of the most awkward analytical boundaries is that between co-ordination and asyndeton, and words like *so* are best treated as part of asyndetic constructions.

Some of these conjunctions allow a 'correlative' word which is attached to the first conjunct: namely, *and* allows *both*, as in *both John and Mary*, *or* allows *either*, and *nor* allows *neither*. Syntactically these do not all behave in the same way, and in particular *either* is different from the other two in that it alone can occur at the start of a main clause (compare *Either John dances or Mary sings* with **Both John dances and Mary sings* and **Neither John dances nor Mary sings*).

The examples given have involved only two conjuncts each, but *and* and *or* allow any number of conjuncts, even without layering. There are two patterns of distribution for the conjunctions among three or more conjuncts: either the conjunction occurs just once, between the last pair of conjuncts (e.g. *John, Bill, Fred, Jack and George*), or it occurs between every adjacent pair (e.g. *John and Bill and Fred and Jack and George*). I assume that a mixture of these two patterns is not possible without layering, so that a string like *John and Bill, Fred, Jack and George* must be given a layered interpretation; and I also assume that the conjunctions cannot be mixed without layering (see p. 222).

As far as meaning is concerned, the meaning of the co-ordinate structure is obviously a function of the meanings of its conjuncts, but the precise relation varies. Some of this variation is signalled explicitly by the choice of conjunction, but there is further variation which may lead to ambiguity, or may be due to the presence of other words. In particular, *and* allows at least three different interpretations when it links phrases. Take *John and Mary ate an apple and a pear*. I assume that we need three separate semantic structures, according to whether they ate an apple and a pear each, or they ate an apple and a pear between them, or John ate an apple and Mary ate a pear. The ambiguity can be removed by the addition of the words *each, between them* and *respectively*,

respectively. (This ambiguity recalls the ambiguity found with plural nouns which we noted on pp. 197 – 202.)

Finally, there is the question of the internal structure of the individual conjuncts. In the examples given so far, the conjuncts are all syntactically complete, in the sense that they are strings of words which could occur, with the same meaning, without the co-ordinate structure – a verb and all its modifiers (a 'clause') or a noun and all its modifiers (a 'noun-phrase'), for example. There are some cases, however, where this is not so, and a conjunct is not complete in this sense. One such case is 'gapping', as in *John tried to invite Mary to the party and Bill, Elizabeth*, where the second conjunct is *Bill, Elizabeth*, with the meaning 'Bill tried to invite Elizabeth to the party.' Outside a co-ordinate structure, *Bill, Elizabeth* cannot occur as a complete clause or phrase, let alone with the meaning given. The term 'gapping' is unfortunate, because it implies that the missing bits of the conjunct constitute just a gap between the overt bits, but the example is chosen deliberately to show that this need not be the case: the missing bits come both before and after *Elizabeth* in the paraphrase.

Another case of incomplete conjuncts is illustrated by *He drinks coffee with milk at breakfast and cream in the evening*, where the second conjunct is *cream in the evening*, meaning 'he drinks coffee with cream in the evening.' (Examples like this were pointed out to me by David Dowty, who learnt of them from Greg Stump.) Again, the second conjunct is syntactically incomplete in that it consists of a string of words with no shared head inside the conjunct, so it could not occur outside a co-ordinate structure, and its meaning has to be recovered from the first conjunct. I shall call such structures 'reduced conjuncts'.

Lastly we have 'right-node raising', where the incomplete conjunct is the first one, as in *John likes, but Mary hates, the food they serve in UCL refectory*. Strictly speaking, these cases are irrelevant to co-ordinate structures because they need not involve co-ordination. For example, the *and* of the above sentence could have been replaced by *while*, which is not in any sense a conjunction: *John likes, while Mary hates, the food they serve in UCL refectory*.

I have not given any references to the literature on co-ordination in the above survey, but most of the phenomena are well known, even if I may have presented some of them in a somewhat controversial way. The literature on co-ordination includes a number of papers by me, in which I give references to other discussions, so I prefer to refer readers to these earlier papers rather than repeat all the references here –

namely, Hudson 1970, 1973, 1976c, 1982. Many of the analyses that I shall espouse here are based on those for which I argue in these earlier papers, but some are different, and of course all of them are different in that I have never before incorporated the analyses into a word grammar.

Overview of the analyses

We shall gradually build up a set of entries to cover all the various types of co-ordinate structure detailed above, but it may be helpful to give an overview of the structures that this partial grammar will assign. We can start with the cases where the conjuncts are all complete, reserving cases of gapping and reduced conjuncts till later.

Take an example like *I know Mary dances and John sings*. We shall recognize both the co-ordinate structure and its conjuncts as constituents, i.e. as units to which the grammar refers, and we can show their boundaries by means of the bracketing system introduced earlier:

I know {(Mary dances) and (John sings)}:

It will be seen that the conjunction *and* is not included among the conjuncts, nor would the correlative *either* in *I know either Mary dances or John sings*:

I know {either (Mary dances) or (John sings)}

However, although we recognize the whole co-ordinate structure as a constituent, this is only for the sake of the rules of co-ordination. As far as the structure's external relations to the rest of the sentence are concerned, these are shown as relations between *know* and one word in each conjunct, namely the word in each conjunct on which all the other words depend (*dances* and *sings*). We can call these words the *conjunct heads*. Thus we say that *know* has just one post-modifier, which is a set of conjunct heads, *dances* and *sings*. This analysis has the advantage of ensuring that each of the conjuncts is compatible with the verb's valency, because the latter is stated in terms of single words (in this case, finite verbs). We can show this set as a branching in the dependency arrow pointing to the object of *know*.

(1)

I   know   [(Mary   dances)   and   (John   sings)]

It will be seen from this example that conjunctions (and correlatives) are exceptional in not having any dependency connections to the rest of the sentence. Instead, they are integrated into the total structure via the co-ordinate structure. (This analysis seems preferable to any of the current ones based on nothing but constituency in that we can recognize the special status of conjunctions as simple markers of co-ordination; it has always been a problem for constituency grammarians to decide exactly how to fit conjunctions into their trees.)

Similarly, the meaning of the whole co-ordinate structure is simply the set consisting of the meanings of the individual conjunct heads. If the co-ordinate structure is a modifier, then this set of referents acts as the argument supplied by that modifier. For example, the set consisting of John and Mary is the 'agent' of *John and Mary drew a picture*, because the syntactic subject is the co-ordinate structure *John and Mary*. (This set-structure is the same as for a plural noun – see p. 199.) However, this leaves open the possibility of two interpretations, according to whether a single act of 'drawing a picture' is involved, or a separate act for each of John and Mary. I see no reason for assuming a syntactic ambiguity here, and indeed we already have a mechanism for generating two distinct semantic structures, in the entry for words with multiple referents (entry (1), p. 200). This says that, optionally, a head (e.g. *drew*) may have the number of its referents determined by the number of referents of one of its modifiers (e.g. *John and Mary*).

We can now turn to the constructions in which all but one conjunct is incomplete. I shall have very little to offer in the way of an analysis of right-node raising (see pp. 235 – 6), so we can assume that the complete conjunct is always the first one. The question is then how we can generate structures in which a second (or later) conjunct is incomplete, either without a gap (reduced conjuncts) or with one (gapped conjuncts).

A reduced conjunct is one which shares some part of the first conjunct. For example, the second conjunct of {*(John came in) and (sat down)*} shares the subject of the first one. The parts of the first conjunct that are shared in this way are always before whichever parts are not shared, so we can mark the boundary between them, with a ' + ' sign: {*(John + came in) and (sat down)*}. The analysis for reduced conjuncts is quite simple, because all it has to do is to allow the shared part of the first conjunct to count towards all the later conjuncts as well. However, we cannot redefine the later conjuncts by saying that they 'really' include the shared part of the first conjunct, because that will make the rules for distributing conjunctions among the conjuncts impossibly complicated. Instead, we shall assume a conjunct which is different from any conjunct shown in the syntactic structure of the word-string itself, but which is reconstructed on the basis of this structure. It is this imaginary conjunct which contains the shared words as well as the words actually in the non-initial conjunct, so we assume an imaginary second conjunct for our sentence *John sat down*. The actual word-string is generated by defining its relations to this imaginary conjunct.

A similar analysis is assumed for gapped conjuncts, but with a difference. In reduced conjuncts, the imaginary conjunct consisted of the actual shared words plus the actual words in the reduced conjunct. But for gapped constructions, the imaginary conjunct is a string of imaginary words, which contain the actual words of the gapped conjunct mixed up with them. Take the sentence {*(John tried to invite Mary to the party) and (Bill, Elizabeth)*}, for example. Here, we have to assume an imaginary conjunct *Bill tried to invite Elizabeth to the party*, but we cannot cobble this together simply by combining an easily defined part of the first conjunct with the whole of the gapped conjunct. Instead, we start by making a copy of the whole of the first conjunct, and then we replace two parts of this copy: its subject, and some other dependent of the verb. These are supplied by the two elements of the gapped conjunct. So we have to replace *John* by *Bill*, as subject of *tried*, and *Mary* by *Elizabeth*, as distant dependent of *tried*. Each of these replacements could lead to a change in the other words of the imaginary conjunct – for example, replacing a singular subject by a plural one could lead to changes in verb agreement – so it has to be a copy of the first conjunct, and not just the first conjunct itself.

The status of these imaginary conjuncts is rather similar to the status of the imaginary active word-string which we assumed in the analysis of passives (see p. 119). They allow us to generate a surface string by matching it against an abstract string which is different from it in certain specified ways, and which can itself be generated by the ordinary rules. Their relation to the underlying structures of transformational grammar deserve thorough investigation, of course, but there are some fairly major differences, as we shall see (p. 228 – 9).

Constituent structure

In view of the position taken in the rest of this book, the most striking feature of the above analyses is probably the fact that they make use of constituent structure, shown by the brackets. As may be imagined, I have tried hard to find a way of doing without this constituent structure, but since I have failed, I must explain why it seems to be necessary, and what implications it has for my general rejection of constituency-based analyses.

In order to explain why constituent structure has to be recognized for co-ordinate structures, I must start by outlining the kind of constituency-free analysis that seems most promising. First we must ignore the cases where conjuncts are incomplete, so that we are dealing only with structures where each conjunct has a separate conjunct head, such as *I like {(red apples) and (green plums)}*, where the conjunct heads are *apples* and *plums*. In such cases, we could dispense with constituent structure by making use of sets: thus, the object of *like* is the set consisting of *apples* and *plums*, whose referent is of course the set consisting of the referents of these two words. Given that we make use of sets in the rules of the grammar (especially in the semantics – see pp. 197 – 210), there is no reason in principle why we should not do the same in sentence structure – and indeed we shall do so even in the constituency-based analysis to follow. Without using brackets, then, the structure for this sentence would be:

(1)

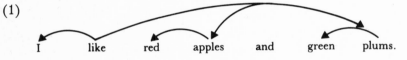

I   like   red   apples   and   green   plums.

The problems with this kind of analysis are as follows:

(a) It provides no satisfactory link between the conjunction and the rest of the sentence; and it is very hard to formulate satisfactory rules for locating conjunctions among multiple conjuncts, because it is hard to identify 'the last pair of conjuncts in the co-ordinate structure' if one cannot refer to 'the co-ordinate structure' as such. (It might seem that *and* could simply be made to depend on the last conjunct head, as a modifier, but this would not do because there is no way of guaranteeing that it will come before all other modifiers of this word.)

(b) It cannot be generalized to cover cases where conjuncts are incomplete, especially when there is more than one incomplete conjunct. For example, take a gapping structure like *John invited Mary, Bill Elizabeth and Tom Sue*. If we use sets instead of constituent structure, we can show that the subject of *invited* is the set of *John, Bill* and *Tom*, and its object is the set of *Mary, Elizabeth* and *Sue*; but there is no way of showing that *Bill Elizabeth* constitutes one conjunct (e.g. from the point of view of the rules which locate *and* between the last pair of conjuncts). The problem is that we cannot identify the notion 'conjunct' with 'conjunct head plus all its dependents' precisely because such conjuncts have no overt conjunct head.

Assuming, then, that constituent structure is necessary for co-ordinate structures, is this the thin end of the wedge whose other end is standard phrase-structure grammar? The answer is clearly no, because the cases where constituent structure is most needed are precisely those cases where it is most of a problem for phrase-structure grammar, because the constituents needed for co-ordinate structures are incomplete (as in gapping and reduced conjuncts). This is no problem for word grammar, because constituent structure is not used for any other purposes, so there is no conflict between the constituents recognized as incomplete conjuncts and those generated for other constructions. Similarly with the other reason for recognizing constituent structure, namely because it provides a good home for conjunctions: as we have seen, conjunctions are one of the things for which the phrase-structure grammar treatment is least impressive, because it is hard to decide whereabouts to put them in a phrase-marker.

Another major difference between my use of constituent structure and its use in phrase-structure grammar is that the constituents are used in word grammar *only* for generating co-ordinate structures, and not at all for linking these structures to the rest of the sentence. As we have seen, the referent of the whole co-ordinate structure is just the set of referents of its conjunct heads, so there is no need to attach this referent to the co-ordinate structure as well as to the set of conjunct heads. And since the external relations all involve just the conjunct heads, there is no need to let them involve the whole co-ordinate structure as well.

One consequence of this is that we do not need to classify the whole co-ordinate structure (because it does not need to satisfy any rules of the grammar except those for co-ordinate structures as such). For example, in *I like red apples and green plums* we recognize *red apples and green plums* as a co-ordinate structure, but we do not classify it syntactically to show that it is a noun, because there is no need to: the fact that it is compatible with *like* is already shown by saying that each of its conjunct heads, *apples* and *plums*, is a noun and therefore compatible with *like*. This amounts to a denial of the usual claim that co-ordinate structures are endocentric, so that the whole structure bears the same category label as its conjuncts. Although this may seem perverse at first sight, it has considerable justification, such as the fact that sentences like *He is happy and in a good mood* are possible. Assuming that in a phrase-structure grammar *happy* is an example of an adjective phrase and *in a good mood* is a prepositional phrase, it is very hard to see how the whole co-ordinate structure would be labelled.

One of the attractions of the endocentric analysis of co-ordinate structures is that it generates layered structures without any special mention of them; but we can achieve the same effect by simply requiring the conjunct heads to be compatible with the same external environment, so that some slot in the latter may be filled by the set consisting of all the conjunct heads. The possibility of layered structures then follows automatically from the fact that a set may itself be a member of a set, as in *I like red apples and green plums, or yellow pears*. The conjunct heads are words 4, 7 and 10, so the postmodifier slot of *likes* can be taken as filled by the set $\{(4 \ \& \ 7) \ \& \ 10\}$, and the corresponding semantic slot by $\{(4^* \ \& \ 7^*) \ \text{or} \ 10^*\}$. As long as we impose no other constraints on the contents of the conjuncts, then, the possibility of layering follows automatically.

THE RULES
The distribution of conjunctions among conjuncts

To start with, we can ignore the internal structure of the conjuncts, and also their external relations to the rest of the sentence, and concentrate on generating strings of conjuncts and conjunctions. For simplicity, we shall illustrate most of these strings with examples where the conjuncts are nouns, but most of them could equally well have been exemplified with strings of clauses.

The easiest pattern to generate is one in which a series of conjuncts has just one conjunction, and this occurs between the last pair of conjuncts (e.g. *John, Bill, Fred and Sam*). I shall use C as a variable to stand for conjuncts, and little c for a conjunction, so the rule needed will allow an indefinite number of C's, with just one instance of c. (For the sake of a later rule, I shall call this c_n.) We shall need to distinguish the different conjuncts from one another later, so I shall assign a subscript to each one, and tie the numbers in the subscripts to linear order (so that C_i must have a lower subscript than C_j if C_i is uttered before C_j). Here is the entry, with z standing for the whole co-ordinate structure:

(1) composition (z): $C_1 \ldots c\ C_n$, model(c): conjunction, $C_i < C_j$, $i < j$

The membership of the category 'conjunction' will be defined in the usual way, by treating 'conjunction' as a model for the words concerned – *and, or, but, nor* and *then*. The entry for each conjunction will then have to add whatever features are idiosyncratic, notably the effect on the total semantic structure, and the internal phonological structure of the conjunction itself.

One of the ways of complicating a co-ordinate structure is by including a correlative (*both, either, neither* being the most obvious examples). These occur before the first conjunct (with some qualifications to which we shall return), but they are also linked to the conjunction, because *both* only occurs with *and*, and so on. Now it may be that many of these connections will be dealt with anyway by the semantics, in that the correlative has a semantic effect which must be compatible with that of the conjunction. For example, *either* can be restricted to occurring only when the referent of the co-ordinate structure is a disjunction, so it will not be able to occur with *and*. However, it may be necessary to impose more specific constraints which do not follow from the semantics – for example, from a semantic point of view it is not clear why *both* should not occur with *but*, and yet it is clear that they cannot occur together (e.g. *He is rich but stupid* and *He is both rich and stupid* contrast with **He is both rich but stupid*). The easiest way to establish this kind of lexical link between two words is to assume a dependency relation between them, so I shall analyse correlatives as modifiers of their conjunctions.

The entry for introducing correlatives is the following:

(2)   modifier (conjunction): $\emptyset$ or m, model (m): correlative,
$$m < C_1, C_1 \ldots \text{conjunction } C_n, n = 2$$

This locates the correlative not next to its head, as we should normally expect, but next to the first conjunct in the relevant co-ordinate structure. Again, the list of correlatives can be defined by the entries for *both, either* and *neither*, all of which will have 'correlative' as their model. The lexical connections mentioned above will be shown by requiring the head word of each correlative to be a particular conjunction; so for example the entry for *either* will be as follows:

(3)   model (*either*): correlative
      head (*either*): h, model (h): *or*.

The qualification that I promised above is to do with the position of the correlative. A correlative either comes at the start of the whole co-ordinate structure, or it occurs in the 'adverb' position in the middle of the first conjunct. It is possible to question the grammaticality of the second construction, but the last sentence illustrated it, so if the last sentence passed unnoticed, we should accept the construction as one to be generated. The position to which we need to refer is next to the 'conjunct head' (defined on p. 215) of the first conjunct, when the conjunct head is a verb. Anticipating the later analysis, we can call the conjunct head of the first conjunct $C_{1/h}$, so the position of the correlative is either one word before or one word after $C_{1/h}$. This alternative needs to be added to the entry for correlatives given in (2), so we can revise this as follows:

(4)   modifier (conjunction): $\emptyset$ or m, model (m): correlative,
                             $\{m < C_1 \text{ or } m = C_{1/h} - 1 \text{ or } C_{1/h} + 1\}$,
                             $C_1 \ldots \text{conjunction } C_n, \, n = 2$

The next question is how to allow more than one conjunction in the string – e.g. *John and Bill and Fred and Sam*. It could in fact be argued that such strings have a layered structure, and that no single layer of co-ordinate structure ever contains more than one conjunction; but I shall assume that this is not so, for lack of clear evidence for semantic bracketing in such strings. On this assumption, then, we need to give a structure to *John and Bill and Fred and Sam* which recognizes just a single co-ordinate structure, containing four conjuncts and three conjunctions. It might seem that we could allow this kind of structure very easily, by making 'conjunction' optional between each non-initial pair of conjuncts, but this would make it possible for the option to be taken up sporadically throughout a long series of conjuncts, without imposing a layered interpretation. In fact, though, a string like *John and Bill, Fred and Sam* always seems to call for a layered interpretation: {[John and Bill], Fred and Sam}. This seems to show that we must not allow more than two possibilities: either every non-final pair of conjuncts has a conjunction between them, or none of them does. Furthermore, if there are multiple conjunctions, they must all be the same conjunction, as any mixing of conjunctions always indicates a layered interpretation (e.g. John and Bill or Fred and Sam).

To show these two restrictions on non-final conjunctions, we make them depend on the final conjunction (just like the correlative), require them to be the same word as their head, and require one of these modifying conjunctions before each of the intermediate conjuncts. Here is the entry:

(5) $\text{modifier}^n \bar{0}^2(c_n)$: $\emptyset$ or c_i, $c_i < C_i$, all i $1 < i < n$,

$$\text{model}(c_n): x, x = \textit{and} \text{ or } \textit{or},$$
$$\text{model}(c_i): x$$

What we can generate with the entries given so far is a variety of strings of subscripted C's, with conjunctions and correlatives distributed as required and linked to one another by dependency links. We have not yet said anything about how these structures interact with the dependency structures generated by the rest of the grammar, but it may be helpful to give some examples of the abstract structures generated:

(6)

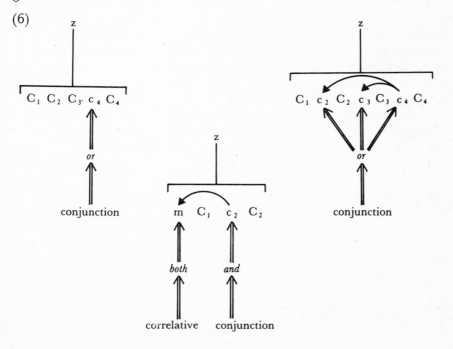

These structures would be suitable for expressions such as *John, Bill, Harry or Sam, John or Bill or Harry or Sam*, and *both John and Bill*, respectively.

The structure of complete conjuncts

We now look at the internal structure of each of the conjuncts, consisting of a string of words. The relations among these words are already defined by the dependency structure, and indeed the rules for co-ordinate structures are such that the relations among the words in a conjunct are always coherent as far as dependency structure is concerned. This is so even when the conjuncts are incomplete, in the sense described earlier, but in this subsection we are concerned only with complete conjuncts, where the internal coherence is very easy to define. To be precise, a conjunct is complete if it contains a conjunct head, which is defined (see p. 215) as a word on which all the other words in the conjunct depend. For example, the conjuncts in {*(the long red pole with the flag on it) and (a little bucket for putting eggs in)*} are both complete, and their conjunct heads are respectively *the* and *a*. As I explained earlier, it is tempting to try a completely different analysis of co-ordinate structures, in which the conjuncts are not strings of words, but just single words, namely the conjunct-heads; but this analysis faces insuperable difficulties (specified on p. 218). So our task now is to define the relations between the conjuncts, the conjunct-heads, and the rest of the words, in a suitable way for inclusion in the formal rules.

Our first requirement is a method for referring to the individual words in each conjunct, in a completely general way (i.e. without regard to their dependency status, their category membership, or anything else). Having solved this problem, we can then define the conjunct head in such a way that we can guarantee that every conjunct has one, which in turn will guarantee the structural coherence of conjuncts. We shall also be able to refer to the conjunct head in later entries.

So far we have represented each conjunct as C_i, meaning the i-th conjunct in the co-ordinate structure. But each conjunct has a composition consisting of a string of one or more words, so we can number these words within each conjunct, and represent the number by another subscript, which we can show abstractly as j. We can then combine the two systems of subscripts into a compound subscript which will uniquely identify each word in a co-ordinate structure; $w_{i/j}$ represents the j-th word in the i-th conjunct. The index for the word *bucket* in the example just quoted would be $w_{2/3}$, meaning 'the third word in the second conjunct', and so on.

We can now generate a structure for each conjunct showing this string of indexed words, but we can build the definition of 'conjunct head' into it as well. To do this, we define a word $w_{i/h}$ (where *h* stands for 'head') as a word on which all other words in the conjunct depend, and which is among the words in the conjunct:

(1)   composition (C_i): $w_{i/1} \ldots w_{i/m}$,
                $1 \ll h \ll m$, model(w): word,
            head $(\ldots w_{i/j})$: $w_{i/h}$, all j, j = h

In words, each conjunct C_i consists of a string of at least one word, which must include the first word $(w_{i/1})$, the last word $(w_{i/m})$, and the conjunct head $(w_{i/h})$, on which any other words depend.

Having ensured that each conjunct is syntactically coherent, we can use the source of this coherence – the conjunct head – for other purposes. We shall be able to use it to give a very simple semantic structure to the co-ordinate structure, because the referent of *z* (the co-ordinate structure) in the earlier diagrams is simply a set containing the referents of all the individual conjunct heads, related by '&' or 'or', according to the conjunction (see p. 236). However, we can continue the syntactic analysis by using the conjunct head to carry the conjunct's external relations.

In particular, we need to make sure that, in some sense, all the conjuncts in a co-ordinate structure have the same external relations; or in transformational terminology, any propositions about their external relations must apply 'across the board'. If we mix up conflicting external relations, the result is zeugma (e.g. *He came in {(a hurry) and (a taxi)}*, where the conjuncts require conflicting meanings of *in*), or sheer incoherence (e.g. *I ate potatoes and in the kitchen*). Most if not all of the problem sentences will be ruled out if we require all the conjunct heads to have no head of their own, or all of them to have the same head; and if furthermore we arrange the semantic rules in such a way that the referent of the whole co-ordinate structure must fit into a single semantic slot (which is in any case the most natural way to arrange the semantic rules).

To achieve this effect, we must supplement the entry just given, by adding another condition: 'head $w_{i/h}$: k, all i' – that is, all conjunct heads must have the same entity *k* as their heads – 'k = $\emptyset$ or h, model (h): word' – i.e. this entity must be either nothing at all, or some word *h*.

Notice that this analysis does not contain any proposal for directly limiting the types of word that can be co-ordinated, in contrast with the majority of current analyses of co-ordination. It is often assumed that conjuncts must be of the same syntactic category, and on the basis of this assumption it is further suggested that co-ordinate structures can be generated by a rule-schema which simply copies all the syntactic features of one node onto a string of nodes beneath it (the conjuncts). The assumption is false, however (as I observed on p. 220). We have already noted that the valency and other constraints on predicatives leave their syntactic realizations unrestricted, so if we make no extra requirements on the syntax in the rules for co-ordinate structures, there is no reason to expect co-ordinated predicatives to be similar in anything but their meaning; and this is what we find, as in *He is well and in good spirits* (co-ordinated adjective and preposition). Similarly, *ask* takes a semantic question as its complement, without regard to whether this is realized as an interrogative clause (e.g. *He asked how late the train was*) or as a definite noun-phrase (e.g. *He asked the scheduled time of the train*); so once again we predict that the two kinds of complement can be co-ordinated, as indeed they can: *He asked the scheduled time of the train and how late it was*. This example, like the earlier one, is predicted to be ill-formed by any grammar which uses a rule-schema for copying identical syntactic features onto conjuncts. Moreover, such a grammar would be very hard to 'patch up' in order to provide a single syntactic category for these co-ordinate structures with syntactically conflicting conjuncts.

To summarize the analysis, I am identifying one word in each (complete) conjunct as its conjunct head, and then I am allowing these conjunct heads to have an external head, provided they all have the same external head. There is just one more point to add. The conjunct heads not only have the same head, but they constitute a single modifier of this head. We cannot allow them to fill separate modifier slots, because this would result in their filling different slots in the semantics as well, and would in every way give the wrong results. The entries given so far do not exclude this possibility, so we must add another condition, that some modifier slot for the shared head h must be filled by a list which includes all the conjunct heads: 'modifier (h): . . . & $w_{i/h}$, all i'. We can add this condition, and the one given above, to the entry for conjunct-structures given in (1), producing the following consolidated entry:

(2)   composition(C_i): $w_{i/1}$ . . . $w_{i/m}$,
             $1 \leqslant h \leqslant m$,

model (w): word,
head (. . . $w_{i/j}$): $w_{i/h}$, all j, j = h,
    head ($w_{i/h}$): k, all i,
  k = $\emptyset$ or h, model(h): word,
  modifier (h): . . . & $w_{i/h}$, all i:

Lastly, we need a notation for showing dependency structures in which two words jointly act as a single modifier. The obvious device is to use a branching dependency arrow, with a single 'base' and multiple arrow-heads. Using this notation, we can give the structure for the sentence *He ate an apple and some grapes* combining both dependency and co-ordinate structures. In this diagram I have separated the dependency structure and the constituency-based co-ordinate structure by writing the latter below the word-numbers; this has the advantage not only of reducing the complexity of the diagram, but also of emphasizing the difference between the two kinds of structure.

(3)

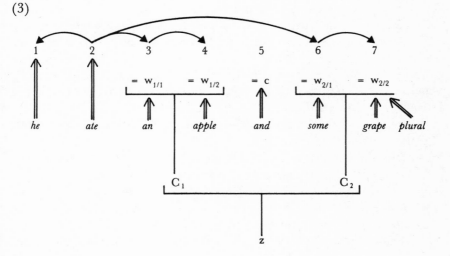

The structure of reduced conjuncts

In the informal discussion on pp. 216 – 17 I distinguished three kinds of co-ordinate structure in which one or more conjunct is incomplete: reduced conjuncts, gapping and right-node raising. We shall devote one subsection to each type, starting with reduced conjuncts.

The characteristic of reduced conjuncts is that (like gapped ones) the reduced conjunct is a non-initial one, but (unlike gapped ones) the reduced conjunct can be made complete simply by adding to it some words from the start of the intitial conjunct. For example, *sat down* is the second conjunct in {*(John came in) and (sat down)*}, and to make it complete we must take the first word of the first conjunct, *John*, and add it to the start of the second conjunct, giving *John sat down*. (Putting the same thing in a different way, *John* is shared, as a modifier, by both *came* and *sat*.) More complicated examples follow the same general principle: {*(John thinks of Mary in the morning) and (Jane in the evening)*} has an incomplete second conjunct which can be completed by adding the first three words of the first conjunct, *John thinks of*, and when we complete it we find that *Jane* is a modifier of *of*, while *in (the morning)* is a modifier of *thinks*. This example shows that the division between what is expressed in the second conjunct and what is 'borrowed' from the first conjunct need not respect the dependency structure (*Jane* and *in* modify different words), although it must respect the order of words (e.g. we could not borrow *in*, as that would involve a discontinuous borrowing, *John thinks of . . . in*: **John thinks of Mary in the morning and Jane the evening*).

The reason why examples such as these present problems is because the strings of words defined by the co-ordinate structures are not suitable for dependency structures, so the ordinary rules for generating dependency structures will not generate the structures needed here. However, it is not difficult to bridge the gap between the dependency and co-ordinate structures, because the discrepancies are quite simple in principle, and can be covered by a few general rules. The best way to formulate these rules is by referring to 'hypothetical conjuncts' – conjuncts similar to the ones contained in the sentence structure, except that they are complete. For example, the reconstructed conjunct in *John came in and sat down* is *John sat down*, in which we have made up a complete conjunct by combining the incomplete one with the first part of the first conjunct. Similarly, the hypothetical conjunct for *John thinks of Mary in the morning and Jane in the evening* is *John thinks of Jane in the evening*.

The grammar uses these hypothetical conjuncts in generating the incomplete ones, as follows. First we define the permitted relations between actual conjuncts and hypothetical ones; and then we let the ordinary rules of the grammar define the permitted structures for hypothetical conjuncts. This approach is very similar, of course, to the transformational approach, and it may be that my rules linking actual and hypothetical conjuncts are formally equivalent to transformations.

However, we already know that language processors reconstruct word-strings which they do not actually hear; for example, in understanding the one-word utterance *who?* you have to work out what word-string the speaker is taking for granted (e.g. A says *I'm getting someone to write my thesis for me*, and B says *Who?*); and you can only understand why someone refers to an object as *they* if you know that the word for referring to that object is syntactically plural, such as *trousers* or *scales*. So all I am doing is to allow the grammar to formalize the way in which this kind of operation can be applied to co-ordinate structures. But the processes referred to here are very different from those for which transformations are generally used – for example, the material underlying the sentence-fragment *Who?* cannot be recovered from the sentence itself, but it is widely accepted that material deleted by transformation should be recoverable in this sense.

Once we have accepted hypothetical conjuncts, the relevant entry is quite easy to write. More precisely, what we shall be writing is simply an 'appendix' to the entries for co-ordinate structures which we have already given, defining the internal compositions of the conjuncts. We start by repeating the entry of (1) on p. 225, which defined the internal composition of complete conjuncts; but we pair it with a slightly different alternative structure, in which the words are divided into two substrings: those before and including some word (arbitrarily numbered *g*), and those after it.

(1) composition (C_i): $w_{i/1} \ldots w_{i/m}$,

$$1 \ll h \ll m,$$

model (w): word,

head $(\ldots w_{i/j})$: $w_{i/h}$, all j, j = h,

or $w_{i/1} \ldots w_{i/g}$ & $w_{i/k} \ldots w_{i/m}$,

$$1 \ll g < k \ll m$$

This entry will allow us to refer to the bipartite structure of the first conjuncts in the examples we have discussed above; so for example the first conjunct of *John thinks of Mary in the morning and Jane in the evening* has seven words, of which the first three are shared with the second conjunct, so in this conjunct g = 3. However, the entry will also allow us to refer to the bipartite structure of gapped conjuncts, such as the second conjunct in *John drank beer and Mary, wine*; and indeed it helps to explain why gapped conjuncts must not have more than two overt constituents.

We can now add the rules for reconstructing a hypothetical conjunct.

If the conjunct which is incomplete is C_i (where i is of course some figure greater than 1), then its hypothetical counterpart can be called C_i'. C_i' is made up out of all the words in C_i, plus all those in the first section of the first conjunct, C_1. Here is the formalization, to be added to the entry just given:

(2) $C_i = C_i'$, all i $1 \leqslant i \leqslant n$
      composition (C_i': $w_{1/1} \ldots w_{1/g}$ & $w_{i/1} \ldots w_{i/m}$ ^

I.e. if one of the non-initial conjuncts is incomplete, they must all be (so I am assuming that sentences like the following are ungrammatical: *John came in, sat down, and his face lit up*).

With this modification, we can already generate all the constructions I have called 'reduced conjuncts'. It has the effect of producing multiple fillers for both head and modifier slots, similar to those which we generated in the previous subsection. For example, take *John came in and sat down*. The reconstructed conjunct is *John sat down*, in which *John* is not just a second instance of the word *John*, but the same instance as we find in the first conjunct. Accordingly, this word has not only *came* but also *sat* as its head, so the structure for the sentence will have to contain a branching dependency line with the branch on the tail end, instead of the head end (in contrast with structure (3) on p. 227).

(3)

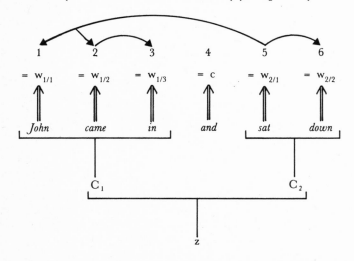

Similarly, we can already generate sentences like *John thinks of Mary in the morning and Jane in the evening*, via the hypothetical conjunct *John thinks of Jane in the evening*. Since the first three words of the sentence are part of the hypothetical conjunct as well as of the first conjunct, they will be linked in dependency to both of the complete conjuncts. But in this case we get more than one multiple dependency, because *of* has two modifiers, and so does *thinks*:

(4)

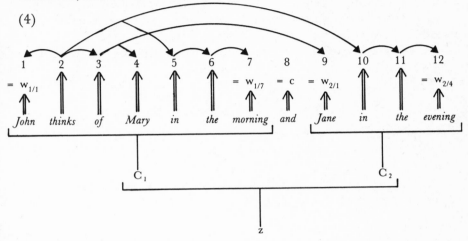

The only defect of the entry as it stands is that it is too permissive. Say we had a first conjunct consisting of *In Rome it's hot*; according to our entry we ought to be able to split this after *in*, and let the second conjunct share the *in*, giving **In Rome it's hot and London it's cool*; but of course this is not possible. This is because of a general restriction on dependency relations crossing the division between the parts, which the example infringes because of the dependency of *London* on *in*.

To be precise, only the following dependency relations are allowed within the hypothetical conjunct, between words in the part borrowed from the first conjunct and words taken from the incomplete conjunct. If the conjunct head (of the hypothetical conjunct) is in the first part, then any dependencies are permitted – provided, of course, that every word in either part depends ultimately on the conjunct head. Hence the possibility of examples like (4) above, where the conjunct head is *thinks*. But if the conjunct head is in the second part, then the only dependencies crossing over the division are those leading directly to the conjunct head itself. Thus we cannot have *London* depending on *in* in the example sentence just given, because the conjunct head is *'s*, in the second part of the hypothetical conjunct, so no word other than *'s* may be linked by any kind of dependency to any word in the first part. We thus need to add the following proviso to the entry:

(5)   head $(\ldots w_{i/j})$: $w_{1/h}$, all j, $j \neq h$,
               or head $(w_{1/j})$: $w_{i/h}$, or $w_{1/y}$, all j, $y \neq j$

In words, either the conjunct head is provided by the first conjunct, and every other word depends on it without further restriction, or else every word in the first conjunct depends directly either on some other word from the first conjunct, or on the conjunct head. Put more simply, it is only when the conjunct head is provided by the first conjunct that dependencies are free of special constraints.

The structure of gapped conjuncts

Having dealt with reduced conjuncts, we shall find it a relatively straightforward matter to bring in gapped conjuncts. The basic fact about gapping is that each non-initial conjunct consists of just two constituents, each of which contrasts with one constituent in the first conjunct. (I am of course using 'constituent' in the usual informal way, to refer to a word and its dependents.) For example, in *John invited Mary to the party, and Bill, Sue,* the second conjunct contains just two words, and these contrast respectively with *John* and *Mary*. Once again, we can best generate the structures of gapped conjuncts by assuming a hypothetical conjunct in which all the 'missing' bits have been provided by the first conjunct; or, putting it another way, the hypothetical conjunct is the same as the first conjunct, except that two constituents have been replaced, each by one of the constituents in the gapped clause. Thus the hypothetical clause in the above example would be *Bill invited Sue to the party*.

We have already provided an entry for hypothetical conjuncts – entry (2) – so we can make use of this for gapped conjuncts too. To show that gapping is an alternative to reduction as a way of structuring an incomplete conjunct, we can link the two formulae with 'or'. The formula for gapping starts off more simply than the one for reduced conjuncts, because it just requires straightforward identity between the hypothetical conjunct and the first conjunct, but we shall then have to add two qualifications to this identity. So we start with the basic entry for gapping, linked disjunctively with the one for reduction in an expanded version of entry (2).

(6) $C_i = C_i'$, all i, $1 < i \leqslant n$,
               composition $(C_i' : w_{1/1} \cdots w_{1/g}$ & $w_{i/1} \; \cdots w_{i/m}$,
               or $\{\, C_i' = C_1$, composition (C_i'): $\ldots w_{i/h} \ldots \}$

In words, each conjunct other than the first is matched by a hypothetical conjunct with the same subscript (C'^i), and either this hypothetical conjunct is made up out of the whole of the actual conjunct plus the initial words of the first conjunct, or it is the same as the first conjunct. In the latter case, its structure must (of course) contain a conjunct head, which we can call $w'^{i/h}$, following the established convention for conjunct heads; we shall have to refer to this conjunct head later.

Between them, these two alternative conditions exhaust all the possibilities for incomplete conjuncts (apart from right-node raising, which I am ignoring for the present). However, the whole of this entry should of course be taken as an alternative to the entry for complete conjuncts given in the previous subsection (entry (2) on p. 230).

There are two main conditions to be added to the entry for gapping, which have the effect of distinguishing the hypothetical conjunct from the first conjunct. Each has to do with one of the two constituents which together made up the gapped conjunct, and both the conditions must make sure that the constituents are true constituents – i.e. one word plus all its dependents. In addition, the first condition requires the word concerned to be the subject of the hypothetical conjunct head. As far as the second constituent is concerned, it makes no difference what its dependency relation to the conjunct head is (so long as it has one, of course). Thus we can construct acceptable examples where the second constituent is very distantly related to the conjunct head – e.g. *John tried to give up eating chocolates, and Mary, sweets.* However, since both constituents must be dependents of the conjunct head, this cannot itself be part of the gapped conjunct; and since the first constituent must be its subject, it must be the kind of word that may have a subject. Pending a radical extension of the use of subject (such as I sketched on pp. 163 – 7), this means that the conjunct head must be a verb or an adjective, which is just the right restriction on the distribution of gapping (the 'gap' must always include a verb or adjective).

All that remains is to give the formalization for these two conditions. In this formalization we shall be able to take advantage of the two-part division of conjuncts which I introduced in entry (1) on p. 229, just as we did in the case of reduced conjuncts; but for gapped conjuncts, it is the gapped conjunct itself whose two-part structure is relevant, whereas it was the first conjunct's when we were dealing with reduced conjuncts. The following conditions are to be added to the entry in (6), and should be included within the bracket following 'or'. To make this clearer, I have included the last line of entry (6) here:

(7)   = (6),
    or $\{C_i'$ $= C_1,$
        composition (C_i'): . . . $w_{i/h}'$ . . .,
        subject $(w_{i/h}')$: $w_{i/f}$, $1 < f < g$,
                head(. . . $w_{i/j}$): $w_{i/f}$, all j, $1 \leqslant j \leqslant g$, $j = f$,
        X (. . . $w_{i/h}'$): $w_{i/1}$, $i < k < m$,
                head(. . . $w_{i/j}$): $w_{i/l}$, all j, $k \leqslant l \leqslant m$, $j = 1\}$

In prose, these two conditions apply to the hypothetical conjunct, C'^i, and respectively require its subject and some other entity (X) to be supplied by the words in the gapped conjunct (C_i). The subject is a word in the first part of the gapped conjunct $(w^{i/f})$, which extends up to the g-th word, and the X is a word in the second part $(w^{i/f})$, between the k-th word and the m-th. The lines starting 'head (. . . ' ensure that all the other words in each part depend on the word concerned, so that each part is a single constituent.

The way in which this entry helps to generate the surface structure, then, is by defining a hypothetical complete conjunct C_i, which is a modified copy of the first conjunct, C^1, but which is also shown as similar to the gapped conjunct (by the part of entry (2) which says 'C_i = C'_i'), to the extent that this is compatible with what is known already about the gapped constituent. But we already know, from entry (7), that the first part of the gapped constituent is the subject of the verb or adjective in the hypothetical conjunct, and the second part is some other dependent of the same word, so since there are no more words in the gapped conjunct, there must be a 'gap', in relation to the hypothetical conjunct.

As far as the structures that are generated are concerned, there is an important difference between the structures for gapped conjuncts and those for reduced conjuncts. As we saw in the structure diagrams of (3) and (4) (p. 230), reduced conjuncts are fitted into the dependency structure for the first conjunct, by allowing the dependency arrows to branch in the same way as we did for complete conjuncts. This is not possible for gapped conjuncts. Take a simple problem: verb agreement. I have not tried to formalize verb agreement in this book, though it raises some interesting problems (Hudson 1977). However, we must allow plural verb-forms if the subject is a co-ordinated string of nouns (e.g. *John and Mary work/*works hard*). But if we treat the subject in a gapped clause as part of the subject of the first clause, we shall have problems with this rule because it ought to produce plural verb-forms in sentences like *John likes/*like Mary and Bill, Sue*, on a par with *John and Bill like/*likes Mary*.

Because of problems such as this one, we must leave the constituents of the gapped conjunct unrelated to the dependency structure for the first conjunct. This means that the relation, in terms of dependency structure, between the two conjuncts is just the same as the relation between a response and the sentence on which it is based (e.g. *Who?* in response to *Someone came to supper last night*): they are related only via a hypothetical word-string which is based on the full sentence and contains the response fragment. A useful notation for showing this kind of relation is the following, where the hypothetical words in the hypothetical conjunct are represented by numbers taken from the first conjunct, with a prime to show that they are hypothetical.

(8)

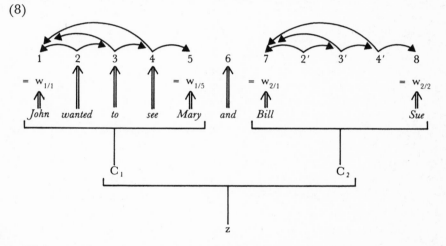

This completes the discussion of gapping, though a few loose ends are still hanging – for example, for some reason gapped conjuncts cannot be linked by *but*, nor is *and* possible if the first conjunct is negative (e.g. **John invited Mary but Bill, Sue; *John didn't invite Mary and Bill, Sue*). However, I hope to have shown that a revealing and fairly simple analysis of gapping is possible in word grammar, and it seems quite likely that the extra details could be fitted into this framework.

Right-node raising

What I have to offer for right-node raising is less than satisfactory, and it must be recognized as an outstanding research problem for word grammar. One problem arises from the nature of the data themselves, since I find most examples of the construction rather stilted and literary, so I comfort myself in the face of my failure to produce a satisfactory analysis with the thought that it is a rather unnatural construction. However, this is a suspiciously easy escape route, and for the time being at any rate we must accept the need to generate strings like *John adores, though Mary can't stand, unripe tomatoes cooked in jam*. Moreover, as I have already pointed out these constructions are not strictly relevant to the analysis of co-ordinate structures because they can occur in other structures (e.g. the example just quoted is not a co-ordinate structure). (Similar remarks would apply, for example, to 'verb-phrase anaphora', although this is sometimes discussed as though it had some connection with co-ordinate structures.)

The best I can offer at present is a rule which overgenerates, and which allows any two syntactically related words to share a postmodifier:

(1)   modifier (a): m
       modifier (b): m,   X(. . . a): b,
                               $a < b < m$

It may be that what we need is some rule more similar to the rule for reduced conjuncts, which would allow us to factorize a pair of constituents, so that one part of one constituent counts as part of the other as well. This was possible for reduced conjuncts, because each of the conjuncts is in fact a constituent, even in word grammar; but we cannot extend the same treatment to right-node raising because we cannot take pre-existing constituents for granted in the same way.

Semantic structures

So far we have paid very little attention to semantic structure, but the syntactic analysis will in fact make it very easy to provide suitable semantic structures for each of the three co-ordinate constructions.

If the conjuncts are complete, then the semantic structure for the whole co-ordinate structure is just a set consisting of all the referents of the individual conjunct heads. For example, if the referents of *John* and *Mary* in *John and Mary* are 1* and 3* respectively, then the referent of the whole structure is '1* & 3*'; and if the conjunction had been *or*, it would have been '1* or 3*'.

Now, we have already seen that the semantic structures of plural nouns consist of a set of entities, whose membership is represented by a row of dots (see pp. 197 – 202), so the semantic structures for plural nouns and for conjoined strings are very similar. This is a very satisfactory state of affairs, because we sometimes need to generalize across them (e.g. in dealing with verb agreement, as I noted above). Similarly, we have seen that the semantic structures for words like *any* contain a disjunctive set, whose members are again represented by a row of dots (p. 209), so their semantic structures are very similar to those for co-ordinated strings with *or* in them. Again, this is a satisfactory conclusion, because there are similarities (e.g. *any of John, Bill and Harry* means the same as *John, Bill or Harry*).

Because of this similarity between the semantic structures for co-ordinate structures and those for plural nouns, the ambiguities which arise in one case may also be expected to arise in the other. For example, *They own a house* allows two interpretations, according to how many distinct states of house-owning are referred to; but the same is true of *John and Mary own a house*. There is no need to change the entry on p. 200 in order to make it apply also to co-ordinate structures.

Nor is there any need to make special provision for semantic structures in the entry for co-ordinate structures, because it is the conjunct heads, and not the co-ordinate structure itself, which are related externally to the rest of the sentence; and if we say that some modifier slot is filled by a set of conjunct heads, it automatically follows that the corresponding slot in the semantic structure must be filled by the set of referents for these individual conjunct heads. Take the example structure given in (3) on p. 227 for *He ate an apple and some grapes*. Here, the object modifier is filled by the conjunct heads, 3 (for *an*) and 6 (for *some*); so the slot which shows the thing eaten in the semantic structure is filled by the set '3* & 6*'. Alternatively, if the referent of *ate* is taken as a set, with a different act of eating for the apple and for the grapes, then 3* will fill the relevant slot in one structure, and 6* will fill the same slot in the other structure.

Reduced conjuncts too are covered by the above remarks, to the extent that each conjunct has a separate conjunct head. For example, {(*John came in*) *and* (*sat down*)} has two conjuncts heads, *came* and *sat*, and the fact that these share a modifier (*John*) is irrelevant as far as the semantics is concerned. However, some reduced conjuncts share a single conjunct head, namely that of the first conjunct (e.g. {(*John thinks of Mary in the morning*) *and* (*Jane in the evening*)}, whose shared conjunct head is *thinks*). In such cases, the referent of the conjunct head has to be a set; but multiple referents for a single word are already allowed for, provided some dependent also provides a multiple referent to pair its members with. However, we need to make special provision for reduced conjuncts, because the words in each conjunct must all be related to the same referent. For example, we have to make sure that *thinks* in the sentence quoted above has just two referents, one mentioning 'Mary' and 'in the morning', and the other mentioning 'Jane' and 'in the evening'.

The rule needed for doing this matching of semantics and syntax can be added to the entry for reduced conjuncts given in (5) on p. 232. This entry already distinguishes the two kinds of reduced structure mentioned above, so we can attach the following to the part of this entry which deals with cases where there is just one conjunct head, in the first conjunct; for convenience, I repeat the relevant line of the entry:

(1)   = (5), p. 232,
       $\{$head$(\ldots w_{i/j})$: $w_{l/h}$, all j, j$\ ' =$ h,
            reference $(w_{l/h})$: $w^*_{l/h}$, $w^*_{l/h} = \ldots \ldots x_i$, all i,
            $X(\ldots x_i)$: $w^*_{i/j}$, all j$\}$
       or . . .

In words, if the conjunct head of the first conjunct is also conjunct head of all the other conjuncts, then this conjunct head $(w_{1/h})$ must have a multiple referent, in which each member (x_i) is linked to a conjunct (the *i*-th conjunct), and every word (the *j*-th word, for all *j*) in that conjunct must be linked semantically to that particular entity, x_i.

For gapping, the semantic structure is somewhat easier to derive from the syntactic structure because we have postulated a conjunct head for each of the conjuncts, even though the conjunct heads for non-initial conjuncts are just hypothetical words. Since we have these hypothetical words in the structures, we can refer to them for the semantics, and let each of them provide a separate referent for the semantics. Thus the structure given for *John wanted to see Mary and Bill, Sue* contained two conjunct-heads, numbered 2 and 2' respectively (see diagram (8) on p. 235); so the referent of the whole co-ordinate structure is the set consisting of 2* and 2'*. All we need to add to the grammar, in order to make this clear, is the condition that 'referent$(w_{1/h})$: $w^*_{1/h} \ldots$ $w'^*_{i/h}$, all i': that is, the referent of the only overt conjunct head is the set consisting of the referent of this word itself, as derived in the ordinary way, plus the referents of each of the hypothetical conjunct heads.

Other complications are possible. For example, the word *respectively* requires a complex cross-matching of distinct modifiers, to produce a set of referents for the verb (e.g. *John and Mary met Bill and Sue respectively* has two referents for *met*, in one of which John met Bill and in the other Mary met Sue). No doubt the entry for this word would be fairly complex, as far as its semantic effects are concerned, but I think it could exploit the analyses already given.

Some problems

The analysis of co-ordinate structures outlined above has solved most of the well-known and much discussed problems, such as the treatment of gapping and the provision of multiple referents. However, it would be unrealistic to pretend that there are no outstanding problems. I have mentioned a few such problems in the course of the above discussion, but there are more, so I shall finish with a list of the ones of which I am most keenly aware.

(a) Various conjunctions are subject to rather mysterious constraints on the syntactic structures into which they can fit. For example, *then* can link nouns, but only if they are non-subjects: *I saw John then Mary*, compared with **John then Mary came in*. Similarly, *but* can link nouns, but only if they are predicatives: compare *He was a good linguist but a bad father* with **I know a good linguist but a bad father*.

(b) What are the semantic effects of the conjunctions other than *and* and *or*? In particular, what is the semantic difference between *and* and *but*? Should we distinguish between inclusive and exclusive interpretations of *or*?

(c) Do examples like *Try and work harder* involve co-ordination at all, or should it rather be taken as a modifier (as suggested on p. 122)? And what about examples like *He bent down and picked up his stick*, which allow 'extraction' from just one of the verbs (e.g. *The stick which he bent down and picked up*)?

(d) Which words cannot be co-ordinated, and why? For example, why cannot we co-ordinate *my* with *your*, to give **my and your ideas*?

(e) What constraints do the constructions described here place on intonation? For instance, does gapping require 'parallelism' of intonation between the contrasted elements? And how should the constraints be stated formally?

(f) What are the relations between co-ordinate structures on the one hand, and on the other (i) asyndeton (e.g. *I know* – *let's run away together*) and (ii) subordinate structures involving dependency (e.g. *John is tall whereas Mary is short*)?

6

Spoken and Written Utterances

UTTERANCE-EVENTS

The structure of utterance-events

Most linguistic theories have little to offer in the study of the events in time which we tend to call 'utterances', but which I shall call 'utterance-events'. This is partly because of the distinction between sentences and utterances which is widely accepted by linguists, and which encourages linguists to restrict their analysis to sentences; partly because of the pervasive influence of writing on linguists' conception of language, which encourages them to analyse linguistic structures in isolation from the contexts in which they are used; and partly because of the stress which many linguists place on the distinction between linguistic and non-linguistic knowledge, which leaves knowledge of utterance-events on the 'wrong' side of the boundary. In contrast, word grammar makes no use of the distinction between sentences and utterances (see pp. 21 – 3), nor of the distinction between linguistic and non-linguistic knowledge (see pp. 35 – 42, and passim), and I shall try to take the differences between speech and writing seriously in the next section. So word grammar allows us to analyse the structure of utterance-events in terms of similar structures to those used in the grammar; indeed, it encourages one to do so, in the same way that it encourages one to explore the structure of cognition beyond the 'strictly linguistic' parts of word meaning.

The reason for preferring the term 'utterance-event' for this analysis is that 'utterance' is ambiguous in an important way. On the one hand it may mean the sounds themselves, i.e. that which is uttered; but it could also be used to refer to the action of uttering (compare the ambiguity of *decision* between the event and the product, and similarly for many other English words). The term 'utterance-event' is meant to remove this ambiguity, and will leave us free to use the term 'utterance' to refer just to the sounds that are produced.

As its name implies, an utterance-event is an instance of an event, so we can apply the same kind of analysis to utterance-events as we did to the semantic structure of *chase* (see pp. 157 – 60). This is important because in both cases we are dealing with the structure of our knowledge, and my assumption throughout this book has been that our knowledge constitutes a single, somewhat modular, network which is exploited in various different ways. In particular, I assume that the semantic structure for a general word which can refer to utterance-events (e.g. *say*) is the *same* as the structure for the area of knowledge which we exploit in processing and remembering utterance-events. For example, if we can postulate the semantic role 'speaker' in describing the structure of a sentence containing the verb *say*, then we can also take it for granted in our analysis of utterance-events; and vice versa.

What then is the structure of an utterance-event, as perceived and remembered by a human observer? Various details remain to be worked out, but at least we can say the following with some confidence:

(a) It is an *event*, so it has a time structure in which the state of affairs changes with time (for this analysis, and the following, see the table in (3) on p. 159); this is obviously true of utterances, because the state of affairs varies both rapidly and regularly with time (e.g. different sounds are produced at different moments).

(b) It is an *action*, so it involves an actor – i.e. an entity which supplies the energy and is the main locus of variation through time (namely, the speaker).

(c) It is a *deed*, so the actor is in control of the changes, and has a purpose.

It is true that some utterance-events deviate from this pattern – e.g. the speaker might be known not to be in conscious control – but we are concerned here only with the normal pattern, and as always deviations can be accommodated.

This analysis could be taken further in detail; for example, we must probably recognize various kinds of deed according to the location of the change within the actor's body, so we could relate speaking to eating (because both involve one's mouth), and contrast it with knitting, walking, and so on. More generally, however, we need to recognize that some kinds of event are defined as having a particular effect, while others are not; and in terms of this contrast, speaking is 'effective', along with singing and building, but in contrast with eating and inspecting. The effect which is produced in the case of speaking is the utterance itself. Similarly, we need to show that utterance-events are an instance of communication, like the act of writing but (I assume) unlike most types of singing. I take it that this can be shown partly by defining the purpose more precisely (though I am not too clear on exactly what the content of this definition should be) and partly by defining a 'receiver'. Presumably 'communication' is an instance of 'deed', so the network of models into which 'utterance-event' fits is as shown here:

(1)

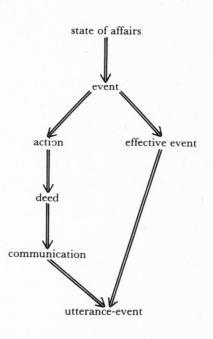

These various models combine to produce the following set of roles for an utterance-event:

(a) speaker = controller = actor;
(b) addressee = receiver;
(c) time, including an internal time structure corresponding to the internal structure of each word;
(d) place;
(e) purpose;
(f) product = utterance – i.e. one or (maybe) more words.

It may be that other elements need to be recognized for certain specific types of utterance-event – e.g. 'hearer' may need to be distinguished from 'addressee' in some public genres, such as radio interviews or cross-examination before a judge and jury. The above list will be sufficient for our present purposes, however.

One question which I have not yet addressed is how long each utterance-event is. One of the difficulties in discourse analysis is in segmentation, and we also have to decide how to segment discourse into units which would be suitable for analysis as utterances. Various possibilities suggest themselves, but none are obviously suitable: sentences and 'turns' (i.e. everything said by one speaker before handing over to another speaker) are unsuitable, for example, because in both cases the purpose can change within the unit. (Remember that we have analysed the meaning of imperative verbs as defining the speaker's purpose, so if we have a mixture of imperative and non-imperative verbs, or two different imperative verbs, we must have a change of purpose.) The only unit for which all the elements are likely to stay constant is the word, so this is the unit which I shall take as the 'utterance'. Accordingly, we can define the utterance as being an instance of 'word', which will take us straight into the grammar and vocabulary of some language.

At first sight, this definition will no doubt seem perverse, because 'utterances' are usually assumed to be much longer than single words. After all, things such as speakers and purposes stay constant from one word to the next. However, one thing does not stay constant, namely time; so if you want to announce the time to the nearest second, you have a communication problem. (E.g. if I say *The time is 12.57 and twelve seconds*, then the proposition must be false for at least some words in the sentence – a curious consequence of technological advance.) We have in fact exploited this fact in dealing with the linear order of words in a string, because each word is given a number which represents a point in time, and the order of words is achieved by ordering these points in time (see pp. 103 – 6); so we have already assigned the 'time' part of our utterance-event structure to individual words.

How then are we to capture the fact that the other elements of utterance-events tend to stay constant from one word to the next? The answer is simple, now that we have the apparatus of word grammar. All we need to do is to require each utterance-event to be the same as the preceding one, except in any respects which are marked as different (which must include time). This can be formalized as follows:

(2)   utterance(u_i): i, utterance (u_h): h, h = i − 1,
$$u_i = u_h,$$
$$\text{time}(u_h): t_h,$$
$$\text{time}(u_i): t_i, h < i$$

In words, the utterance-event in which some word *i* is uttered must be the same as the utterance-event in which the preceding word *h* is uttered, except for the difference in time between them.

The relevance of utterance-events for word structure

The analysis of utterance-events which we have just considered would be necessary if our aim were the complete analysis of cognitive structure, just because we obviously do understand this part of our experience along the lines of this analysis. For example, if you ask someone to tell you about some utterance-event which they experienced, then they will certainly feel obliged to supply information about speaker, addressee, time, place and so on, and this information must be stored, in a structured way, in their memory. However, our need for this kind of analysis is more pressing, as it is essential to a proper analysis of properly 'linguistic' structure (i.e. of word structure). In this subsection I shall list some reasons why this is so.

(a) *Deictic semantics*. The semantic analysis of words with deictic meanings must, by definition, refer to elements of the utterance-event containing the word concerned. For example, the personal pronouns refer crucially to the speaker and the addressee, demonstratives have at least some meanings which refer to the place or time (e.g. *this/that room, this/that year*), many nouns and adverbs have referents which are related to the time or place (e.g. *here, now, ago, today*). Of course, it would be possible to take these elements of the utterance-event as primitives, as I did earlier when I took NOW as a primitive (see pp. 146, and 185), but we can now do better than that, and define NOW in relation to the utterance-event concerned.

The parts of semantic analysis to which the utterance-event is relevant are not restricted to the traditional areas of pure deixis, however. I argued on pp. 180 – 6 that definiteness should be defined in terms of the knowledge of the speaker and the addressee, and then I extended this type of analysis to mood on pp. 186 – 97; so if these arguments were valid, the semantic analysis for these parts of the grammar must refer to the speaker and addressee, both of which are defined in relation to the utterance-event. Moreover, we had to define the knowledge concerned as what these participants have at a time just before the utterance-event, so time is relevant; and for imperatives I argued that purpose was crucial, because the purpose of an imperative utterance is to make the content of that utterance true. Thus large areas of semantic structure seem to be inextricably intertwined with the structure of the utterance-event – not a surprising conclusion, of course, in view of the fact that words always occur embedded in utterance-events, but an uncomfortable one for supporters of the distinction between semantics and pragmatics. Furthermore, it is interesting to note that recent studies of child language (e.g. Barrett 1983) have shown that the first 'meanings' that children attach to words are tied to particular types of utterance-event, so the 'referent' only gradually becomes distinct from the 'utterance-event' in the child's mind.

(b) *Metalanguage*. Ordinary language includes a very large number of words for referring to different kinds of utterance-event. Some of these words refer to the purpose of the event (its 'illocutionary force', in Austin's terms), such as *promise* and *advise*; others refer to its consequences (its 'perlocutionary force'), such as *persuade* or *deceive*; others refer to the manner of utterance (e.g. *whisper, gabble*), and so on. Such words are of interest partly because they provide evidence for the general claim I made above, about the structured way in which we perceive and remember utterance-events – if this claim were false, we could never understand or use these words. However, they are also important because they show that we should have to engage in a detailed analysis of utterance-events just for the sake of this area of word-meaning, even if we held that the structure of utterance-events was really a matter of pragmatics rather than semantics. The categories that I listed above as elements in utterance-events would certainly be included among the structures we produced for the meanings of these words, though other elements (e.g. manner, consequence) would also be needed.

Performative verbs are a particularly interesting subclass of metalinguistic word, because they can be used to define the type of utterance-event in which they themselves are involved (in much the way that imperatives define the purpose of their utterance-events). For example, *promise* may be uttered as a promise, in strings like *I promise to help you*. This is easy to formalize, because we simply allow the referent of *promise* to be the same entity as the utterance-event containing it as an utterance. Its referent is in any case some entity which is an utterance-event, so it would be hard to prevent it from being used to refer to its own utterance-event.

What both deictic words and performatively used performative verbs have in common is that they have semantic structures which are linked directly to the structure of the utterance-event in which they occur. In particular, some entity in the former is identified with some entity in the latter. For example, the referent of a performative verb is identified with its own utterance-event, and the referent of a personal pronoun is identified with the speaker or addressee in this utterance-event. We can show these relations diagrammatically by using a convention which we have defined (see p. 9) but not yet used; the squiggly line connecting a word to its utterance-event. We can represent the structures for *I* and for a performative use of *promise* like this:

(1)

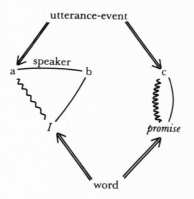

(c) *Stylistic restrictions*. There is no doubt that any native speaker of English knows the difference between words like *try* and *attempt*, or *cat* and *pussy*, so the network must be able to accommodate such knowledge. We might call it 'stylistic knowledge', but really we have to do here with a range of knowledge much broader than what is traditionally called stylistic. For example, if I know that some kind of word is typically used by some type of person, then this knowledge will fall under my 'stylistic' category. This is meant to include any knowledge that we have about the utterance-events in which words occur, other than the types which we have already discussed (deictic and metalinguistic or performative). Some such knowledge involves one or the other of the participants, or both, some involves the classification of the utterance-event itself for type (e.g. 'religious service', 'committee meeting', 'football match'), and so on. The range of phenomena are well known in sociolinguistics, and there should be no need to rehearse them here (see Hudson 1980a for details). As yet, we have seen very few attempts to explore the place of these types of knowledge in a theory of language structure, and it is time some serious work was done in this area.

It may be that non-categorical, quantitative constraints could also be analysed in the same way, in relation to the knowledge of utterance-events and their properties. Presumably all the quantitative data which have been discovered by Labov and his followers (summarized in Hudson 1980a, chapter 5) has some kind of basis in the knowledge of the speakers concerned, and one of the main challenges for theoretical linguists these days is to develop a total theory which is compatible with these findings. It is still an open question whether the quantitative and variable nature of the data requires similarly quantitative knowledge-structures, as was implied in the theory of variable rules, or whether it could be reconciled with a categorical knowledge-structure in which various components interact in such a way as to produce these quantitative data. It seems reasonable to hope that word grammar will provide at least as good a framework for such work as any other current theory.

WRITING
The relation of written texts to utterance-events

What follows is meant to make just two simple points, rather than to represent even the beginnings of a proper theory of written language, in spite of the pressing need for such a theory. The first point is that the structure of our knowledge of written words is different from that for spoken words, and similarly for the written equivalent of the utterance-event. The second is that the structure of writing is at least to some extent derivative from that of speech.

One of the main differences between speech and writing is that the latter replaces the dimension of time by that of space. It is typical of the ambivalent attitude of linguists to the difference between speaking and writing that we so often speak of rules applying 'from left to right', of the 'left-hand end of the sentence' and so on; without writing, such expressions would be meaningless. However, it is not just the analytical apparatus that is different – even the words used in the two channels are different, to reflect the different dimensions. For example, in writing one uses expressions such as *above* and *below*, in the rather abstract sense in which *above* can mean either literally higher up on the same page, or on an earlier page; but it would be nonsense to use either of these words, in a comparable sense, in speaking.

Another gross difference is that writing is organized in a strictly hierarchical way, at least in the kind of writing which is published and which one learns to produce as part of formal education: words are grouped into sentences, sentences into paragraphs, paragraphs into sections, sections into chapters. This is clearly a very difficult thing to learn, and there seems to be virtually nothing similar in spoken language. In particular, I have devoted a large part of this book (especially pp. 92 – 8) to arguing against a hierarchial organization of word-strings, and I have argued elsewhere (Hudson, 1980a:131) that discourse structure in speech is 'floating' rather than hierarchical. Once again, it is at least tempting to suspect that the attractions of hierarchical analysis for linguists lie in its relevance for written rather than spoken language.

Besides differences like these, however, there are similarities between speech and writing which suggest that writing is parasitic on speech (as one might expect, in view of the phylogenetic and ontogenetic priority of speech). For example, the time dimension can be invoked in writing although not strictly relevant (e.g. *now*, *earlier*), and certain spelling rules have to refer to pronunciation (e.g. the rule for choosing between *a* and *an* refers to phonological consonants and vowels, so that a word like *university* takes *a* although it starts with an orthographic vowel). It seems that when we learn to read and write we must work out for ourselves a large number of rules for converting information about spoken words into a form which makes it relevant to written words. For example, any rule which refers to 'speaker' must be translated into one with 'writer' instead; and so on.

In terms of our overall knowledge structures, our knowledge of written language must be related to our knowledge of other kinds of static patterns, such as pictures, maps and road-signs, whereas spoken words are presumably more closely related to other types of deliberately made sounds, such as music. These different relations help to explain some of the gross differences, and at least some of the connections can presumably be explained by treating spoken words as the model for written words, so that a written word is assumed to have the same properties as some spoken model, except for whatever differences follow from the channel difference.

Knowledge of written words as part of 'language'

For some time linguists have tended to exclude written forms from their subject matter by fiat (e.g. 'the spoken forms alone constitute the object of linguistics' – Saussure 1916/1959:24). More recently, however, it has become acceptable to include knowledge of written forms among the kinds of knowledge which belong to one's 'linguistic knowledge'. Nathan 1979 is a particularly rich collection of arguments for this position, but it is also accepted by Miller (1978), McCawley (1980) and Matthei and Roeper (1983), for example. Of course, whether or not one includes knowledge of writing as part of language depends on one's definition of language, and I have already expressed a deep lack of interest in such questions. However, it is interesting to see how knowledge of spelling interacts with knowledge of pronunciation, and affects pronunciation, so what follows are some examples of this kind of interaction, to show that even an account of speech must take account of spelling if the speaker is literate.

For my first example I turn to the use and non-use of /r/ in some varieties of Southern British English. The accents in question are non-rhotic (i.e. allow /r/ only when it is followed by a vowel), but unlike most non-rhotic accents, they avoid so-called 'intrusive /r/' – an /r/ sound which does not correspond to an *r* in the spelling. Intrusive /r/ is commonly found in other accents in strings like *saw it*, and even in single words like *sawing* (which is then homophonous with *soaring*). The speakers of interest to us are those who frown on such pronunciations, and avoid them studiously in their own speech. How do they do this? How do they know that *soar* can alternate between having no /r/ (e.g. *soared*) and having /r/ (e.g. *soaring, soar up*), but that *saw* cannot, but must always lack the /r/? One possible answer is that they have learned it by listening to others, and this may indeed by a partial explanation. However, it seems much more likely that they make use of the spellings of these words, and may even have been told at some point, 'You mustn't pronounce /r/ if it is not in the spelling.' Since they have this knowledge already, it would be most surprising if they did not use it to determine their pronunciation.

The second example is based on an observation by S.R. Anderson (1981). He points out that if we wanted to form an adjective from the name *Fulton*, we would pronounce the adjective with /ou/ in the second syllable (*Fultonian*), in spite of the fact that the second syllable of the name is pronounced with a schwa, and there is no evidence from pronunciation that this schwa alternates with /ou/. Anderson assumes that the alternation is evidence that the relation between the two vowels must be shown in an abstract phonological representation shared by them, and then goes on to argue that such abstract representations must be learned from the spelling. But surely there is a much simpler explanation: there is no abstract phonology, and the pronunciation of a word like *Fultonian* is derived from the spelling? The rules for mapping spellings onto pronunciations would be quite straightforward to work out, and it would be most surprising if a literate adult did not know at least some such rules. Similar explanations could presumably be offered for a lot of the abstract phonological alternations which have been widely assumed to show the need for shared phonological representations.

The conclusion is that spelling knowledge interacts with knowledge of pronunciation in deciding how a speaker pronounces a word. This is something which literate speakers are well aware of, so it is hardly a surprise, but it is surprising that so little attention has been paid in linguistics to such phenomena. The two examples of how knowledge of spelling can help to explain facts about pronunciation nicely illustrate the most general theme of this book: that if we are really interested in explaining why the structure of language is as it is, then we must look for similarities and connections with areas of knowledge which have traditionally been considered 'outside language'. Maybe we shall fail to find such explanations for some parts of language which do call for explanation, and in that case we shall be entitled to conclude that the true one must lie elsewhere, perhaps in some property unique to language; but until we have looked for explanations in the most obvious places, we shall never know.

References

Allerton, D. J. (1982) *Valency and the English Verb*. London: Academic Press.

Anderson, J. M. (1971) *The Grammar of Case: Towards a localistic theory*. Cambridge: Cambridge University Press.

(1977) *On Case Grammar. Prolegomena to a theory of grammatical relations*. London: Croom Helm.

Anderson, J. R. (1976) *Language, Memory and Thought*. Hillsdale, N. J.: Lawrence Erlbaum.

(1980) *Cognitive Psychology and its Implications*. San Francisco: Freeman.

Anderson, S. R. (1977) On the formal description of inflection. *Papers from the Thirteenth Regional Meeting of the Chicago Linguistics Society*, 15 – 45.

(1981) Why phonology isn't 'natural'. *Linguistic Inquiry* 12, 493 – 540.

Atkinson, M., Kilby, D. and Rocca, I. (1982) *Foundations of General Linguistics*. London: George Allen & Unwin.

Bach, E. (1968) Nouns and noun-phrases. In E. Bach and R. T. Harms (eds) *Universals in Linguistic Theory*. London: Holt, Rinehart & Winston.

Baker, C. L. (1979) Syntactic theory and the projection problem. *Linguistic Inquiry*, 10, 533 – 81.

Barrett, M. D. (1983) Scripts, prototypes and the early acquisition of word meaning. *Working Papers of the London Psycholinguist Research Group*, 5, 17 – 26.

Bartsch, R. and Vennemann, Th. (1972) *Semantic Structures. A study in the relation between semantics and syntax*. Frankfurt: Athenäum.

Beaugrande, R. de and Dressler, W. (1981) *Introduction to Text Linguistics*. London: Longman.

Berman, A. (1973) A constraint on Tough-movement. *Papers from the Ninth Regional Meeting of the Chicago Linguistics Society*, 34 – 43.

Bierwisch, M. (1981) Linguistics and language errors. *Linguistics*, 19, 583 – 626.

Blake, B. J. (1983) Structure and word-order in Kalkatungu. The anatomy of a flat language. *Australian Jnl Linguistic* 3, 143 – 75.

Bolinger, D. L. (1971) *Meaning and Form*. London: Longman.

Botha, R. (1981) A base rule theory of Afrikaans synthetic compounding. In M. Moortgat, H. v. d. Hulst and T. Hoekstra (eds) *The Scope of Lexical Rules*. Dordrecht: Foris.

Brame, M. (1983) Bound anaphora is not a relation between NPs. *Linguistic Analysis*, 11, 139 – 166.

Bresnan, J. W. (1976) Evidence for a theory of unbounded transformations. *Linguistic Analysis*, 2, 353 – 93.

(1978) A realistic transformational grammar. In M. Halle, J. Bresnan and G. Miller (eds) *Linguistic Theory and Psychological Reality*. Cambridge, Mass.: MIT Press.

Bresnan, J. W., Kaplan, R. M., Peters, S. and Zaenen, A. (1982) Cross-serial dependencies in Dutch. *Linguistic Inquiry*, 13, 613 – 35.

Carroll, J. M. (1978) Creative neologism as a dynamic process in language evolution: a case study from English. *Proceedings of the Berkeley Linguistics Society*, 4, 397 – 417.

Cattell, R. (1976) Constraints on movement rules. *Language*, 52, 18 – 50.

Charniak, E. (1981) The case-slot identity theory. *Cognitive Science*, 5, 285 – 92.

Chekili, R. (1982) *The Morphology of the Arabic Dialect of Tunis*. London University PhD dissertation.

Chomsky, N. (1957) *Syntactic Structures*. The Hague: Mouton.

(1965) *Aspects of the Theory of Syntax*. Cambridge, Mass.: MIT Press.

(1970) Remarks on nominalization. In R. A. Jacobs and P. S. Rosenbaum, (eds) *Readings in English Transformational Grammar*. London: Ginn.

(1974) Questions of form and interpretation. *Montreal Working Papers in Linguistics*, 6, 1 – 42.

(1977) On wh movement. In P. W. Culicover, T. Wasow and A. Akmajian (eds) *Formal Syntax*. London: Academic Press.

(1981) *Lectures on Government and Binding*. Dordrecht: Foris.

Clark, E. V. (1974) Normal states and evaluative viewpoints. *Language*, 50, 316 – 32.

Clark, H. H. and Clark, E. V. (1977) *Psychology and Language: An introduction to psycholinguistics*. London: Harcourt, Brace, Jovanovich.

Collins, A. M. and Quillian, M. R. (1969) Retrieval time from semantic memory. *Journal of Verbal Learning and Verbal Behavior*, 8, 240 – 7.

Comrie, B. (1981) *Language Universals and Linguistic Typology*. Oxford: Blackwell.

Covington, M. A. (1979) The syntactic theory of Thomas of Erfurt. *Linguistics*, 17, 465 – 96.

Cutler, A. (1981) The reliability of speech error data. *Linguistics*, 19, 561 – 82.

Clark, H. H. and Haviland, S. E. (1977) Comprehension and the Given – New contract. In R. O. Freedle (ed.) *Discourse Production and Comprehension*. Norwood, N. J. : Ablex 1 – 40.

Dahl, Ö. (1976) What is new information? In N. E. Enkvist and V. Kohonen (eds) *Reports on Text Linguistics: Approaches to word-order*. Abo: Finnish Academy.

(1980) Some arguments for higher nodes in syntax: a reply to Hudson's 'Constituency and dependency'. *Linguistics*, 18, 485 – 8.

Davison, A. (1980) Peculiar passives. *Language*, 56, 42 – 66.

Diehl, L. G. (1981) *Lexical-generative Grammar: Toward a lexical conception of linguistic structure.* Indiana University PhD dissertation.

Dik, S. C. (1978) *Functional Grammar.* Amsterdam: North Holland.

Dowty, D. R. (1979) *Word Meaning and Montague Grammar. The semantics of verbs and times in Generative Semantics and in Montague's PTQ.* Dordrecht: Reidel.

(1980) Grammatical relations and Montague grammar. Duplicated.

Ebert, R. P. (1973) On the notion 'subordinate clause' in Standard German. In C. Corum, T. C. Smith-Stark and A. Weiser (eds) *You Take the High Node and I'll take the Low Node.* Chicago: Chicago Linguistics Society, University of Chicago.

Evans, G. (1980) Pronouns. *Linguistic Inquiry*, 11, 337 – 62.

Ferguson, C. A. (1979) Phonology as an individual access system. In C. J. Fillmore, D. Kempler and W. S-Y. Wang (eds) *Individual Differences in Language Ability and Language Behavior.* London: Academic Press.

Fillmore, C. J. (1968) The case for case. In E. Bach and R. Harms (eds) *Universals in Linguistic Theory.* New York: Holt, Rinehart & Winston.

Gazdar, G. and Pullum, G. K. (1981) Subcategorization constituent order and the notion 'head'. In M. Moortgat, H. v. d. Hulst and T. Hoekstra (eds) *The Scope of Lexical Rules.* Dordrecht: Foris.

(1982) Generalized phrase structure grammar: A theoretical synopsis. Duplicated; distributed by Indiana University Linguistics Club.

Gruber, J. (1965) *Studies in Lexical Relations.* MIT PhD dissertation; distributed by Indiana University Linguistics Club (1972).

Haas, W. (1973) Review of John Lyons, *Introduction to Theoretical Linguistics. Journal of Linguistics*, 9, 71 – 114.

Haegeman, L. (1983) Complementiser-agreement in West Flemish. Paper read to Linguistics Association of Great Britain, Sheffield.

Haiman, J. (1980) Dictionaries and encyclopedias. *Lingua*, 50, 329 – 57.

Hale, K. (1981) On the position of Walbiri in a typology of the base. Duplicated; distributed by Indiana University Linguistics Club.

Halliday, M. A. K. (1967) Notes on transitivity and theme in English, Part 2. *Journal of Linguistics*, 3, 199 – 244.

(1970) Language structure and language function. In J. Lyons (ed.) *New Horizons in Linguistics.* Harmondsworth: Penguin.

Hankamar, J. and Sag, I. (1976) Deep and surface anaphora. *Linguistic Inquiry*, 7, 391 – 428.

Hawkins, J. A. (1976) On explaining some ungrammatical sequences of article + modifier in English. *Papers from the Twelfth Regional Meeting of the Chicago Linguistics Society*, 287 – 301.

(1978) *Definiteness and Indefiniteness.* London: Croom Helm.

(1980) On implicational and distributional universals of word order. *Journal of Linguistics*, 16, 193 – 235.

Hays, D. G. (1964) Dependency theory: A formalism and some observations. *Language*, 40, 511 – 25.

Hendrick, R. (1981) Subcategorization: its form and functioning. *Linguistics*, 19, 871 – 910.

Heny, F. (1977) Review of N. Chomsky, *The Logical Structure of Linguistic Theory*, *Synthese*, 40, 235 – 91.

Herbst, T., Heath, D. and Dederding, H. M. (1980) *Grimm's Grandchildren: Current topics in German Linguistics*. London: Longman.

Heringer, H. J. (1970) *Theorie der Deutschen Syntax*. München: Max Hueber.

Hietaranta, P. S. (1981) On multiple modifiers: a further remark on constituency. *Linguistics*, 19, 513 – 16.

Hoard, J. E. (1979) On the semantic representation of oblique complements. *Language*, 55, 319 – 32.

Hockett, C. F. (1961) Linguistic elements and their relations. *Language*, 37, 29 – 53.

Hogg, R. M. (1977): *English Quantifier Systems*. Amsterdam: North Holland.

Huddleston, R. D., Hudson, R. A., Winter, E. O. and Henrici, A. (1968) *Sentence and Clause in Scientific English*. University College London: mimes.

Hudson, R. A. (1977) On clauses containing conjoined and plural noun-phrases in English. *Lingua 24*, 205 – 53.

(1971) *English Complex Sentences: An introduction to systemic grammar*. Amsterdam: North Holland.

(1973) Conjunction-reduction. *Journal of Linguistics*, 9, 303 – 5.

(1974) A structural sketch of Beja. *African Language Studies*, 15, 111 – 42.

(1975) The meaning of questions. *Language*, 51, 1 – 31.

(1976a) *Arguments for a Non-transformational Grammar*. Chicago: University of Chicago Press.

(1976b) Regularities in the lexicon. *Lingua*, 40, 115 – 30.

(1976c) Conjunction-reduction, gapping and right-node raising. *Language*, 52, 535 – 62.

(1977) The power of morphological rules. *Lingua*, 42, 73 – 89.

(1980a) *Sociolinguistics*. Cambridge: Cambridge University Press.

(1980b) Constituency and dependency. *Linguistics*, 18, 179 – 98.

(1980c) A second attack on constituency: a reply to Dahl. *Linguistics*, 18, 489 – 504.

(1981) A reply to Hietaranta's arguments for constituency. *Linguistics*, 19, 517 – 20.

(1982) Incomplete conjuncts. *Linguistic Inquiry*, 13, 547 – 50.

(forthcoming) Some basic assumptions about linguistic and non-linguistic knowledge. *Quaderni di Semantica*.

Hust, J. R. (1978) Lexical redundancy rules and the unpassive construction. *Linguistic Analysis*, 4, 61 – 89.

Jackendoff, R. S. (1972) *Semantic Interpretation in Generative Grammar*. Cambridge, Mass.: MIT Press.

(1975) Morphological and semantic regularities in the lexicon. *Language*, 51, 639 – 71.

(1976) Toward an explanatory semantic representation. *Linguistic Inquiry*, 7, 89 – 150.

(1977) *X Syntax: A study of phrase structure*. Cambridge, Mass.: MIT Press.

(1978) Grammar as evidence for conceptual structure. In M. Halle, J. Bresnan and G. Miller (eds) *Linguistic Theory and Psychological Reality*. Cambridge, Mass.: MIT Press.

(1981) On Katz's autonomous semantics. *Language*, 57, 425 – 35.

Kac, M. (1974) Autonomous linguistics and psycholinguistics. *Minnesota Working Papers in Linguistics and Philosophy of Language*, 2, 42 – 7.

(1978) *Corepresentation of Grammatical Structure*. London: Croom Helm.

(1980) Corepresentational grammar. In E. A. Moravcsik and J. R. Wirth (eds) *Current Approaches to Syntax = Syntax and Semantics*, 13, London: Academic Press.

Kaisse, E. M. (1983) The syntax of auxiliary reduction in English. *Language*, 59, 93 – 122.

Keenan, E. L. and Comrie, B. (1977) Noun phrase accessibility and universal grammar. *Linguistic Inquiry*, 8, 63 – 99.

Kiparsky, P. and Kiparsky, C. (1971) Fact. In M. Bierwisch and K. Heidolph (eds) *Progress in Linguistics*. The Hague: Mouton.

Kiparsky, P. and Staal, J. F. (1969) Syntactic and semantic relations in Panini. *Foundations of Language*, 5, 83 – 117.

Klein, E. (1980) The interpretation of adjectival comparatives. Duplicated.

Labov, W. (1972) *Sociolinguistic Patterns*. Oxford: Blackwell.

Lakoff, G. (1970) Global rules. *Language*, 46, 627 – 39.

(1977) Linguistic gestalts. *Papers from the Thirteenth Regional Meeting of the Chicago Linguistics Society*, 236 – 87.

Lakoff, G. and Thompson, H. (1975) Introducing cognitive grammar. *Proceedings of the Berkeley Linguistics Society*, 1, 295 – 313.

Langacker, R. W. (1978) The form and meaning of the English auxiliary. *Language*, 54, 853 – 82.

(1982) Space grammar, analyzability and the English passive. *Language*, 58, 22 – 80.

Levinson, S. C. (1983) *Pragmatics*. Cambridge: Cambridge University Press.

Li, C. (1976) *Subject and Topic*. London: Academic Press.

Lyons, J. (1968) *Introduction to Theoretical Linguistics*. Cambridge: Cambridge University Press.

(1977) *Semantics*. Cambridge: Cambridge University Press.

McCarthy, J. J. (1981) A prosodic theory of non-concatenative morphology. *Linguistic Inquiry* 12, 373 – 418.

McCawley, J. D. (1968a) Concerning the base component of a transformational grammar. *Foundations of Language*, 4, 243 – 69.

(1968b) Lexical insertion in a transformational grammar without deep structure. *Papers from the Fourth Regional Meeting of the Chicago Linguistics Society*, 71 – 80.

(1977) Acquisition models as models of acquisition. In R. W. Fasold and

R. W. Shuy (eds) *Studies in Language Variation*. Washington D.C.: Georgetown University Press.

(1980) An un-syntax. In E. A. Moravcsik and J. R. Wirth (eds) *Current Approaches to Syntax = Syntax and Semantics*, 13, London: Academic Press.

(1981) *Everything that Linguists have Always Wanted to Know about Logic *but were ashamed to ask*. Oxford: Blackwell.

(1983) What's with *with*? *Language*, 59, 271 – 87.

Mackay, D. G. (1974) On tense and the internal lexicon. In S. A. Thompson and C. Lord (eds) *Approaches to the Lexicon = UCLA Papers in Syntax*, 6, UCLA Linguistics Dept.

McNamer, P. F. (1975) A hierarchy of quantified noun phrases. In R. W. Fasold and R. W. Shuy (eds) *Analyzing Variation in Language*. Washington D.C.: Georgetown University Press.

Matthei, E. and Roeper, T. (1983) *Understanding and Producing Speech*. London: Fontana.

Matthews, P. H. (1974) *Morphology: An introduction to the theory of word-structure*. Cambridge: Cambridge University Press.

(1979) *Generative Grammar and Linguistic Competence*. London: Allen & Unwin.

(1981) *Syntax*. Cambridge: Cambridge University Press.

Miller, G. A. (1978) Semantic relations among words. In M. Halle, J. Bresnan and G. A. Miller (eds) *Linguistic Theory and Psychological Reality*. Cambridge, Mass.: MIT Press.

Miller, G. A. and Johnson-Laird, P. N. (1976) *Language and Perception*. Cambridge: Cambridge University Press.

Nathan, G. S. (1979) Towards a literate level of language. *Parasession on the Elements*. Chicago: Chicago University Linguistics Society.

Newmeyer, F. J. (1980) *Linguistic Theory in America. The first quarter-century of transformational-generative grammar*. London: Academic Press.

Percival, W. K. (1976) On the historical source of immediate constituent analysis. In J. D. McCawley (ed.) *Notes from the Linguistic Underground = Syntax and Semantics*, 7, London: Academic Press.

Perlmutter, D. (1971) *Deep and Surface Structure Constraints in Syntax*. New York: Holt, Rinehart & Winston.

Pike, K. L. (1982) *Linguistic Concepts: An introduction to tagmemics*. Lincoln and London: University of Nebraska Press.

Plank, F. (1980) Reconstructing the concept of subject. Duplicated.

Postal, P. M. (1966) On so-called 'Pronouns' in English. In F. Dinneen (ed.) *Monograph on Languages and Linguistics*, 19, Washington D.C.: Georgetown University Press.

Potts, T. C. (1978) Case-grammar as componential analysis. In W. Abraham (ed.) *Valence, Semantic Case and Grammatical Relations*. Amsterdam: Benjamins.

Pullum, G. K. (1979) *Rule Interaction and the Organization of a Grammar*. London: Garland.

Pullum, G. K. and Wilson, D. (1977) Autonomous syntax and the analysis of auxiliaries. *Language*, 53, 741 – 88.

Pulman, S. G. (1983) *Word Meaning and Belief*, London: Croom Helm.

Quirk, R., Greenbaum, S., Leech, G. and Svartvik, J. (1972) *A Grammar of Contemporary English*. London: Longman.

Radford, A. (1981) *Transformational Syntax. A student's guide to Chomsky's Extended Standard Theory*. Cambridge: Cambridge University Press.

Raskin, V. (1981) Script-based lexicon. *Quaderni di Semantica*, 2, 25 – 34.

Rivero, M-L. (1975) Referential properties of Spanish noun phrases. *Language*, 51, 32 – 48.

Robinson, J. J. (1970) Dependency structures and transformational rules. *Language*, 46, 259 – 85.

Romaine, S. (1980) The relative clause marker in Scots English: Diffusion, complexity and style as dimensions of syntactic change. *Language in Society*, 9, 221 – 47.

Rosch, E. (1976) Classification of real-world objects: origins and representations in cognition. In S. Ehrlich and E. Tulving (eds) *La Mémoire Sémantique*. Paris: Bulletin de Psychologie.

Ross, J. R. (1969) Adjectives as noun phrases. In D. Reibel and S. Schane (eds) *Modern Studies in English*. New York: Prentice-Hall.

       (1970) On declarative sentences. In R. A. Jacobs and P. S. Rosenbaum (eds) *Readings in English Transformational Grammar*. London: Ginn.

       (1973) A fake NP squish. In C. J. Bailey and R. Shuy (eds) *New Ways of Analyzing English*. Washington D.C.: Georgetown University Press.

Rouveret, A. and Vergnaud, J-R. (1980) Specifying reference to the subject: French causatives and conditions on representations. *Linguistic Inquiry*, 11, 97 – 202.

Sampson, G. (1975) The single mother condition. *Journal of Linguistics*, 11, 1 – 12.

Saussure, F. de (1916/1959) *Course in General Linguistics*. New York: McGraw-Hill.

Schank, R. and Abelson, R. (1977) *Scripts, Plans, Goals and Understanding. An inquiry into human knowledge structures*. Hillsdale, N. J.: Lawrence Erlbaum.

Selkirk, E. O. (1981) English compounding and the theory of word structure. In M. Moortgat, H. v. d. Hulst and T. Hoekstra (eds) *The Scope of Lexical Rules*. Dordrecht: Foris.

Seuren, P. A. M. (1969) *Operators and Nucleus: A contribution to the theory of grammar*. Cambridge: Cambridge University Press.

Small, S. (1980) *Word Expert Parsing: A theory of distributed word-based natural language understanding*. University of Maryland PhD dissertation.

Smith, N. V. (1979) *The Acquisition of Phonology: A case study*. Cambridge: Cambridge University Press.

Smith, N. V. and Wilson, D. (1979) *Modern Linguistics: The results of Chomsky's revolution*. Harmondsworth: Penguin.

Sommerstein, A. R. (1972) On the so-called definite article in English.

Linguistic Inquiry, 3, 197 – 209.

Sperber, D. and Wilson, D. (1982) Mutual knowledge and relevance in theories of comprehension. In N. V. Smith (ed.) *Mutual Knowledge*. London: Academic Press.

Starosta, S. (1978) The one per sent solution. In W. Abraham, (ed.) *Valence, Semantic Case and Grammatical Relations*. Amsterdam: Benjamins.

(1979) The end of phrase-structure as we know it. *University of Hawaii Working Papers in Linguistics*, 11, 59 – 76.

(1982) Case relations, perspective and patient centrality. *University of Hawaii Working Papers in Linguistics*, 14, 1 – 33.

Steedman, M. (forthcoming) On the generality of the nested dependency constraint and the reason for an exception in Dutch. *Linguistics*.

Stockwell, R. P., Schachter, P. and Partee, B. H. (1968) *Integration of Transformational Theories on English Syntax*. Duplicated; published (1975) as *The Major Syntactic Structures of English*. New York: Holt, Rinehart & Winston.

Sullivan, W. J. (1980) Syntax and linguistic semantics in stratificational theory. In E. A. Moravcsik and J. Wirth (eds) *Current Approaches to Syntax = Syntax and Semantics*, 13, London: Academic Press.

Tasmowski-De Ryck, L. and Verluyten, S. P. (1981) Pragmatically controlled anaphora and linguistic form. *Linguistic Inquiry*, 12, 153 – 4.

Tesnière, L. (1959) *Éléments de Syntaxe Structurals*. Paris: Klincksieck.

Van Langendonck, W. (1982) Passive in a semantic-syntactic dependency network. *Communication and Cognition*, 15, 407 – 28.

Vendler, Z. (1967) *Linguistics in Philosophy*. Ithaca, N.Y.: Cornell University Press.

Warburton, I. P. (1977) Modern Greek clitic pronouns and the 'surface structure constraint' hypothesis. *Journal of Linguistics*, 13, 259 – 301.

Wasow, T. (1976) McCawley on generative semantics. *Linguistics Analysis*, 2, 279 – 301.

Williams, E. (1980) Predication. *Linguistic Inquiry*, 11, 203 – 38.

(1981) On the notions 'lexically related' and 'head of a word'. *Linguistic Inquiry*, 12, 245 – 73.

Wilson, D. (1975) *Presuppositions and Non-truth-conditional Semantics*. London: Academic Press.

Winograd, T. (1975) Frame representations and the declarative/procedural controversy. In D. G. Bobrow and A. Collins (eds) *Representation and Understanding. Studies in cognitive science*. London: Academic Press.

(1976) Towards a procedural understanding of semantics. *Revue Internationale de Philosophie*, 30, 260 – 303.

Young, D. J. (1980) *The Structure of English Clauses*. London: Hutchinson.

Name Index

Subject Index